Religion, Realism and Social Theory

Theory, Culture & Society

Theory, Culture & Society caters for the resurgence of interest in culture within contemporary social science and the humanities. Building on the heritage of classical social theory, the book series examines ways in which this tradition has been reshaped by a new generation of theorists. It also publishes theoretically informed analyses of everyday life, popular culture, and new intellectual movements.

EDITOR: Mike Featherstone, *Nottingham Trent University*

SERIES EDITORIAL BOARD
Roy Boyne, *University of Durham*
Mike Hepworth, *University of Aberdeen*
Scott Lash, *Goldsmiths College, University of London*
Roland Robertson, *University of Aberdeen*
Bryan S. Turner, *University of Cambridge*

THE TCS CENTRE
The *Theory, Culture & Society* book series, the journals *Theory, Culture & Society* and *Body & Society*, and related conference, seminar and postgraduate programmes operate from the TCS Centre at Nottingham Trent University. For further details of the TCS Centre's activities please contact:

Centre Administrator
The TCS Centre, Room 175
Faculty of Humanities
Nottingham Trent University
Clifton Lane, Nottingham, NG11 8NS, UK
e-mail: tcs@ntu.ac.uk
web: http://tcs.ntu.ac.uk

Recent volumes include:

Critique of Information
Scott Lash

Liberal Democracy 3.0
Stephen P. Turner

French Social Theory
Mike Gane

The Body and Social Theory, 2nd Edition
Chris Shilling

Religion, Realism and Social Theory

Making sense of society

Philip A. Mellor

 SAGE Publications
London ● Thousand Oaks ● New Delhi

SAGE Publications Ltd
1 Oliver's Yard
55 City Road
London EC1Y 1SP

SAGE Publications Inc
2455 Teller Road
Thousand Oaks, California 91320

SAGE Publications India Pvt Ltd
B-42 Panchsheel Enclave
Post Box 4109
New Delhi – 100 017

British Library Cataloguing in Publication data

A catalogue record for this book is available from the British Library

ISBN 0 7619 4864 3
ISBN 0 7619 4865 1

Library of Congress Control Number: 2004095881

Printed and bound in Great Britain by Athenaeum Press, Gateshead

Contents

Acknowledgements

There are a number of people I would like to thank for their encouragement and support. Jim Beckford, Grace Davie, Mike Gane, Robert Alun Jones, David Lyon, Richard Roberts and Kenneth Thompson have all been supportive, while my work has also undoubtedly benefited from the convivial and always rewarding discussions at the British Centre for Durkheimian Studies in Oxford. I would like to thank Bill Pickering, especially, but also Nick Allen, Mike Hawkins, Willie Watts Miller, Robert Parkin, Susan Stedman Jones and all the other participants in the Centre. I have also appreciated the support of my colleagues in Theology and Religious Studies at the University of Leeds, particularly that of Kim Knott and Nigel Biggar, who offered comments on early drafts of parts of the book, and I would like to record my thanks for the conversations, criticisms and questions offered by a number of my doctoral students (Louise Child, Jonathan Fish, Martin Hobson and Sylvia Watts), all of which have helped this book to develop in the form it has. At Sage, Chris Rojek has also been very supportive and I acknowledge my gratitude to him. This book is the first to follow a long period of collaborative work with Chris Shilling, and I owe a particularly great debt to him: not only did he offer constructive criticisms of most of the manuscript, but the book could not have developed in the way it has without the stimulus of our joint work in the preceding years, and the staunch friendship and consistent encouragement he has provided. None the less, the responsibility for the arguments developed here rests entirely with me. Finally, Lucie (our own little emergent phenomenon) and Francesca provided (mostly) welcome distractions and reminders that some things are more important than books, while Murielle did that yet also gave me the unfailing love and support that made this book possible. My greatest debt of gratitude is unquestionably to her.

For Murielle

1

Introduction: Real Society

The purpose of this book is to develop a theoretical account of society that will not only help illuminate important dimensions of the transformations and developments that are shaping many contemporary forms of social life, but will also make a contribution to broader debates about the general characteristics of human societies. Contrary to those who argue that 'society' is now an outmoded basis upon which to develop sociological analysis, the argument of this book is that the idea of society needs to be re-examined, and developed, rather than abandoned. It may be an exaggeration to say, as Anthony Giddens (1987a: 25) has done, that 'society is a largely unexamined term in sociological discourse', but it is clear that there has been a lack of theoretical clarity about the term, that the significance of historical and religious influences on notions of society has rarely been grasped fully, and that there has often been a failure to address ontological questions about social life directly. A sociological tendency to overemphasise the unique features of modern and postmodern social life has exacerbated these problems, as have those 'post-societal' and 'post-social' sociologies, philosophies and cultural theories that urge the abandonment of 'society' as an abstract, archaic and arbitrary construction of sociological discourse. Against these, a systematic reassessment of the nature of society, which illuminates its key dimensions and characteristics, can help reconnect contemporary social theory to its classical tradition, draw more creatively and constructively from developments in other disciplines, and refocus the sociological project upon real human beings in their embodied being-in-the-world.

This reappraisal of society is built on a form of social realism: contrary to some influential forms of the 'cultural turn' in sociological theorising it takes seriously the reality of people, society and the world. Postmodernism has been particularly influential in promoting the idea that any notion of reality is arbitrary and culturally specific, but such an implication is evident in a broad range of sociological and cultural theories. In fact, Berger and Luckmann's (1966: 14) argument that sociologists cannot possibly remove the quotation marks from 'reality', since the meaning of this term is always socially and culturally constructed in specific contexts, seems to have become a widespread norm in sociological theory, even if, like Berger and Luckmann, an appeal to 'empirical evidence' is often used to forestall a slide into complete cultural relativism. Taken to their logical extreme, such arguments severely limit the possibility of understanding any society or culture other than our own, and certainly deprive us of any solid ground on which to challenge social or cultural practices that seem to us oppressive, immoral or dehumanising. They also suggest a wildly dualistic view of humans: on the one hand, humans are incapable of having any contact with, or grasp of, anything real or true because they are so firmly in the grip of a specific culture; on the other hand, human powers are so immense that the world has no reality apart from the ways in which we conceive it. Against such arguments, which reduce sociology to a philosophically incoherent form of cultural interpretation, this book frees reality from its quotation marks, and seeks to develop a view of humans that depicts them as neither feeble dupes of culture nor masters (or mistresses) of the universe. What it rejects is the widespread tendency to conflate questions of knowledge with questions of being, and a related tendency to judge both in relation to what is empirically observable: it builds upon the recognition that the real and the empirical are not identifiable (Archer, 1995), and that social realities are far more complex than extreme forms of constructionism suggest (Byrne, 1998).

The social realist position developed here draws on a critical analysis of Émile Durkheim's sociology, conducted in dialogue with a broad range of contemporary social and cultural theories, and it is focused on the elementary significance of religion for how we make sense of society. Durkheim has often been singled out as offering a particularly unsatisfactory and 'archaic' understanding of society in our 'post-societal' age (Touraine, 1989; Lemert, 1995; Urry, 2000; Bauman, 2002). None the less, attempts to consign his understanding of society to a 'classical' stage of sociology look hasty and ill judged. It can be noted, for example, that Durkheim's work resonates with some of the most radical scientific developments of recent times, since his focus on the inherent complexities of social realities as emergent phenomena has intriguing parallels in chaos and complexity theory (Byrne, 1998), post-Newtonian reconceptualisations of the temporal dimensions of the world (Adam, 1990), and contemporary non-reductionist philosophies of the mind (Sawyer, 2002). Furthermore, in contrast to the implicit cognitivism of much postmodern philosophising, it can be noted that Durkheim illuminates social theory's need to get to grips with social complexity in a way that accounts for the embodied potentialities and limitations of human beings, prefiguring many recent developments in the sociology of the body (Mellor and Shilling, 1997). Durkheim's (1995: 315) suggestion that a 'society will die' if the idea of it is not kept alive within individual minds offers a particularly valuable point of departure from which to begin a reassessment of the concept.

In the late modern West, where the 'beliefs, traditions, and aspirations of the collectivity' no longer seem to be felt and shared by many individuals, it is pointless to deny that society is, in some respects, 'under siege' (Durkheim, 1995: 315; see Bauman, 2002; Freitag, 2002). In Durkheim's view, however, this would not legitimate the notion of a 'post-societal' form of sociology. For Durkheim, *particular* forms of society may die if their beliefs, traditions and aspirations are no longer alive within individuals, but there can be no question of a post-societal form of human existence since society is not, in the first instance, a *particular* set of institutions, practices or beliefs, but a collective way of being emergent from, and expressive of, what it is to be human (Durkheim, 1982a: 57). Viewed in this light, as Karl

Polanyi (2001) emphasised in his magisterial account of the inhuman consequences of trying to obliterate society in the name of free market economics, questions about the nature and reality of society have unavoidable moral dimensions. It is in this sense, at least, that Durkheim's sociology remains of immense value for contemporary social theory. For him, society is the necessary context for the development and flourishing of human potentialities, a view that reflects his vision of sociology as a moral project. In a world increasingly characterised by the imperialism of market forces, dehumanising technological developments, global conflicts and religious violence, questions about a common human basis for the emergence of society look more, not less, important today than in the periods in which Durkheim and Polanyi sought to explore them. It is in the light of these concerns that the four main arguments developed throughout this book originate. These are as follows.

First, social theory must be built on sound ontological arguments concerning the human beings who populate those social forms that social theorists seek to understand and explain. In postmodern thought in particular, but also in other areas of social theory, there is a tendency to argue that humanity (along with 'society' and more or less everything else) is a cultural construction with no essential characteristics or potentialities. This ignores the fact that a common human species exists across different social and cultural contexts, characterised by the same embodied condition, even if human embodiment is engaged with through a multiplicity of different social and cultural forms. The specific argument developed here is that humans are endowed with embodied capacities for an emotional, cognitive, moral and religious engagement with others and the world, and that these capacities constitute the embodied basis upon which the emergence of distinctively social realities, and the development of humans as social beings, occurs. In the light of this argument, 'society' cannot be evacuated from social theory any more than human beings can, since human embodiment not only acts as a medium for its emergence but, in a sense, necessitates this emergence: humans' practical engagement with the world stimulates the collective development of emotional, cognitive, moral and religious capacities, gives rise to collective representations of human ideas and experiences, and produces collective social arrangements for the satisfaction of human needs and desires.

Second, however, as an emergent phenomenon, society has *sui generis* qualities and powers that cannot be reduced to the individuals who constitute it or be understood simply as the aggregate of its individual constituents. This is not simply because all individuals confront an already existing social reality, or that the shape of the social reality we help to constitute bears a tangential, or even contradictory, relationship to our goals, projects and intended actions (Archer, 1995). Rather, a society has qualities and powers all of its own because human relations stimulate and develop distinctively social forces that have the power to reshape individual and collective actions, identities and experiences in specific ways. Reflection upon these forces helps us to understand why it is that individuals, who have the same human capacities and potentialities, can, because of their participation in different societies, grow up to have radically different views of themselves and their place in the world, and divergent understandings of the moral obligations and religious duties they have towards others. In short, society has a holistic character transcendent of the individuals who constitute it. As Byrne (1998: 3) has noted, although 'holism' is currently an unfashionable concept in the social sciences, one of the most significant aspects of post-Newtonian science has been the recognition that 'the whole is greater than the sum of its parts'. Such recognition is also implicit in many critical realist accounts of the 'emergent properties' of social realities (Archer, 1995, 2000), but Durkheim's vision of society as a *sui generis* phenomenon makes this explicit, and demands that contemporary accounts of social 'networks and flows' (Urry, 2000) are placed in a more holistic context.

Clarifications of the precise nature of those social forces that circulate within social life, and examinations of how these give rise to the emergent, *sui generis* reality of society, have, none the less, often proved elusive. Sawyer (2002), for example, while embracing Durkheim as a theorist of emergence, offers a structuralist analysis of different levels of emergent strata without actually seeking to clarify the precise nature, and broader societal context, of social currents and forces. A third key argument of this book, however, is that a useful and illuminating way of understanding the character of these distinctively social forces is to examine them in relation to what Durkheim (1974a) has called a 'hyper-spirituality' specific to collective life. Throughout Durkheim's work he attempts to make sense of what have aptly been called the 'compulsions that order the social', those forces that precede and are given form in social life (Jenkins, 1998: 85). The notion of hyper-spirituality, which has been neglected by social theorists until now, can be used to capture a sense of how these *sui generis* social forces, which are emergent from the embodied potentialities and characteristics of humans, come to constitute a specific ecology within which the social aspects of our humanity are nurtured and developed. Furthermore, it directs our attention to the fact that fundamental dimensions of social life cannot be understood within the framework of empiricism, since social reality is not a one-dimensional phenomenon to be apprehended only through 'hard data', but is complex and multi-layered, with some non-empirically observable elements which can be known only through their causal effects (Archer, 1995: 50; Sayer, 2000: 15). In this respect, the notion of hyper-spirituality also draws attention to the importance of social theory: society cannot be understood entirely through empirical studies.

The fourth key argument of this book is that grounding social theory in an engagement with society as a phenomenon emergent from the relations of embodied humans, and characterised by a specific hyper-spirituality, allows for the development of a fresh understanding of the sociological importance of religion. Focusing especially upon the historical and contemporary significance of Christianity for how we make sense of society in the

Western world, I shall argue for a non-reductionist understanding of the social significance of religion. Although Durkheim (1995) went on to develop his arguments about the *sui generis* aspects of society in his account of the fundamental importance of the 'sacred' in all societies, it is possible to move beyond his view that religions are simply symbolic expressions of social energies, and to understand that religion, as a phenomenon *emergent from but not reducible to* the hyper-spirituality of society, also expresses a broader human engagement with what Zygmunt Bauman (2002: 53–4) has called the 'transcendental conditions of human togetherness'. In this regard, a social realist approach can establish a rapprochement with those forms of theological realism that have, more than many forms of social and cultural theory, grasped the significance of chaos and complexity theories for illuminating the ontologically stratified nature of the world, where 'an immanent structure comprises a hierarchy of levels of reality which are open upward but not reducible downward' (Torrance, 1998: 20). From a sociological point of view, this approach opens up the possibility of engaging with the real significance of religion for society rather than 'explaining' it as an epiphenomenon of, or mask for, something deemed to be more important, such as economics, power interests or psychological needs.

This focus on religion may look odd to those who have come to take modern assumptions about 'secularisation' for granted (even if the post-September 11th world suggests the need for a more complex picture of the relationship between religion and society), but, as Charles Lemert (1999: 240) has commented, 'It is possible that social theory's troubles are, in part, due to its refusal to think about religion.' What I shall argue, in fact, is that many of the social and cultural conflicts of the present, including those surrounding the 'decline' of society, can properly be understood as religious conflicts, despite their apparent secularity. In this regard, I build on Kierkegaard's suggestion, dating from the revolutions of 1848, that 'What looks like politics and imagines itself to be politics, one day will show itself to be a religious movement' (Hollier, 1988: xxv). Indeed, I shall suggest that while Western societies, following the Reformation, became *post-Christendom* societies, they have never become fully *post-Christian*. Secularisation theorists tend to concentrate their arguments upon factors such as the decline in church attendances (Bruce, 2002), the disappearance of certain types of Christian discourse (Brown, 2001) or, more broadly, patterns of structural and functional differentiation, wherein religion becomes restricted to a socially insignificant 'sub-system' of contemporary societies (Dobbelaere, 1999). What such studies do not engage with satisfactorily is the fact that social realities are complex, multi-layered phenomena with religious aspects that are so deeply rooted that they not only tend to be unacknowledged, but may also be expressly denied (Durkheim, 1977; Taylor, 1989; O'Donovan, 1999; Siedentop, 2000). In Western societies, these roots have a specifically Christian character and I shall argue that this not only helps make sense of many contemporary characteristics of, and conflicts within, these contexts, but also throws fresh light upon conflicts with those Islamic social movements that appear to manifest an endemic hostility to Western societies.

Throughout this book a large number of different visions of society, together with various 'post-societal' or 'post-social' theories, will be examined critically in relation to the four core arguments outlined above. The purpose of the rest of this chapter is to introduce these core arguments in more detail, and to establish the theoretical necessity of focusing on society as a *real* phenomenon. This necessity is evident not only with regard to the wide range of sociological perspectives (considered in detail in the following chapter) that see society as, in various senses, an 'inhuman' or 'hyper-real' phenomenon, but also with regard to some broader sociological misconceptions about the nature of society. These include the tendency to identify society with the historically and culturally specific phenomenon of the nation-state, and, at another extreme, the tendency to reify 'Society' as something independent of all human beings. A brief account of some of the problems with these views can help establish the importance of focusing on society as a real, human phenomenon.

(Un)real society

The infamous declaration, in the 1980s, by the then British Prime Minister, Margaret Thatcher, that 'There is no such thing as society' reflected her indebtedness to a liberal philosophical heritage, and to neo-classical economics, where 'society' is, at best, an aggregate outcome of individual actions or, at worst, simply an empty piece of rhetoric (see Strathern, 1998: 65). Although in other respects they make unlikely bedfellows, Thatcher's rejection of society found support from theorists of postmodernity such as Baudrillard (1983, 1990a, 1990b), Deleuze (1979), Lyotard (1984) and Derrida (1991). Rather than rejecting the notion of society in favour of a strong view of the individual, these theorists directly or indirectly challenged both notions on the grounds that they do not refer to *real* phenomena, but are simply culturally relative constructions masking the endemic plurality and indeterminacy of the world. Attempts to eliminate the notion of society from sociology by writers such as Alain Touraine (1989, 1995, 2003) and John Urry (2000, 2003) offered a further challenge to sociology's traditional object of study: rather than offering philosophical objections to society in general, they simply suggested that its time had come and gone, that what we used to call society has vanished into the global networks and movements of a new era, thus necessitating a new 'sociology beyond societies'.

These attacks on the reality of society stem from diverse philosophical and sociological traditions, and offer a range of different explanations as to why society is a concept best abandoned. All of them, however, tend to promote the idea that sociological conceptions of society are not only historically and culturally specific, but also, in some cases at least, abstract products of the imagination rather than reflections of anything real. In this regard, these contemporary social theories are succumbing to a broader tendency evident within Western societies where, as Slavoj Zizek (2002) has suggested, the inability to grasp any sense of the real apart from specific cultural constructions of it seems to have become a defining feature of contemporary life. In its sociological form, this involves unmasking the social realism of writers such as Durkheim as a myopic cultural imperialism that confuses historically and culturally contingent modern phenomena with general social characteristics. In self-consciously 'post-societal' forms of sociology, and others that attempt to grapple with some of the social and cultural changes that are central to the arguments of post-societal approaches, this is narrowed down further to a mistaken identification of society with the nation-state.[1]

Norbert Elias (1978: 241) may have been correct in noting that 'Many twentieth century sociologists, when speaking of "society", no longer have in mind … a "bourgeois society" or a "human society" beyond the state, but increasingly the somewhat diluted ideal image of a nation-state' (see Billig, 1995: 52–4). Although Urry (2000: 8–9) builds on Elias's insight by drawing attention to the historical and cultural specificity of this particular association, he then compounds the problem identified by Elias in linking their mutual decline. Amongst other things, this identification of society with the nation-state robs it of any reality independent of this historically specific form or, at worst, simply reduces it into modern sociological imaginings about that form. Bauman (2002: 43), for example, associates Durkheim's emphasis on the reality of society with an act of imagination supported by the empirical data of the time ('the threshold of the now bygone century'). Aside from the fact that this reduction of society to an imaginative act serves to endorse the individualistic rhetoric of Thatcher's attack on the notion, which would surely make Bauman uncomfortable, it also depends upon some questionable assumptions concerning the contemporary and historical development of society. Here, two points are particularly worth noting.

First of all, arguments concerning the decline of the nation-state, which see it as being 'eroded from without' by globalisation and 'eroded from within' by pluralism, tend to have a highly speculative character (Habermas, 1996). Giddens (1987b: 256) has noted that nation-states have, for a long time, been reflexively constituted through a global system of relations, while Robertson's (1992) influential account of globalisation balances recognition of the continuing significance of nation-states with an analysis of global developments transcendent of them. A number of recent detailed studies of the changes wrought by globalisation have also emphasised the continuing importance of the nation-state rather than its decline (for example, Albrow, 1996; Fulcher, 2000), while Tiryakian's (2003) Durkheimian account of the effervescent revitalisation of the post-September 11th USA suggests the still powerful emotional, symbolic and moral vitality of the nation-state for many. It can also be noted that the USA's current, unparalleled global political influence is hardly suggestive of a world in which nation-states are no longer important.

With regard to 'internal' threats to the nation-state, which see its decay as a result of increasingly diverse ethnicities, religions, values and lifestyle choices, it can also be noted that these are often wildly overstated. It is now customary to refer to Britain, for example, as a 'pluralist', 'multicultural' society, or even as a 'loose federation of cultures' (Commission, 2000; see Beckford, 2003: 91). Such views, however, are often expressive of commitments to a post-Christian and post-national vision of how Britain ought to develop, rather than an objective account of what it currently is. In fact, according to the Office of National Statistics (2001), nearly 70 per cent of the population of England and Wales defines itself as white and Christian, while 71 per cent of black people also define themselves as Christian. In the light of this data, the limits of claims about the decline of the nation-state because of pluralism look fairly clear and, indeed, it is not surprising that studies have shown how, globally, pluralism within societies is often more apparent than real (for example, Hjerm, 2000; Gvosdev, 2001). It is also easy to leap to the conclusion that immigration weakens nation-states, but, again, there is little evidence for this so far. In a detailed empirical study of immigration and multiculturalism in Britain and Germany, Koopmans and Statham (1999), for example, found little to support arguments about the decline of the nation-state and found that immigrants and ethnic minorities had to adjust to specifically *national* models of citizenship. From such studies it is not unreasonable to conclude that the nation-state remains an important institutional expression of society (see also Alexander, 2001; Beaman, 2003; Beyer, 2003).

A second point worth noting, however, is that, regardless of the strengths or weaknesses of nation-states, the sociological focus on society cannot be tied inextricably to these particular forms anyway. Contrary to the postmodernist idea that sociology simply invented its object of study, it has to be acknowledged that reflections upon society predate modern sociology: they are found in the writings of Plato and Aristotle (Frisby and Sayer, 1986), for example, and form a significant component of medieval theology too (Beckwith, 1993). Indeed, Milbank (1990) has suggested that theological reflections upon, and attempted radical reconstructions of, society predate, and will postdate, modern, sociological interpretations with their focus on 'secular' and political dimensions of social life. More radically, Bossy (1985), Taylor (1989) and O'Donovan (1999) have illuminated how modern conceptions of society actually have their origins in theological visions of social life rather than representing a clear break with a religious past. The Protestant assumptions also lurking behind Thatcher's prioritisation of individuals above 'society', perhaps reflecting her Methodist upbringing, are of significance in this regard. None the less, it is also important to note that premodern reflections on the nature of society are not specific to Western social and cultural contexts. Thousands of years ago Indian religious philosophy also became engrossed with the nature of individuals' commitments to, and duties within, society, despite also pre-figuring the postmodernist idea that much of what we take to be reality is actually illusion (Dumont, 1970). In fact, it is difficult, if not impossible, to think of a single example of a social, cultural or religious context where some sort of reflection upon the nature of society is not apparent.

The pervasiveness of reflections upon society across different times and cultures not only calls into question the restriction of the term's significance to modern nation-states, however, but also raises doubts about a contemporary sociological tendency to overemphasise the distinctiveness of present social realities in relation to the past. Writers such as Giddens (1990, 1991a) embody this tendency to stress the radical disjunction between (future-oriented) modern and (past-oriented) premodern societies, while postmodernism's key defining feature is the idea of an end to modernisation processes and the appearance of some sort of new age. The spiralling development of various other 'post-isms', all of them eager to mark out some new radical disjunction from the past, exacerbates the sense that sociology has an increasingly flimsy grasp upon the notion of historical development. As Kumar (1995: 17–18) has noted with regard to information society and post-industrial theorists, they tend to work with a very short-sighted historical perspective that attributes 'to the present developments which are the culmination of trends deep in the past'. In this respect, it is also worth noting that Urry's (2000) 'post-societal' sociology draws extensively from Adam's (1990) account of temporal complexity, but ignores her arguments about the need for historical factors to be examined in a vast, evolutionary perspective. As Byrne (1998: 44) has suggested, although postmodernists have adopted some of the language of complexity theory, particularly in relation to temporality, there is something fundamentally *atemporal* about their understanding of the world, since the location of something in the past is often apparently sufficient to render it outmoded: the past is always *passé*.

Interestingly, however, such short-sightedness was not, in general, a characteristic of the classical sociological theorists. Indeed, while they were attentive to the specific characteristics of modern societies, they were also rather more circumspect about these than many contemporary writers, and certainly did not use the term society only, or even largely, with regard to modern nation-states. In Marx's writings, society tended to be a 'residual category' rather than a fully developed concept, but it is clearly central to his vision of communism and not confined to modernity (Gouldner, 1980: 12; Burawoy, 2003:197). For other major classical theorists, the notion of society is used in relation to a broad range of social and historical contexts. Weber (1965), for example, while having a particular interest in modern societies, also studied ancient Indian, Egyptian, Chinese and Babylonian societies. Similarly, although Simmel (1997), of all the classical theorists, expressed the most reservations about the term 'society', he was able to identify and examine distinct religious patterns of interaction within society in Christian and early Islamic contexts. It can also be noted that Bauman's (2002: 43–4) association of Durkheim's conception of society with the empirical existence of the coercive power of the modern nation-state ignores the fact that his greatest book concerns Aboriginal societies, not nation-states (Durkheim, 1995). Consequently, while it is one thing to acknowledge that the sociological focus on society (and what it has understood as society) emerged out of a specific historical, social and cultural context (Shilling and Mellor, 2001), it is another thing entirely to suggest that it is meaningless to talk about society outside this context.

While challenges to the idea that sociology is the study of society have focused on the contextual specificity of Durkheim's account of society, however, they have also offered the (somewhat contradictory) argument that he promotes a 'reified' vision of society (Lukes, 1973: 20–23). Here, rather than the sociological vision of society being too context-specific, it is deemed to be far too general. Touraine (1989, 1995), Lemert (1995) and Urry (2000) single out this reification of society as *the* most influential source of sociology's 'anachronistic' concern with society. In each case it is understood as something insensitive to the dynamic patterns of contemporary change. For Touraine (1989: 7), Durkheim's understanding of society crystallises the classical sociological concern with integration and order. For Lemert (1995: 48), Durkheim's vision of an organic, ordered society ignores the divisions and differences of modernity: it is, simply, 'a lost world he constructed in his sociological imagination'. Similarly, Urry argues that the central organising principle of sociology has been Durkheim's identification of an autonomous realm of the 'social', distinguished from the 'natural', as the core object of sociological analysis (Urry, 2000: 10). For Urry (2000: 26), the fluidity, sensuousness and positive embrace of *différance* characteristic of contemporary social life render the 'static' Durkheimian concept of society redundant.

Yet the Durkheim such writings reject is often something of a sociological parody, wherein his arguments are characteristically reduced to a neo-Parsonian concern with the Hobbesian 'problem of order' (see Mellor, 1998, 2002; Morrison, 2001). This understanding of Durkheim appears to be an established part of sociology's collective memory, but is unsustainable on the basis of a direct and detailed reading of his work. Contrary to the view that Durkheim identifies society as a realm entirely autonomous from nature (Urry, 2000: 10), he actually, for example, argues for sociology being focused on society as 'a specific reality', but also notes that this has to be contextualised within a recognition that 'man and society are linked to the universe and can be abstracted from it only artificially' (Durkheim, 1995: 432; see Jones, 1997: 154). Furthermore, it can be noted that, in his inaugural lecture at Bordeaux in 1887, he emphasised that an abstract, reified conception of 'Society' (such as he associated with Comte) should not be the focus for sociological analysis (Durkheim, 1974c: 197; Strenski 1997: 158–9). Instead, sociology should concern itself with the constitution and development of societies in the dynamic interrelationships of people in their everyday lives and across time; an understanding reflected in a wealth of sociological, anthropological and philosophical works by his followers, many of which demonstrate a good sense of the complexity, dynamism and fruitfulness of his conception of society (for example, Caillois, 1950; Hertz, 1960; Mauss, 1969; Turner, 1969; Bataille, 1991, 1992; Maffesoli, 1996).

In fact, although Durkheim is often accused of promoting an abstract conception of society, it is the post-societal view, with its dissipation of questions about embodied being into cultural processes and flows, that tends towards an abstractionism Durkheim can help prevent. In particular, it is the Durkheimian tradition that expresses most forcefully the idea that being part of society is inextricably tied to our humanity, offering a vision of the irrepressibly vital social energies that characterise human encounters and relationships, nurturing and sustaining solidarities, bonds, moral obligations and collective symbols. It is on this basis that it is possible to see how a critical engagement with this tradition can prove an invaluable source of assistance if we are to continue to study what societies really are.[2]

Human society

As Margaret Archer (2000: 2) has observed, constructing a social theory that takes sufficient account of the actions, cares and concerns of embodied human beings has become a defensive project in an academic environment where modernity's 'Death of God' has now been matched by postmodernism's 'Death of Humanity'. This death has been announced, and often celebrated, in a broad range of post-structuralist and postmodern philosophy (Foucault, 1970; Baudrillard, 1983; Rorty, 1989; Derrida, 1991), but is also apparent in many other influential forms of social theory. Manuel Castells's (2000: 21) account of a contemporary 'culture of real virtuality', for example, where the 'autonomous ability to reprogramme one's own personality' becomes the dominant mode of identity-construction, exemplifies the implicit evacuation of the human from sociological theory. A similar evacuation is evident in Urry's (2000: 40–1) 'post-societal' presentation of the Internet as the principal metaphor for the fluid character of contemporary social life, and in Donna Haraway's (1991) promotion of the biotechnological image of the 'cyborg' as a liberating way of making sense of social life in an age of global networks constructed through systems of electronic communication.

Turner and Rojek (2001: 228) have challenged such dehumanising perspectives on the empirical grounds that their appeal for certain social theorists is not matched by their relevance for the majority of people. A more crucial challenge, however, rests on the question of ontology, the theory of being underpinning them. Often, the most basic of ontological questions – are human beings *really* like this? – is not even addressed directly. Rather, Richard Rorty's (1991) argument that we must avoid the 'embarrassments' of foundational claims about the inherent, natural characteristics of human beings seems to have been widely accepted. In particular, the epistemological focus of postmodernism, which precludes the possibility of access to a real world or to truth because of its overriding concern with culturally specific constructions of meaning, renders basic ontological questions pointless. None the less, such perspectives manifest what Bhaskar (1979) has called the 'epistemic fallacy', where epistemology (the theory of knowledge) becomes conflated with ontology. Against this fallacy, it can be emphasised that while human knowledge, meaning and identity may indeed be characterised by a great deal of contingency, it is an entirely different thing to say that this means there is no real world (and real human beings) of which we can have any knowledge. This is important for two reasons.

First, despite cultural differences, our embodied being-in-the-world means that all humans share certain basic capacities to feel hunger, pain, joy, desire and a broad range of other emotional and sensual phenomena. We also have the capacity to act, to do things, and to think reflexively about ourselves, our actions and the world around us. It is clear, of course, that the development of these capacities, the individual and collective experience of them, and the theories we construct to account for them can all vary significantly between different cultures. Even so, the failure to take them seriously, along with the unavoidably mortal character of humans, does not look like a very sound basis for social theory. Even in the global information age envisaged by Castells, it may be the case that a 'global elite' can imagine itself as inhabiting 'cyberspace', and that it has the cultural and financial resources to minimise the territorial identifications, economic burdens and social commitments that might otherwise constrain its life-projects (Bauman, 2002: 235), but the ability to access computers, use satellite information systems and build 'virtual communities' depends on a physical body that feels pleasure and pain, that has cognitive capacities, and that, at some point, will inevitably die. The reduction of humanity and society to virtuality by writers such as Castells and Baudrillard seems to ignore this.[3]

Second, and following from this, an attention to ontological issues is important because, without it, visions of the endlessly constructible characteristics of humans encourage moral concerns to lose all substance. In his discussion of environmentalist ethics, for example, Urry talks about the extension of rights from humans to animals, but does not explain how such rights can be 'extended' if humanity, as he claims, has no essence, inherent potentialities or emergent powers worth respecting and protecting (Urry, 2000: 169). More broadly, Bauman's (1993: 243) suggestion that the vociferousness of contemporary appeals to 'human rights' often masks what is simply a self-interested appeal to 'the right to be left alone', illuminates the dissipation of moral concern into cultural relativism that tends to accompany a failure to ground notions of rights in anything real. Furthermore, as Turner and Rojek (2001: 109) note, 'Arguments about cultural relativism can be, and have been, manipulated and abused by authoritarian governments to justify various forms of state violence under the banner of cultural authenticity.' As they suggest, a vision of universal human rights must start with the ontological reality of the body, otherwise there is no solid basis upon which to challenge the violence, degradation and oppression inflicted upon people across different cultures.

The grounding of social theory in a satisfactory account of what it is to be human has to extend further than paying attention to the body in a narrow sense, however, and must also involve an engagement with the collective contexts that humans, as *social beings*, live and develop within. Urry's (2000: 187) discussion of the obligations and duties of contemporary citizenship recognises the importance of collective contexts, but he does not associate them with 'society', only with patterns of 'global homogenisation, consumerism and cosmopolitanism'. Leaving aside the question of how extensive and influential such processes actually are, it is clear that Urry is denying society any ontological reality. In fact, although there is some ambiguity about what he means by 'society' (he sometimes implies it existed in the past), he tends overall to refer to it as a 'metaphor' for social patterns and processes that should now be abandoned in favour of metaphors of fluids and flows. When Urry (2000: 22) seeks to resist relativism through his argument that the 'productivity' of various metaphors can be assessed in relation to empirical evidence, however, he proposes an essentially *anthropocentric* view of the world, despite his rejection of the idea of an essential humanity. The conflation of the empirical with the real is, as Bhaskar (1998: 42) states, anthropocentric in that it equates what humans experience with what actually exists. As Archer (1995: 69) notes, however, the reality of some things might only be established by the effects they have on other things. It is in this regard that Durkheim's notion of society as a *sui generis* reality is particularly important and useful.

Sui generis society

Robert Bellah (1973) has suggested that there is no word more widespread and yet more difficult in Durkheim's work than 'society', and grasping 'the many meanings of that word and its many levels of meaning would be almost equivalent to understanding the whole of Durkheim's thought'.[4] In fact, rather than simply accepting the reality of society as an empirical fact, Durkheim's entire body of work can be read as an attempt to get to grips with the irreducible complexity of social life, and the many levels of social, psychological and material forces, observable and non-observable, that constitute its reality. This is why it has been suggested that, for Durkheim, society constituted a 'research horizon', a 'problematic', rather than 'a positively determined given' (Karsenti, 1998: 71). This conception of society as a research problem has, perhaps, been lost in much subsequent sociology, which might explain Giddens's (1987a: 25) comments about society being a 'largely unexamined term'. In the work of Durkheim, none the less, society is examined and reconsidered repeatedly, contrary to suggestions that Durkheim never actually defines the term (Lemert, 1995: 26; Poggi, 2000: 84).

As Steven Lukes (1973: 21) observes, Durkheim defined it in a number of ways: society was the social or cultural transmission of beliefs and practices, the existence of association, the imposition of socially prescribed obligations, the object of thought, sentiment and action, and, sometimes, a concrete society (such as nation-state), or groups or institutions within it. In general, however, and linking all Durkheim's different uses of the term, the concept of society is used to address the 'supra-individual' elements in social life relating to social actions, feelings, beliefs, values and ideals (Lukes, 1973: 115). As Bellah (1973: ix) suggests, 'Not only is a society not identical with an external "material entity", it is something deeply inner'. Durkheim's (1995: 12–18) critique of empiricism is significant in this regard, since he argues that reducing reality to experience inevitably results in a denial of the truth, meaning or value of anything outside the specific individual or social constructions placed upon phenomena: in other words, the deepest strata of human, social and natural forms of life are simply argued away. Contrary to such reductions, he identifies society with 'an immense cooperation that extends not only through space but also through time', combining ideas and feelings in a rich and complex set of processes through which we become 'truly human' (Durkheim, 1995: 15–16).

For Durkheim (1973: 149, 162), since society arises from human *relations* it cannot be explained as 'the natural and spontaneous development of the individual', but it also cannot be conceived of in isolation from the individuals who constitute it. Society depends on the individuals who constitute it, but it is not reducible to them because, as an emergent *sui generis* reality, it has the power to transform human beings in significant ways.[5] Acknowledging this power is important, because, otherwise, it is easy to overestimate the scope and potentialities of individual agency, and thereby to underestimate the challenges and constraints that face individuals in their day-to-day lives.

It is notable that, in this respect, Giddens (1976, 1984) has criticised Durkheim's notion of a *sui generis* reality above and beyond individual agency, believing that it encourages an unsupportable vision of societies as clearly delimited entities characterised by high levels of integration. As Stephen Turner (1983) has shown, however, this involves a misinterpretation of Durkheim's realism, and the reduction of his position to functionalism. When Giddens (1990: 64) suggests that sociologists have placed far too much emphasis on 'society' he is identifying it with functionalist notions of a 'bounded system', to which he contrasts his own concern with the chronically reflexive processes through which patterns of modern social life are endlessly reconstructed. Like Durkheim, he aims to offer an 'ontology of social life', but he rejects notions of any 'reified' emergent properties or *sui generis* realities to propose a focus on recurrent social practices and their transformations (Giddens, 1991b: 203). Consequently, his vision of social life is essentially processual, with everything in 'fluid process of becoming', but he sees nothing emerging out of these processes other than some unintended consequences of actions (Archer, 1995: 95–6). Even 'structural properties', the 'rules and resources' that enable and constrain agency, have no existence outside their instantiation by agents, having only a 'virtual existence' in the heads of social actors (Archer, 1995: 97–8; see Craib, 1992: 42).

Kilminster (1991: 101) has argued that this vision of social life tends to underestimate the affective dimensions of humans that allow us to bond with others, endorsing a highly rationalistic view of humans as reflexively monitoring actors, but it also attributes humans with immense powers in terms of shaping social realities (whose existence is 'virtual' outside their actions).

In contrast to Giddens, Bhaskar (1989: 77) and Archer (1995: 139) emphasise that 'society pre-exists the individual': 'the church-goer or language user finds their beliefs or language *ready made at birth*' (emphasis in original). With regard to religion, rather than something such as Christianity having only a virtual reality 'instantiated' through actions, Christians find themselves *constrained* by the systems of belief and practice that may date back thousands of years. Some, of course, can feel repulsed rather than attracted by the demands these might place upon individuals, and seek to 'pick and mix' from available traditions or even seek to invent new forms, but this can only be done within already existing constraints that, minimally, allow the use of the term 'Christian' at all. Furthermore, as Durkheim (1982a: 51) suggested, 'I am not forced to speak French with my compatriots, nor to use the legal currency, but it is impossible for me to do otherwise … Even when in fact I can struggle free from these rules and successfully break them, it is never without being forced to fight against them.' Here, Durkheim is establishing the reality of social facts through their causal effects upon action (Bhaskar, 1998: 220). However, the idea that society is an emergent reality is not simply dependent upon notions of constraint: the emergence of society is also expressed through the stimulation of ideas, feelings and moral bonds that transcend the utilitarian calculation of self-interest (Durkheim, 1995: 209). This is where the notion of 'hyper-spirituality' is particularly useful.

Hyper-spiritual society

Durkheim's dynamic picture of social life is reflected in his interest in the pre-contractual foundations of the 'organic solidarity' that, in his earliest book, he believed to be characteristic of modern societies (Durkheim, 1984).[6] What he was suggesting was that the more formal contractual and institutional dimensions of society depended on the circulation of pre-existing social forces, energies and obligations, an idea that Rowan Williams (2000: 58–9), via an assessment of the continuing value of Bossy's (1985) notion of the 'social miracle', has recently emphasised as being crucial to a satisfactory understanding of what societies essentially are. Although Durkheim later abandoned the distinction between 'mechanical' and 'organic' forms of solidarity, his interest in these pre-contractual forces continued, and they are at the heart of what he means by 'hyper-spirituality'. What is of particular note about this notion is that it expresses the idea that, emerging from the relations between individuals, there is a specific social ecology within which individual identities are reshaped and developed in far-reaching ways.

Durkheim's argument is that the simple aggregation of the biological and mental components of an individual human cannot account for the distinctive consciousness, predispositions and personality of that individual: rather, these distinctive characteristics are aspects of an individuality emergent from the processes and interactions, in totality, of all the different components of individual life. Anticipating twenty-first century philosophies of the mind (Sawyer, 2002), Durkheim argued that these *sui generis* characteristics constitute the particular 'psychic life', or 'spirituality', of the individual. By analogy, he argues that society, as a *sui generis* phenomenon emergent from relations between individuals, has its own specific hyper-spirituality and that this represents the distinctive object of sociological study (Durkheim, 1974a: 27–8, 34). In short, what we call 'society' is not simply an empirical or pragmatic phenomenon constructed with the aim of meeting certain economic, political or philosophical needs, but a *sui generis* 'enhancement of being' that imbues social life with its transcendent character (Freitag, 2002). Consequently, the notion of hyper-spirituality is of fundamental sociological importance because it helps illuminate the ontological depth of social reality, pointing towards a holistic context for human action, belief and experience that escapes empirically focused sociologies.

Georges Gurvitch (1964, 1971) expanded upon Durkheim's work in this regard by developing a form of 'depth level analysis' that aimed to study observable social phenomena in relation to what Korenbaum (1964: xiii) calls 'the very deepest, most obscured and veiled layers of social reality'. These deepest layers were found in emergent forms of collective consciousness, characterised by an inherent dynamism that shaped societies in subtle but far-reaching ways (Thompson, 1971: xvi). In more contemporary studies such a systematic approach to these deeper layers of social reality is notably absent, though there are some intriguing suggestions that such phenomena remain significant. Indeed, a useful way of expanding upon the importance of Durkheim's notion of hyper-spirituality is to note the presence, in a range of social theories, of an under-theorised reference to a holistic substratum of social energies or forces that underpin a society's more institutionalised dimensions. Virilio, for example, identifies a subterranean 'social drama' within everyday life that often eludes institutionally focused forms of sociology (Armitage, 2000: 43). This idea is also found in the work of de Certeau (1984: xi), who talks of 'the obscure background of social activity', as well as in the Durkheimian arguments of Maffesoli (1996) concerning the 'social divine'. Bauman (2001: 3–4), in fact, also refers to the 'life-juices' of society, which provide a sort of 'metacapital' that binds individuals into particular social orders. In each case, the nature and significance of this social substratum are not articulated in a developed way, and in Bauman's work, in particular, this substratum appears to be of decreasing sociological significance.

While Gurvitch's (1964: 1) focus on the 'pluri-dimensional' characteristics of social phenomena is a great deal more systematic than many of these more recent studies, however, and clearly focused upon their enduring sociological importance, what his work lacks is a detailed engagement with the moral and the religious implications of these 'veiled' layers of social reality. More helpfully, though, the philosopher of science Michael Polanyi (1958, 1967) has also talked of a social substratum of knowledge, a 'tacit dimension', that not only shapes human thought but also projects it beyond the empirical towards a fuller grasp of the nature of reality. Here, as Torrance (1985: 113) suggests, it is possible to appreciate how human life has an inherently social and moral character that reveals to us the world in its ontological depth. Our human embodiment, which enables us to transcend the limits of individual existence through our interactions with others in society, integrates us within a 'spiritual reality' that thereby builds an open-ended transcendent relation into our personal and social reality (Polanyi, 1967: 53ff.; Torrance, 1985: 111; see also Bossy, 1985, Williams, 2000).

Polanyi's notion of an emergent, tacit 'spiritual reality' and Durkheim's notion of an emergent societal 'hyper-spirituality' have a great deal in common, as is clear in relation to Durkheim's account of the *homo duplex* character of humans. He emphasises this *homo duplex* nature in two senses: first, human identities have individual and collective sources; second, their 'rational' dimensions arise out of a 'non-rational' stimulation and circulation of social energies within the *sui generis* reality of society (Durkheim, 1974b). The causal significance of hyper-spirituality within his vision of societal complexity is manifest in this power of society to suggest, and, indeed, impose, certain ways of acting and thinking upon individuals (Durkheim, 1982b: 248). It is also manifest, however, in the fact that this fundamental 'coerciveness' of society co-exists with the stimulus to an open-ended investigation of social reality in all its ontological depth. It is in the context of this duality that sociology, which is rooted in the attempt to investigate this ontological depth, becomes possible: it is itself emergent from hyper-spirituality, but comes to explore this hyper-spirituality systematically (Durkheim, 1953; Lukes, 1973: 416).

Postmodernist theories, however, even if they do not reject the idea of the social *per se*, tend to reject the idea of any holistic dimension to social relations, focusing on processes of fragmentation or segmentation. Deleuze and Guattari (1988: 208), for example, return to Durkheim's fiercest contemporary critic, Gabriel Tarde, to help emphasise their key principle of the segment taking precedence over any notion of an organic whole (Gane, 2003: 148). None the less, it is important to note that, for Durkheim (1974b: 24), the hyper-spirituality of collective life is not only manifest in the relations between individuals and a 'total society', but between individuals and 'secondary groups' within a larger social whole. This is evident even in relation to small-scale social groupings such as families, where enduring social relations can produce distinctively collective realities which have a profound effect upon the consciousness and actions of the individuals within them, for good or ill.[7] The notion of hyper-spirituality is not, therefore, meant to refer to *one* form of overarching collectivism that contains all individualities within its vast embrace. On the contrary, it refers to a quality of human relations emergent from our embodied being-in-the-world, facilitating the birth and flourishing of the distinctively social aspects of our humanity at various emergent levels that embrace intimate relations, small groups, nations and even global relations.

This is not to say that such a flourishing is in all respects desirable, however, since social energies and forces have an *ambiguous* quality. This helps us understand how it is that social forces can promote heroism, loyalty and self-sacrifice as well as racism, fascism and barbarism (Durkheim, 1995: 213; Fields, 1995: xlii). As something that arises from the hyper-spiritual dimensions of society, religion too has often manifested this ambiguity, stirring up violence and war as well as nurturing profound insights into the nature of life and human destiny. Even so, as an emergent phenomenon concerned with the transcendental conditions of human togetherness inherent within humanity's embodied being in the world, religion is a uniquely important social phenomenon worthy, as Durkheim recognised, of very serious sociological attention.[8]

Religious society

There has been a recent upsurge of academic interest in a range of phenomena that have been labelled 'religious'. In fact, many writers are now beginning to draw attention to the spread of religious factors across many social and cultural domains, including 'techno-science' (Virilio, 1996), everyday social interactions (Maffesoli, 1996), consumerism (Featherstone, 1991; Ritzer, 1999), communications media (Lyon, 2000) and postmodernist philosophy (Wernick, 1992). The fact that many studies of these new religious phenomena draw on Durkheim's work suggest the continuing value of his view that 'the religious life of a people is a manifestation of its profoundest being' (Hertz, 1983: 87). Like Luckmann's (1967) notion of 'invisible religion', however, these uses of Durkheim tend to work with very broad conceptions of what can count as 'sacred', so that more or less anything can be seen in 'religious' terms. This has the advantage of illuminating common features between apparently 'secular' phenomena and more traditional religious forms, and of highlighting the hyper-spiritual context from which both forms emerge. Maffesoli (1996: 73), for example, using Durkheim's notion of the 'social divine', associates the effervescent solidarity exhibited in sexual networks, Internet groups and various sporting and musical groupings with the Christian concept of the 'communion of saints'.

The disadvantage of such approaches, however, is that a focus on common features can ignore fundamental differences: sexual networks come into existence with the utilitarian purpose of facilitating the gratification of specific desires, and do not tend to look further than that; the notion of the 'communion of saints', on the other hand, embraces all sorts of beliefs, arguments and experiences developed over centuries, concerning issues of life and death, human potentiality and limitations, and the nature of the universe. Simply to equate the two is to adopt a sociological strategy that cannot distinguish between the fairly unreflective gratification of immediate desires and serious attempts to grapple with questions about human destiny and the nature of life. In fact, such studies conflate religion with the hyperspirituality of society when they should be seen as distinct, though related, phenomena.

In this respect, it is notable that Lemert (1999), drawing on Durkheim's theories, supplemented by historical studies of Greek society, offers an account of religion that sees it, as Durkheim did, in relation to 'the serious life'.[9] His argument is that the value of an engagement with religion for social theory rests on its illumination of the contingency and finitude of human existence, grounded in the human experience of family and community. As he suggests, religion is a source of social and political realism, in the sense that it reminds us that hope, and the feelings of fellowship and identity that bind us into a society, are inextricably tied to the brute facts of human mortality and interdependence. For Lemert (1999: 260), as for Charles Taylor (1994: 73), the value of religion in this sense is particularly apparent in relation to conflicts surrounding the 'politics of redistribution' and the 'politics of recognition': by accepting that issues of social injustice and cultural difference are rooted in a religious engagement with human finitude, at societal and individual levels, then some of the social, cultural and political conflicts of contemporary societies can be placed in a new, more constructive context.[10]

Nevertheless, Lemert's focus on religion as a reminder of human contingency and finitude robs its emergent cosmological dimensions of any real ontological significance, and reduces it to a pragmatic means of curtailing dangerous forms of social and political utopianism. In contrast, the understanding of religion developed throughout this book holds that it is a phenomenon that expresses, through actions and beliefs, a collective engagement with the possibilities of transcendence emergent from the contingencies, potentialities and limitations of embodied human life. As already noted, Durkheim's notion of an emergent hyper-spirituality suggests that an open-ended orientation towards transcendence is a defining feature of our embodied relations with others in society: it is this orientation that facilitates the emergence and development of those distinctively religious actions, beliefs and forms of knowledge that, with varying degrees of systematisation, subtlety and complexity, reveal further aspects of the world's ontological depth, and thereby place human social life within a broader, characteristically cosmological perspective. It is this 'revelation' of ontological depth that accounts for the social power of religions, evident in the embodied commitment of individual persons to morally, practically and intellectually demanding forms of life (Archer, 2000: 186), and in the structuring of societies according to religious principles. Given that the latter might be regarded as the more problematic of these two examples, since sociology has for a long time taken assumptions about secularisation for granted, it is worthwhile introducing two key points, to be developed later in this book, concerning the specifically Christian influence upon Western societies.

First, assumptions about contemporary Christian decline can all too easily encourage a failure to take seriously the Christian influence upon the historical evolution of Western societies, resulting in a general, and unsupportable, neglect of the immense importance of religious issues. As Trigg (1998: 5) suggests, 'the instant dismissal of the beliefs on which our Western civilisation was founded is neither very sensible nor very scholarly'. In contrast to such short-sightedness, which rests on a simplistic understanding of historical development, writers with a broader grasp of history have demonstrated the central significance of Christianity for the development of Europe (Rémond, 1999), the natural sciences (Torrance, 1984), the social sciences (Shilling and Mellor, 2001; Gane, 2003), and even of modernity itself (Kumar, 1995).

Second, however, the Christian influence upon social life is not only historical but evident in the present too, even if this influence is to a large degree concealed by a discourse of secularity. As Oliver O'Donovan (1999: 247) notes, although the modern liberal technological society appears to be thoroughly 'secular', and often seems to operate as a 'quasi-mechanical system' devoid of specific moral and religious dimensions, this ostensible secularity rests on a 'false self-consciousness': the distinction between the religious and the secular has a specifically Christian character, expressed historically in the separation of the spiritual and the temporal and notions of 'two realms' or 'two cities' (see Taylor, 1989). Further to this, even some of the most distinctive manifestations of modern Western secularity have been underpinned by specifically Christian beliefs. Thus, the First Amendment to the US Constitution, which enshrines the principle of the separation of church and state, 'can usefully be taken as the symbolic end of Christendom' (O'Donovan, 1999: 244). None the less, this doctrine was shaped by ardent Christians who believed that the First Amendment would facilitate the development of 'authentic Christianity', rather than by self-conscious secularists (O'Donovan, 1999: 245).

The sociological significance of the Christian influence upon modern notions of 'secular' society is apparent when we consider that, in contrast to Christianity, Islam, for example, does not have a distinction between 'two realms', which is why Muslims do not tend to see Western secularity as religiously neutral in the way that Westerners tend to (see Rémond, 1999: 196; Siedentop, 2000: 208). This underlines the importance of specifically *religious* differences for the development of society, and points towards some of the dangers in trying to explain away religious factors through forms of economic or political reductionism. In this regard, it is notable how, in post-September 11th assessments of conflicts between Islam and the West, Turner (2002), Fukuyama (2002) and Kellner (2002), following the example of Barber (2001), can all underplay distinctive elements of Islamic belief and practice, and concentrate instead on economic and political issues relating to relative poverty and the global spread of Western consumerism. As Huntington's (1996) 'clash of civilisations' thesis suggests, however, religious differences can have very deep roots within, and immense influence upon, societal forms that are civilisational in scope. Ignoring the religious assumptions underpinning our own 'secular' accounts of society cannot put sociologists in a good position to comprehend societies outside the modern West.

In the light of these arguments, it is possible to appreciate the wisdom of Durkheim's (1995) contention that, at an elementary level, society is always a religious phenomenon, though it also necessary to reject his reductionist understanding of religion as a symbolic expression of social forces, just as he rejects the idea that the *sui generis* reality of society can be reduced into its individual constituents.[11] It is only by embracing the idea that 'downwards reductionism' is theoretically unacceptable that the real social significance of religion, as a causal power affecting people's views, choices and actions, can be appreciated. Although emergent from hyper-spirituality, an idea that has traditionally been addressed by theologians through the subject of 'natural theology' (see Trigg, 1998: 175–182), religion's capacity to engage productively with the orientation towards transcendence that characterises social relationships not only ensures that religion is always 'a fundamental and permanent aspect of humanity' (Durkheim, 1995: 1), but also ensures that religious influences are located at the heart of all societies rather than in the private or epiphenomenal 'sub-systems' envisaged by secularisation theorists. Further to this, a non-reductionist understanding of religion helps clarify the meaning of MacIntyre's (1955: 260) claim that different religions offer 'mutually exclusive ontologies', since the reality of the world's ontological depth is not only revealed in, but inseparable from, the social and historical specificity of particular traditions of belief and practice (see Moore, 2003).[12]

Multi-dimensional society

In the course of this chapter, I have considered some key aspects of the contemporary critique of the notion of society, arguing that the mistaken identification of classical sociological notions of society with the modern nation-state ignores their sensitivity to the historical development of diverse societal forms. In particular, I have argued that such critiques tend to misrepresent Durkheim's thought, and have emphasised the value of building upon his social realism in order to develop a more satisfactory understanding of society. Following this, I have suggested that this new understanding must take account of the following four arguments: first, that society is dependent for its emergence on the embodied characteristics and potentialities of human beings; second, that, as an emergent form, society has a *sui generis* character, transcendent of the individuals who constitute it; third,

that this transcendence can be conceptualised as a distinctive 'hyper-spirituality' that offers a specific ecology within which the social aspects of our
humanity are nurtured and developed; and fourth, that the hyper-spiritual
aspects of social reality imbue it with an open-ended orientation towards
transcendence that allows for the emergence of those religious forms that
come to exercise a defining influence upon social life.

These arguments will be developed throughout the rest of the book with
reference to six dimensions of society that, properly explicated, can help
revitalise its sociological study, and reveal the over-hastiness of those who
seek to abandon it for post-societal forms of sociology. Each chapter is
focused on one of these dimensions, examining society as a *complex, contingent, necessary, temporal, tacit* and *resurgent* reality.

Chapter 2 is concerned with society as a *complex* reality, and contains a
more detailed examination of post-societal perspectives, focusing upon how
the underlying ontological assumptions specific to various contemporary
social and cultural theories are able to deal with moral and religious issues
satisfactorily, and investigating the degree to which the 'hyper-spirituality'
of social realities as emergent phenomena is dealt with adequately, if at all.
Through a critical discussion of various forms of postmodern theory, sociological visions of the technological reconstruction of social and cultural life,
and contemporary theories of consumerism, individualism and market
processes, it is argued that many of these theories engage with social realities in a highly partial manner through various forms of reductionism that
take insufficient account of enduring human characteristics and potentialities. In contrast, it is argued that societies must be seen as complex, non-
reducible phenomena emergent from human relationships.

Chapter 3 extends these arguments further by focusing on the *contingent* character of society. As Archer (1995, 2000) has emphasised, society is not a self-subsistent reality, but one that is dependent for its
emergence upon the human beings who constitute it. In this regard, the
arguments constructed in this chapter emphasise the importance of
developing an embodied understanding of society, and seek to demonstrate that the hyper-spiritual and religious forces that are key features of
social life are emergent phenomena contingent upon, but irreducible to,
human individuals who possess particular potentialities and powers. The
arguments of this chapter are developed through a critical discussion of
a broad range of theorists but are focused specifically upon the social theories of Turner and Rojek (2001), Archer (1995, 2000), Durkheim
(1995) and Bataille (1987, 1991), all of which offer illuminating, though
sometimes problematic, accounts of the embodied basis of society.
Bringing them into dialogue, I suggest, offers a fruitful way forward for
developing a social realist account of the contingent relationship between
embodiment, society, hyper-spirituality and religion.

Chapter 4 complements the discussion of the contingent nature of society by focusing on the fact that it nevertheless imposes itself as a *necessary*
reality. In contrast to theories focused on the plurality of choices and options

facing modern individuals, the first part of this chapter is focused on the analysis of taboo, which, despite the postmodern concern with transgression, can be considered as a central manifestation of the impact of society as a *sui generis* reality upon individuals, in the sense that taboos express some of the obligatory aspects of hyper-spiritual dynamics. Following this, Mauss's (1969) account of gift exchange is considered as a key study of how patterns of reciprocal obligation come to circulate within various types of society, while Bataille's (1991) development of Mauss's arguments in his own account of the 'general' and the 'restricted' economy is discussed as a direct challenge to those postmodern theorists who seek to co-opt Bataille for their own ends. What both Mauss and Bataille demonstrate is that the economy is always embedded in society, an idea that is also the cornerstone of Polanyi's (2001) contribution to the study of modern economic systems. Consequently, the rest of the chapter examines Polanyi's thoroughgoing critique of the market model of humanity and society, which, though originally published in 1944, illuminates tendencies towards an economically driven dehumanisation of social realities that are particularly relevant to the contemporary era of globalisation.

Chapter 5 extends the reappraisal of society further by focusing on the broad *temporal* context within which societies develop, and the distinction between the temporal and the spiritual that has had a major influence upon the development of various theological, philosophical and sociological notions of society. After discussing the value of a social realist account of the significance of time for how we conceptualise society, it is argued that Christian history has provided Western societies with certain cultural contradictions, concerning the temporal and the spiritual, that continue into the present and still affect how we make sense of social life. Following this, it is argued that these contradictions run through influential philosophical accounts of social bonds and contracts, and are present in some key sociological visions of modernity. Throughout, it is suggested that many conventional assumptions about contemporary secularity tend to confuse the way we think about things with the way things really are, and that in this respect the distinction between the temporal and the spiritual can be more analytically precise and useful than that between the secular and the religious.

Chapter 6 is concerned with how the *tacit* dimensions of society are embedded within individual and collective forms of consciousness. The first part of this chapter is devoted to exploring Durkheim's notion of 'collective representations' with regard to this 'embedding' process. Following this is a critical assessment of Serge Moscovici's 'social representations' theory, which adds to Durkheim's work a valuable account of the persistence of certain 'core themata' within the fluid, shifting configurations of social forms and processes that characterise modern life, and the role of social representations in the world-views of even those who claim not to believe in them. The rest of the chapter focuses on three different strata within social reality that are dependent upon tacit forms of knowledge resistant to reflexive deconstruction. First, various attempts to explore the sociological significance of 'everyday life' are discussed in relation to what Bourdieu has referred to as the 'doxic', or taken-for-granted knowledge enfolded in the social habitus (Fowler, 1997: 2). Second, the presence of a tacitly Christian way of structuring conceptions of social life within various modern notions of 'public' and 'private' life is discussed as a key example of how a core sociological dichotomy can rest on a religious substratum. Third, the role of tacit assumptions in inter-societal relations is considered, looking at the different role of Christian and Islamic representations in Said's (1978) thesis on 'Orientalism'. In conclusion, it is suggested that a focus on how the tacit dimensions of societies continue to shape the consciousnesses of individuals calls into question those sociological visions that too readily assume 'a disappearance of the social bond and value breakdown' (Lash and Featherstone, 2001: 17).

Chapter 7 is concerned with society as a *resurgent* reality. Through a critical discussion of the various strategies employed by contemporary social theorists to ignore the specifically religious dimensions of contemporary conflicts between Islam and 'the West', which are, for example, often reduced to economic factors or debates about modernity and its discontents, this chapter argues that a neo-Durkheimian form of social realism is best placed to illuminate the real nature of these conflicts, and to help make sense of the return of theological factors to the social theory of writers such as Virilio. The key point stressed here is that, viewed within a 'stratified ontology' sensitive to emergent hyper-spiritual and religious forces, a fresh analysis of contemporary conflicts between Islam and the West can help us to grasp some of the key challenges facing social theory today; challenges that do not reveal the demise of society, but, on the contrary, its resurgence. Following this, Chapter 8 draws together all the preceding arguments and offers some concluding comments upon why sociology must remain focused upon the study of society.

Notes

1. Bauman (2002: 11, 43), for example, identifies sociology's understanding of 'society' with the emergence of the modern nation-state; an identification reinforced by his description of society as an 'imagined community' in the manner of Anderson's (1991) well-known analysis of the nation-state. Urry's (2000) account of the history of the term 'society' also focuses on its emergence with the rise of the modern nation-state and its subsequent incorporation into European and American visions of the sociological project under the influence of Durkheim and Parsons. None the less, this not only underestimates the subtlety and complexity of many sociological theories of society, including that of Durkheim, but also offers a highly selective account of the history of 'society' as a concept, even within sociology itself.

2. Contrary to the common sociological view of the bold claims Durkheim makes for society, the Durkheimian tradition also offers a useful basis for thinking about society because it can illuminate society's *limits*. The common view ignores the extent to which Durkheim was deeply concerned with philosophical questions of freedom, necessity and determinism, and the fact that he developed a realist rather than idealist form of social theory that sought to take these into account, emphasising that social facts should be studied as real things not as concepts (Jones, 1999: 77). His concern with the embodied character of human beings, and there-

fore of social life, is crucial in this respect, and is the proper context in which to assess his stress on the socially creative role of phenomena such as 'collective effervescence' (Durkheim, 1995: 221). Consequently, I shall argue that, although Durkheim is often held to exemplify what Archer (1988, 1995, 2000) has called 'downwards conflation' (reducing everything into society), he actually proposes a realist form of social theory close to Archer's own (even if her arguments help illuminate certain limitations in Durkheim's thought), and that this offers a productive basis upon which to explore the relationship between society and humanity's embodied being-in-the-world.

3. Furthermore, as Archer (1998: 193) notes, we should remember that the privileges of Western societies have to be placed in broader human context: 'The postmodern experience is not on globally for those needing bread not circuses and seeking freedom of expression not expressive freedom. There are transcendental material requirements for the existence of the Collège de France and for the privileged practice of "playing with the pieces".'

4. Even though this was not his intention, Bellah's (1973: ix–x) comment that 'Durkheim uses the word "society" in ways closer to classical theology than to empirical science' would no doubt be taken as a damning condemnation by those sociologists who believe he reifies society. None the less, Bellah's comment touches upon Durkheim's attempts to invest social realities with sufficient ontological depth.

5. Bhaskar (1998: 211) has sought to distinguish his own 'critical realism' from Durkheim's social realism on the basis that Durkheim associates society's emergent powers with *collective* rather than *relational* phenomena. He argues that, in contrast, collective phenomena must be 'seen primarily as the expressions of enduring relationships'. This misunderstands Durkheim's position, however, which is actually very close to what Bhaskar is proposing.

6. Durkheim's model of society has been described as 'a social body which suffers all the processes of life and death and rebirth' (Gane, 1983a: 229), under the impact of *sthenic* and *asthenic* cycles of social forces (Mauss, 1973: 292). The dynamism inherent to it has also been developed by Victor Turner (1967, 1974) through his notion of *communitas*.

7. This is an especially significant point, however, in relation to contemporary Western societies, which are characterised by such diversity that Touraine (1989: 15), amongst others, can argue that the complex and changing fields of social relations seriously compromise any simple association between individuals and an overarching totality. Here, social groups of many sizes and strengths manifest diverse forms of practical action and varied representational systems that can have a complex and often conflict-ridden relationship with others, as well as with nation-states and global forces and institutions (see Yeatman, 2003). Hyper-spirituality may be an inherent feature of all social relationships, then, but the forms it takes not only vary enormously but can also overlap in different emergent strata, and can thereby provoke social and cultural conflict.

8. The hyper-spiritual substratum of a society is a 'domain of uncertainty', in the sense that all sorts of phenomena can emerge from it to reflect upon the transcendent conditions of human togetherness, such as sociology, philosophy and political theory. The persistent emergence and endurance of religion, however, suggests that this uncertainty and indeterminacy has boundaries, and that religion is, as Durkheim (1995: 1) suggested, a 'fundamental and permanent' feature of social life.

9. Although, as I have already noted, Lemert (1995: 48) has, in the past, been highly critical of Durkheim's understanding of society, his more recent writings have revealed an appreciative and far deeper engagement with Durkheim's thought than many other contemporary critics. This is evident not only in his (1999) discussion of religion and contemporary social theory, but also in his (2003) arguments concerning the presence of Durkheim's 'ghosts' in many contemporary social and cultural theories that ostensibly reject his arguments. For Lemert (2003: 315), Durkheim's enduring legacy rests on the honesty and rigour with which he investigates the tension between the socially constituted character of knowledge and the common human basis upon which different social and cultural forms develop.

10. Anne Warfield Rawls (2001), again drawing on Durkheim's account of religion, also offers an argument that emphasises the value of returning religion to the centre of social the-

ory. She identifies a 'fallacy of misplaced abstraction' that has characterised twentieth-century sociology, exacerbated by the 'cultural turn' in sociological theorising. This fallacy, manifest as the prioritisation of ideas and beliefs over practices, has led, inevitably, to the conclusion, evident in much postmodern theorising and cultural studies, 'that there is no escape from the relativism of competing sets of beliefs, and competing sets of meanings, each of which defines a competing reality' (Rawls, 2001: 63). For her, conflicts concerning phenomena such as oppression, racism and sexism, which, in the light of the 'fallacy of misplaced abstraction', come to be reduced to systems of representations, need to be understood *primarily* as phenomena 'enacted and experienced concretely by real people in real time and in real places' (Rawls, 2001: 63).

11. It is for this reason that social theory must not only engage with theology, but must also resist the temptation to reduce theological realism downwards into social realism: the reality of God, for example, cannot be explained away as a mere symbol of distinctively social phenomena (see Soskice, 1987; Torrance, 1998: 20; Patterson, 1999; Moore, 2003).

12. Further to this, it is inappropriate to suggest that, for example, Christianity and consumerism are comparable 'religious' forms: they may share certain characteristics (e.g. the generation of powerful emotions in relation to shared 'sacred' symbols), but that is because of an analogous hyper-spiritual substratum, not because they are ultimately the same sort of phenomenon. Their engagements with the philosophical, moral and spiritual aspects of the human lot are hardly commensurable, and, of course, phenomena such as consumerism are devoid of any cosmological dimension. It is also inappropriate, however, to assume that religions such as Christianity and Islam are commensurate social forms, given the profound differences in their origins, theology and development over huge periods of time. Consequently, a social realist account of religion, centred on the analysis of emergent dimensions within a 'stratified ontology' (Sayer, 2000: 12), cannot, even if in other respects it is much indebted to Durkheim, adopt the very broad model for what counts as 'religion' that has come to be associated with Durkheimianism: it offers a reductionist interpretation of emergent phenomena that too readily flattens out very significant differences under the weight of purportedly common social functions, and thereby limits the degree to which contemporary differences and conflicts are comprehensible.

2

Complex Society

The purpose of this chapter is to examine some influential 'post-societal' and 'post-social' perspectives more closely, in order to assess the validity and value of their claims in relation to the key arguments about social life at the heart of this book. In this regard, I focus on how the underlying ontology specific to each approach is able to deal with moral and religious issues, and investigate the degree to which the 'hyper-spirituality' of social realities as emergent phenomena is dealt with adequately, if at all. In so doing, it is not my intention to deny that some of the traditions of interpretation discussed here have some important and illuminating things to say about contemporary social and cultural changes. My aim, rather, is to suggest that, even where some valuable insights are developed, these are compromised by a somewhat partial engagement with societal complexity. Consequently, although this chapter explores various post-societal or post-social approaches, it can be read as an attempt to elaborate upon Giddens's (1987a: 33) argument that 'sociologists have failed to come to terms conceptually with fundamental factors which make the societies they analyse "societies" at all', even if, as it will become clear, I disagree with him about what these factors really are. Taken together, the diverse visions of society considered in this chapter testify to the difficulties of grasping social complexity, but a consideration of their underlying tendencies towards various forms of reductionism also helps illuminate how a more satisfactory understanding of society might be possible. At the start, however, it is important to be clear what is meant by a 'complex society'.

Notions of 'complexity' are now increasingly popular in sociology, though many of these are adaptations of ideas developed in the natural sciences (for example, Byrne, 1998; Urry, 2003). Some of these are of potentially great value in assessing the characteristics of social reality, and are discussed later in this chapter. None the less, the notion of a 'complex society' that informs much of this chapter draws principally upon a different tradition of thought, though I believe it has much in common with recent scientific perspectives. In Durkheim's work, 'complexity' is an inherent feature of all societies and, therefore, a key concern for sociology. In fact, although he often made distinctions between 'simple' and 'complex' societies, he nevertheless recognised that a society always manifests a 'complex reality' wherein economic, political and philosophical factors have to be grasped in their totality, and analysed in relation to the religious substratum that allows for the emergence of their particular characteristics (Durkheim, 1953: 62; Gane, 1988: 104). For Gurvitch (1971) too, social reality is a complex totality, composed of various 'depth levels' underpinning various forms of sociality characterised by different degrees of institutionalisation, while a similar notion of a 'complex society' has been used by Karl Polanyi (2001) to account for the interrelationship of diverse elements within society, though he views modern societies as being particularly complex since they are often characterised by forms of economic and philosophical reduction-ism that expressly deny the social and religious realities within which they are embedded. In the following discussion, this understanding of social com-plexity not only helps make sense of the partiality of many contemporary critiques of society, but also helps establish the social realist argument that the difficulties and ambiguities surrounding the study of society need not result in responding to complex questions about social life with the easy answers offered by various form of relativism and reductionism.[1]

The chapter progresses as follows. The first two sections deal with the-oretical approaches to society that link notions of a postmodern transfor-mation of the contemporary world to a post-social fragmentation of human relationships; a link that allies notions of 'hyper-reality' to a thoroughly dis-embodied view of human beings. These arguments have had a significant influence upon the post-societal visions of society as an 'archaic' sociologi-cal notion, but also upon the techno-scientific and consumer-oriented analy-ses of society that are discussed in later sections of the chapter. Sociological analyses of the individualistic, morally indifferent or self-interested charac-teristics of contemporary societies are also discussed, however, as influential accounts of societal fragmentation that resist the logic of postmodernism yet appear to render a social realist argument redundant. In the final section, a brief account of sociological appropriations of scientific notions of com-plexity is offered as a way of illuminating how a realist vision of social com-plexity might develop further. Initially, however, the postmodernist idea that society is now shaped by a hyper-reality rather than a hyper-spiritual-ity can be introduced as a particularly influential post-social perspective.

Hyper-real society

I have already noted that, if the conventional view of sociology as 'the study of society' is being challenged on a number of fronts, many of them tend to con-gregate around the idea that 'society' is an arbitrary construct of certain types of sociology, political ideologies and cultural theories, imposed upon the complex, shifting and infinitely variable patterns of social and cultural existence. Postmodernist philosophy offers an influential post-societal perspective built on this type of argument. Its philosophical genealogy can be traced from Nietszche's proclamation of the 'death of God' and his deconstruction of all claims to truth as manifestations of a 'will to power', through Foucault's 'death of Man' and the reduction of reality to competing discourses representing power interests, to Baudrillard's 'death of the social' and the collapse of reality into the 'simulacra' of the 'hyper-real' (Baudrillard, 1990a: 186). What is notable about this genealogy is the pattern of chronic social constructionism it expresses: the illumination of social forces as the medium through which notions of God and Man are con-structed leads eventually to the revelation that the social itself is actually a con-struction too.

Archer (2000: 87) has discussed postmodernism in terms of the tendency to see our social relations as so overpowering that human beings become reduced to infinitely malleable forms that can be shaped according to society. Here, however, the seeds of social constructionism sown by postmodernism reap a whirlwind of arbitrary significations that destroy society itself, so that postmodernism tends to follow a pattern whereby 'society' is reduced into 'culture', and then 'culture' is reduced into 'language', which becomes a game of significations detached from anything real. Not only Baudrillard (1983, 1990a, 1990b), but also Deleuze (1979), Lyotard (1984) and Derrida (1991) have all encouraged a deep scepticism about society following such a pattern, suggesting that society is simply a culturally relative construction that masks the endemic plurality and indeterminacy of human life. Baudrillard's arguments concerning the 'death of the social' are particularly significant in this respect.

Baudrillard (1983: 4) notes that sociology depends upon a 'positive and definitive hypothesis of the social', but considers three possibilities concerning the social that illuminate its non-existence or current dissolution, thereby marking the death of sociology as well as of the notion of the social. These three possibilities are as follows: first, that things have never functioned 'socially' but 'symbolically, magically, irrationally'; second, that the social is some sort of 'residue' now becoming absorbed into the administrative machinery of society; and third, that the social might once have existed but has now vanished into the simulations, circuits and networks of the information age (Baudrillard, 1983: 68, 73, 83). Baudrillard's own position in relation to these three possibilities is not entirely free of ambiguity, but it is generally accepted that the third position characteristically marks his 'anti-sociology' (Bogard, 2000: 240). Within this anti-sociology, the 'social' is displaced by a *simulation* of the social, just as the real has given way to the hyper-real. Here, there is no ontological basis upon which to ground any notion of the real, or any form of knowledge about anything, since there is only radical, chaotic, meaningless contingency. As Gane (2003: 160) suggests, within this condition of hyper-reality, 'events and phenomena follow a delirious course' since the world is now characterised by 'radical indeterminacy' and 'radical uncertainty'.

None the less, Baudrillard's proclamation of the 'death of the social' in the delirious simulations of the hyper-real implicitly offers some sort of 'holistic' vision of the contemporary world, even though he repeatedly emphasises the impossibility of access to meaning, truth or the real. In this regard, it is of note that he identifies theory with a form of 'exorcism' carried out on the world, suggesting some sort of religious world-view lurking underneath his apparent nihilism (Baudrillard, 1988a: 100). Indeed, it has been noted that in Baudrillard's thought, as in much postmodern thinking, there is, arguably, a 'submerged religious paradigm' (Turner, 1990: 10). Baudrillard's work is characterised by a strong dose of nihilism, yet he also aligns himself with the Jesuits of the Counter-Reformation. He argues that, despite accepting the 'death of God', the Jesuits sought to use the glittering, seductive images of the baroque to offer the promise of redemption. Similarly, he advocates a strategy of immersion in the seductive but meaningless 'simulacra' of the hyper-real in an attitude that veers between an 'immoral stoicism and the hope that something redemptive may yet appear' (Wernick, 1992: 69). If this 'submerged religious paradigm' is really there, however, and Baudrillard refuses to say whether it is or not, then it is an extreme form of negative theology that hopes for religious illumination through the deconstruction and rejection of everything that might offer a source or route for it. 'God', 'society' and 'humanity' are just fictional 'totalisations' imposed upon the meaningless flux of life, and none of them has any inherent meaning or reality.

A 'submerged religious paradigm' that can be identified in Baudrillard's work, nevertheless, is what King (2000: 263) has referred to as a reworking of Descartes' 'hyperbolic doubt'. As King suggests, Descartes (1994: 79) imagined that he was in the power of 'some malicious demon' intent on deceiving him through the reality of external things. To counter the demon, Descartes considered all physical, biological and material phenomena in the universe, and even his own flesh and blood, to be delusions, finding certainty only in his own existence (Descartes, 1994: 79). In *Fatal Strategies* (1990b: 72), Baudrillard draws upon Descartes' 'First Meditation', and the 'epistemic void' it opens up, to talk of 'The Evil Genie of the Social', which, like Descartes' 'malicious demon', seeks to mislead Baudrillard by positing some reality in social life (King, 2000: 263). Here, it might be said that Baudrillard is not trying to get to grips with the complexity of the world at all, but simply avoiding it through a Cartesian strategy of assuming that all apparently real phenomena are some sort of evil trick. Indeed, it is Baudrillard's adoption of this strategy for the elaboration of his notion of hyper-reality, along with other epistemologically oriented forms of postmodernism that deny the real, that leads King (2000: 270) to conclude that 'These theories are not serious but merely impose the uncritical sentiments of disillusioned intellectuals onto the social process as a whole, assuming that their own obscure doubts are widely experienced across the whole of society' (see also Bauman, 1988: 223; 1989: 2). A significant feature of these impositions and assumptions concerns the peculiarly disembodied view of human beings.

Disembodied society

Despite the apparent prominence of the body in many forms of postmodern theory, there are no 'real' embodied human beings only the 'simulacra' of being human, because there is no solid ontological foundation for any emergent social and natural phenomena. Gilles Deleuze (1977), for example, talks of the 'affective foundations' of thought, but what he means is that the truth-value of ideas is determined by the level of emotional intensity they stimulate. The embodiment of humans that makes such emotional intensity possible is, however, only a 'complex interplay of highly constructed social and symbolic forces. The body is not an essence, let alone a biological substance; it is a play of forces, a surface of intensities: pure simulacra without originals' (Braidotti, 1994: 112). Theological advocates of postmodern theorising often express similar views. Don Cupitt (1995: 117–20), for example, in attempting to outline a form of theology after the 'end of Truth', argues that the only thing left is *language* and the 'scattering energies' of the body. Here, the 'body' is simply a site for language 'to ride upon or to modulate', since the world is only a 'stream of language-formed events'. Consequently, theology, like philosophy, can only operate as a form of poetry, employing 'evocative metaphors', myths and reflections upon reflections in the eternal meaninglessness of everything. As for 'humanity', it is simply a construction of language.

Rosi Braidotti's philosophical 'nomadism', which embraces myth-making and the generation of imaginative fictions that allow her to 'think through and move across established categories and levels of experience', is an influential example of this reduction of humanity into a theory of language. 'Nomadism' is 'thinking about thinking in a metadiscursive mode', a 'molecularisation of the self' that reduces the body and society to fictional constructs that can be played with endlessly (Braidotti, 1994: 4, 202, 16). Here, given that all social (and even biological) forms are deemed to be devoid of any reality or substance, the idea that a specific hyper-spirituality could emerge and have a transformative impact upon individual identities is clearly particularly unattractive, even if some such collective reality sometimes appears to lurk at the edges of this nomadic myth-making. The dim suggestion of such as reality, along with a clear testimony to a lack of interest in lived social realities, is indicated, in fact, by Braidotti's (1994: 16) suggestions that the 'nomadic, polyglot writer despises mainstream communication', that notions of 'common sense' are a form of mental 'pollution', and that the nomadic philosopher longs not for social bonds but for the 'radical nonbelonging' of the desert.

The fact that such representations of humans, society and the world exist is no doubt significant: as Giddens (1990, 1991a) has suggested, they may reflect the sense of indeterminacy and insecurity associated with periods of rapid social and cultural change. None the less, how seriously should we take them in their own terms? The answer to this appears to lie within the inherent contradictions of postmodern theory itself. The non-viability of a vision of a human existence free of collective 'pollution' in a state of 'radical nonbelonging', for example, is indicated, it can be noted, in Braidotti's (1994: 35) admission that 'it was not until I found some stability and sense of partial belonging, supported by a job and a permanent relationship, that I could actually start thinking adequately about nomadism'. This type of philosophical orientation does not seem able to make the theoretical link, however, between theory and the real comforts and challenges of embodied being. It simply endorses, and embraces with some enthusiasm, ideas about the 'atomisation' of the social into 'flexible networks of language games' (Lyotard, 1984: 17; Deleuze, 1979; see also Baudrillard, 1983; Rose, 1996). Similarly, Cupitt's belief that we can choose a linguistically constructed fiction to live by ignores the fact that this proposes someone able to make such a choice, and also ignores the fact that if everything is linguistically constructed then language itself would collapse (Trigg, 1998: 158–9).

In broad terms, then, although such forms of postmodernism ostensibly challenge the reductive 'imperialism' of modern, rational thought (Deleuze, 1968, 1969), and thereby seek to engage with the world's complexity in a more open, sensitive way, they actually manifest a thoroughly partial vision of social and cultural life that reduces ontological issues into an epistemological 'playing with the pieces' (Archer, 2000: 316). For MacIntyre (1988: 369), in fact, Deleuze's nomadism, which valorises what Durkheim saw as a social pathology, abandons any serious engagement with society for a self-indulgent immersion in ephemera. As Mike Featherstone (1991: 9) has noted, the implication, for those who take such philosophical positions seriously, is that sociological analysis must be abandoned for 'playful deconstruction and the privileging of the aesthetic mode', since to do otherwise would be to perpetuate the 'grand narratives' and fictional 'totalisations' of modern sociology. Here, the rejection of 'society' or the 'social' involves the reduction of sociology into a highly relativistic form of cultural studies (or literary theory), which, amongst other things, makes 'a fetish of difference and diversity' without being able to deal with the realities of day-to-day lives, let alone broader questions and conflicting claims about moral, political and social justice (Turner and Rojek, 2001: 110). The vision of radically unattached individuals 'thinking about thinking' in the linguistically constructed fictions and arbitrary simulations of the real not only ignores the necessities of food, work and companionship, but offers a highly implausible model for social theory since it massively underestimates the degree to which we cannot simply reinvent the world to suit our own wishes, and that, while we elaborate theories of hyper-reality, real people in real societies have to face social, cultural and political pressures upon their capacities to eat, think and act freely, and form associations that will enable their hopes for themselves and their families to flourish rather than wither.

Archaic society

Despite their disregard for what seem to be unavoidable ontological facts about human beings, however, postmodern forms of philosophy have been incorporated into sociological analysis in various forms, and with varying degrees of acceptance of their ultimate logic for sociology and for moral and political critique. In general terms, they have tended to support the view that there has been a proliferation of centrifugal social and cultural processes that make the notion of an overarching society untenable, and that any newly envisaged conception of sociology needs to account for the complex and fluid configurations of peoples and identities that characterise the current era (see Shilling and Mellor, 2001). While some sociological incorporations of postmodern theorising have accepted the whole package of linguistically based relativism, however, more selective incorporations have tended, rather, to draw on postmodern themes and arguments to account for contemporary social and cultural changes. The changes are, however, deemed to be so radical that the 'society' of traditional sociological discourse looks like an archaic remnant of an earlier age of nation-states and tightly bounded social orders.

Smart (2000: 267) has noted that, although he repeatedly talks of the 'death of the social', the status of the term 'society' in Baudrillard's thought is thoroughly ambiguous and under-theorised. In contrast, he notes that Touraine's critique of the notion of society is far more systematic and historically grounded (Smart, 2000: 268–9). None the less, Touraine's (1989, 1995) focus on social movements that render the idea of 'society' meaningless, and Urry's manifesto for 'sociology *beyond* societies', clearly arise out of an engagement with postmodern philosophy. For Touraine (1989: 15), the complex and changing fields of social relations that mark the present seriously compromise any notion of an overarching totality to which individuals understand themselves to belong. Focusing on the need for a sociology of *change*, Touraine (1989: 11) argues that 'the very idea of *society* should be eliminated'. For him, 'individuals are increasingly determined by their movements rather than by their belonging' (Touraine, 1989: 15). Urry's (2000:1) 'manifesto for sociology' also makes the claim that sociologists should abandon the concept of society. He argues that sociology should, instead, be focused on the analysis of 'global networks and flows' since societies, as sociologists have conceived of them, no longer exist.

Urry (2000: 27–8) draws on the 'nomadism' of writers such as Deleuze and Braidotti to reinforce his post-societal vision, but attempts to resist their relativism: he believes that it is possible to clarify and evaluate the empirical claims implicit in such theories, and that the development of 'nomadic consciousness' must depend upon 'corporeal mobility'. For Urry (2000: 33), however, this mobility renders 'the metaphor of society as *region*' useless: in a world where even the 'global' cannot be conceived as a 'region' but as 'network' and 'fluid', the idea of people being identified with, and studied in relation to, a societal region makes no sense. Urry (2000: 36) argues that these global flows produce a 'hollowing out of existing societies', producing overlapping, disjunctive orders across time and space in 'a kind of hypertextual patterning'. Consequently, we now 'inhabit an indeterminate, ambivalent and semiotic risk culture where the risks are in part generated by the declining powers of societies in the face of multiple "inhuman" global flows and multiple networks' (Urry, 2000: 37).

It is within this essentially postmodernist vision of a 'hypertextual', 'indeterminate, ambivalent and semiotic risk culture' that Urry draws on complexity theories developed in the natural sciences. In this regard it is notable that he relies heavily on Reed and Harvey (1992), but does not fully integrate their interest in emergent patterns of order into his own arguments. For example, where he considers an 'emergent global order' he immediately defines it as 'constant disorder' (Urry, 2000: 208). In fact, the only real source of order he acknowledges within his account of complexity is in relation to the notion of the 'network', in the sense that a 'dynamical net' can serve to channel 'the messy power of complexity' into particular directions (see Kelly, 1995: 25–6). In a later work, *Global Complexity*, Urry (2003: 21) pays greater attention to Priogine and Stengers's (1984: 292) interest in emergent order, but focuses heavily on the idea of 'islands of new order in a sea of disorder'. Consequently, while in this book he is led to offer more cautious arguments concerning the disappearance of society and the decline of the nation-state he still tends to interpret these manifestations of order in terms of 'chaotic effects' (Urry, 2003: 106–8).

Following from this, perhaps, his account of some major 'emergent' phenomena in this global (dis)order tends to be an account of *unintended and unpredictable consequences* rather than 'emergence' as such. Thus, the immense social, technological and cultural significance of the Internet is an unintended consequence of its development for military purposes, global warming is an unintended consequence of driving, and the growth of religious fundamentalism is an unintended consequence of the global spread of Western consumerism (Urry, 2000: 208–9; see also Beck, 2000). Aside from the fact that even ardent devotees of the 'cultural turn' in sociology might baulk at the idea of explaining religious fundamentalism as an epiphenomenon of consumerism, it can also be noted that such a vision of a radically disordered and disorienting world where *anything can happen* finds no justification in complexity theory (Byrne, 1998), and none in social realism, since it lacks a systematic engagement with ontology. Indeed, radical indeterminism, the putative non-existence of society, and the peculiarly disembodied vision of social agency are all linked.

There is an ambiguity in Urry's account concerning whether society is a 'metaphor' or a real phenomenon, albeit with 'declining powers'. The issue of agency is also problematic, given that the importance of corporeal mobility is stressed alongside 'inhuman' flows and networks. In fact, Urry (2000: 14) argues that 'the concept of agency needs to be embodied', but simultaneously suggests that 'there is no autonomous realm of human agency'. Thus, he draws attention to the significance of the senses in relation to the emergence of distinctly modern forms of life and to the experience of contemporary post-societal 'flows and mobilities', but distinguishes this from the assertion of any specifically human society, reality, essence or powers in a world where *inhuman* objects constitute social relations through phenomena such as technologies, texts and machines (Urry, 2000: 14, 77; 2003: 56). For Urry (2000: 15–16), the idea of a 'human agency' that produces a 'social reality' is absurd: 'the ordering of social life is presumed to be contingent, unpredictable, patterned and irreducible to human subjects'.

The only things that appear to have a real existence in this post-societal vision are *machines*: transportation systems, cable and wireless networks, microwave channels, satellites and the Internet are the 'scapes' that 'constitute various interconnected nodes along which the flows can be relayed' (Urry, 2000: 35). 'Real human beings' are no more than ghosts in these machines, which means, for example, that Urry's examination of the notion of citizenship in a post-societal era ('a citizenship of flow') has to skirt around the absence of any ontological foundation for the balance of rights and duties he seems to believe is desirable: if everything is just a series of technologically determined 'flows', and notions of 'humanity' and 'society' are simply outmoded metaphors, then who can say whether one set of social and political arrangements is better than another, and why should we care? Furthermore, it is notable that, although religious issues are hardly mentioned by Urry, his brief references to the Islamic *jihad* against the West suggest that fundamentalist organisations should be seen as 'virtual communities' constructed through cultural discourses and media images (Urry, 2000: 43, 209; see Barber, 1995; Rose, 1996). Here, Al-Qaida is not an embodiment of a radicalised interpretation of Islam, but a 'chaotic' phenomenon representative of the 'emergent global fluid of international terrorism' (Urry, 2003: 132). This easy association of social movements with fashionable notions of virtuality and global 'fluids', which puts Muslim terrorists on a par with New Age newsgroups, is surely a massive simplification of the real social dynamics, and their distinctive hyper-spiritualities, that lead people to identify with such forms. In denying a specifically human agency, it also means that we cannot even begin to consider why such people might be prepared to die, and to kill others, because of the religious values their membership of a particular community entails. Furthermore, such easy associations tend to endorse those forms of social and cultural theory that appear to engage creatively with scientific and technological developments, but effectively abandon any attempt to grapple with social complexity by adopting forms of technological reductionism.

Techno-society

Craig Calhoun (1998: 380) has noted that the excitement of new technology can lead researchers to start with computer-mediated communication and then look for communities associated with it, rather than studying the role of computers and other communications media within communities that already exist. Following this, as Christopher May (2002: 85) suggests, calling communities that have a presence on the Internet 'virtual communities' ignores the degree to which face-to-face encounters, pre-existing traditions and networks, and enduring forms of social solidarity can be much more important than electronic communications media. This excitement about technology is a characteristic feature of many writings about the 'information society'. These writings do not tend to reject the notion of 'society' *per se*, but offer visions of a reconstruction of social and cultural life that is so radical that classical sociological notions of society and humanity have to be abandoned. Daniel Bell's (1974, 1980) account of the increased significance of scientific, technological and informational processes in 'post-industrial society', and Touraine's (1969) arguments concerning the emergence of a new class structure based on the control of knowledge and information in the 'programmed society', were influential early attempts to make sense of this reconstruction.

Where Touraine offered a critical vision of the dehumanising aspects of contemporary social and cultural changes, however, more recent accounts of the information society have exhibited what Calhoun (2000: 47) has called a 'failure of imagination' in their presentation of such changes as *inevitable*. As David Lyon (1988: 8) has suggested, a common orientation that has developed in accounts of the information society is that of *techno-logical determinism*, where human beings have to adapt to changes brought about by technological and scientific developments, resulting in new social and cultural processes and patterns. As he suggests, the danger here is that moral and philosophical questions about the 'human condition' become displaced by assumptions about the technological possibilities of social engi-neering (Lyon, 1988: 158; see also Webster, 1995). Similarly, May (2002: 21) identifies in notions of the information society a 'shift from engagement to passive accommodation ... by presenting these changes as epochal rather than merely taking place *within* contemporary society'. The notion of an 'information age', like that of a 'postmodern age', in fact, thereby manifests a neglect of enduring questions about being human in favour of a focus on novel, large-scale transformations to which people simply must adapt.

Castells's (1996, 1997, 1998) work on the information society is instructive in this regard: he is critical of a number of aspects of 'the infor-mation age', including its tendencies towards social fragmentation and the commercialisation of communication, but none the less believes that poli-tics outside the new communications media is now impossible, and that the powers of individual states necessarily wither in the face of global informa-tion networks (May, 2002: 34, 94, 120). Furthermore, technology now reconfigures time and space. Castells (2000: 15) recognises that 'networks are very old forms of social organisation', but argues that in the information age they have taken on new life 'by becoming information networks, pow-ered by new information technologies'. These networks are characterised by 'timeless time' and the 'space of flows': past, present and future occur in random sequences, and meanings, identities and functions are no longer tied to particular places or localities (Castells, 2000: 13–14).

Thus, the technologically induced reconfiguration of the social also involves a reconfiguration of the human. For Castells, social networks now operate on the basis of humans who are configured like computers and, as such, have no means to make a necessary linkage between knowledge and experience: 'The autonomous ability to reprogramme one's own personal-ity' becomes the dominant mode of identity-construction in 'a culture of real virtuality', 'where all symbols coexist without reference to experience' (Castells, 2000: 21). This is how it is that the Internet becomes the princi-pal metaphor for the contingent, fluid character of contemporary social life (Urry, 2000: 40–1): we can talk about an 'information *society*' if we wish, but the notion of society has been stripped of much of its distinctively human content in favour of the 'programmes', 'nodes', 'grids', 'networks', 'virtuali-ties' and 'hypertexts' of communications technologies. In so far as people figure at all, they are disembodied 'minds' assimilating codes of information and images of representation (Castells, 1997: 84). In this respect it is notable that Castells touches upon *knowledge* and *experience*, but does not grapple with *being*, which might encourage him to question the extent of this transformation of human beings and societies, or, at least, to grasp more fully the de-humanising aspects of some of the processes he considers.[2]

Paul Virilio's (2000) analysis of these developments, on the other hand, while it shares elements of Castells's approach, offers a much more robust critique of contemporary developments, particularly with regard to their dehumanising consequences. Furthermore, he links dehumanising processes with a *corruption* of knowledge that alienates us from our own being rather than simply talking about the circulation of knowledge within technologically constructed domains. In fact, Weber's (1991) concerns about modern science as a stimulus to the dominance of instrumental over value-rational action is multiplied several times over in Virilio's (2000: 1) view of twentieth-century science's 'pursuit of *limit performances*, to the detriment of any effort to discover a coherent truth useful to humanity' (italics in original). Quoting Rabelais's view that 'Science without conscience is mere ruination of the soul', Virilio (2000: 2–4) argues that 'techno-science' is 'gradually wrecking the scholarly resources of all knowledge' as it abandons intellectual adventure for technological adventurism, testing limits for the sake of testing limits: *extreme science*, which now shares a cultural kinship with 'extreme sports', has no connection to any notion of the 'common good'.

For Virilio, this absence of any connection between techno-science and common, human values is relentlessly enforced by the way in which global networks of information increasingly disconnect us from the Earth, bringing about 'an end of geography', as time and space become warped by the cybernetic interactivity of the contemporary world (Virilio, 2000: 9). Within this cybernetic reconstruction of reality, the *global* becomes the centre of things and the *local* the periphery, as virtual geography starts to dominate the real dimensions of the Earth (Virilio, 2000: 10). This domination is apparent in the construction of Internet communities, where the 'neighbourhood unit' is no longer local, but an elective, global association mediated by technology (Virilio, 2000: 59). Such communities operate on the basis of a 'tele-presence', rather than an embodied encounter with others, across virtual time and space.

This lack of an embodied co-presence in our encounters with others means that we are increasingly deprived of our sensuality, and that our old 'animal body' is increasingly out of place in this emerging symbiosis between technology and the human (Virilio, 2000: 40). As Virilio (1997: 20) expresses it, 'getting closer to the 'distant' takes you away proportionately from the 'near' (and dear) – the friend, the relative, the neighbour – thus making strangers, if not actual enemies, of all who are close at hand'. In other words, the whole phenomenology of our embodied encounters with others is not only being displaced by new, virtual encounters, but also these invert, if not destroy, conventional social patterns. The phenomenon of 'cybersex' is an extreme example of this process of divesting human interaction of its embodied basis. Like a 'universal condom', offering contact without contact, cybersex turns an act of the flesh, and an exchange of bodily fluids, into a virtual exchange of information where physicality is reduced to an act of 'remote-control masturbation' (Virilio, 1997: 104). These 'teletechnologies of remote love' are, furthermore, harbingers of a radical reconstruction of male/female relationships and patterns of reproduction. Changes in the relationships between men and women are evident in the fact that 'mutual repulsion is already winning out over attraction, over sexual seduction', as accusations of 'sexual harassment' and serial divorces increasingly mark contemporary sexual relations, but the uncomplicated pleasures of virtual sex, with a technologically created ideal man or woman, threaten to push this divergence of the sexes further. The implications of this for reproduction are immense, not simply in the sense that such developments can be read as 'a furtive form of *remote birth control*', but because of their broader rejection of embodied human love, and the family descendants it engenders (Virilio, 1997: 108–9, emphasis in original).

In broad terms, these developments signal a loss of faith in the *social* and its hyper-spiritual dynamics; a loss of faith also exemplified, and sometimes celebrated, in the more nihilistic elements of postmodern philosophy. This postmodern view, however, is strongly opposed by Virilio, who reasserts the importance of the social in the face of Baudrillard's nihilism, and rejects the concept of 'simulation' in favour of that of 'substitution' (Armitage, 2000: 43). For Virilio, there is no collapse between representation and the real, only the substitution of a virtual reality (with its own, technologically mediated, representations) for the flesh and blood reality of human interaction. This substitution is also, however, a *religious* substitution: the collapse of the social is tied to the gradual elimination of traditional forms of the sacred from the contemporary world, and the emergence of techno-science as a new, surrogate religion. This idea expresses the more apocalyptic strand of Virilio's thought.

As Lyon (1988: 144) notes, new technologies have been infused with religious symbolism at least since the time of Francis Bacon, whose *New Atlantis* (1627) proposed that science and technology could be the means for overcoming the human 'fall' from God's grace. None the less, the immense power, fascination and excitement that technology now seems to hold for many people, added to its capacity to substitute virtuality for reality, expresses for Virilio a new religious form in which nobody can 'behave like unbelievers'. The only way to counter this technological religion is to choose the 'god of transcendence' over the 'machine-god', since all atheists now bow before the miracles of techno-science (Virilio, 1996: 81). This religious rebellion is difficult, however, in a world where genuine religion, along with humanity and society, are being systematically eliminated (Virilio and Lotringer, 1997: 124).

In contrast to many techno-society theorists, then, Virilio's vision is a passionate, immensely powerful depiction of the contemporary *human* lot, which does not simply accept contemporary technologically driven social and cultural changes as inevitable, let alone desirable. Furthermore, in contrast with much postmodern theory, he does not doubt that embodied human beings, natural and transcendental realities, and society have onto-logical substance to them. Likewise, there is a keen sense of the moral capac-ities and potentialities of humans that informs his work, and stimulates the outrage he expresses in relation to many aspects of techno-science. What he shares with writers such as Castells and Urry, none the less, is the belief that a radical reconstruction of such things is taking place. Thus, what alarms him is the dehumanisation, disembodiment and moral anaesthetisation that is now, he believes, accompanying the substitution of virtuality for reality.

The power of Virilio's analysis is evident when we consider those med-ical and scientific practitioners who appear to take a professional pride in leaving others to assess the moral consequences of their actions, those tech-nological developments that encourage people to ignore those around them in pursuit of electronically mediated pleasures and projects, and those changes in military technology that give the annihilation of civilians the appearance of video games. And yet, as challenging and genuinely illumi-nating as this vision is, it tends to underestimate the abilities of people to resist such processes, and the sheer impossibility of this virtual substitution proceeding beyond a certain point. With regard to the former, it can be noted that everyday acts of solidarity, sociability and moral responsibility mark many people's lives, including that of Virilio himself: although his Christian faith has a highly elusive presence in his writings, in his daily life he is closely involved with the Catholic worker-priest movement, working with the poor and the homeless. With regard to the latter, it can be noted that even the electronically mediated thrills of 'cybersex' depend on a sen-suous, material body able to experience arousal and orgasm. Furthermore, Virilio's vision of a world where a real, embodied proximity is being trans-muted into a virtual cyberworld sometimes reflects a social constructionist aspect to his thought that sits uncomfortably alongside his more fundamen-tal convictions about the nature of human beings and the world. Thus, his declaration that 'reality is produced by a society's culture' (Virilio, 1997: 107; Armitage, 2000: 43), contradicts his critique of Lyotard, where he asserts that certain 'grand narratives', such as 'justice', cannot be seen as cul-turally relative constructions (Armitage, 2000: 39).

Consumptive society

I have already noted the connection between Virilio's vision of techno-science and Weber's concerns about the spread of instrumental forms of rationality at the expense of value-rationality. A further influential set of social theories concerned with the 'hollowing out' of society focus more specifically upon this instrumentalism and, rather than seeing social life as technologically driven, tend to see it as increasingly determined by patterns of homogenisation, rationalisation and an economically driven con-sumerism. George Ritzer's (1993, 1998) account of the 'McDonaldization' of society is an influential account of these processes. Alongside 'McDonaldization', however, consumerism has also been associated with a religious pattern of 're-enchantment' rather than a consolidation of the 'disenchantment' Weber associated with the spread of instrumental rationalisation (Ferguson, 1992; Ritzer, 1999; Lyon, 2000). This religious dimension of consumerism is expressed through emotional identifications with powerful symbols in 'cathedrals of consumption', but lacks the moral seriousness of traditional religious forms and their engagement with human potentiality and finitude. Taking both of these aspects of consumerism together, in fact, it is possible to talk not only of a *consuming* society, but also of a *consumptive* society in the sense that such processes can be associated with a chronic enfeeblement of society as a context for human flourishing.

'McDonaldization' is not simply the application of highly rationalised methods of production, distribution and consumption to the fast-food industry, but the spread of these into society as a whole: 'After the McDonaldization of the fast-food industry, these principles have been applied to universities and medicine. McDentists and McDoctors extends the principles of cheapness, standardisation and reliability to the health industry' (Turner and Rojek, 2001: 108). For Ritzer (1998: 68), contemporary capitalism is now geared towards the 'maximisation of consumption', and the spread of efficient, rationally organised and standardised products which, even if they are focused on 'niche' markets, ensure that consumers are guaranteed 'safe', predictable goods, services and experiences. Thus, 'action holidays', for example, are actually carefully ordered simulations of adventure and danger pre-packaged for consumers who desire efficient and controlled breaks from their daily routine (Ritzer, 1998: 146; see Bauman, 2002: 197).

Bryan Turner and Chris Rojek (2001: 219) illuminate some of the embodied aspects of living in 'McSociety' when they note the McDonaldization of maternity units in public hospitals, where the labour of mothers is organised in a highly rationalised manner, expressing an underlying Cartesian view of the body as a machine. This suggests a connection to the values of techno-science discussed by Virilio, but also to the postmodern global networks discussed by Castells and Urry. As Lyon (2000: 78) notes, McDonald's is 'part of the accelerated compression of time and space which is characteristic of the postmodern'. While Barber's (1995) depiction of the confrontation between Islamic *jihad* and 'McWorld' indicates the power of these McDonaldization processes, however, the idea that they have no religious dimension in and of themselves has been challenged. Ritzer (1999: 7) notes that McDonald's and other globally recognised brands such as Disney, have become some of the world's 'most powerful icons', and are part of the re-'enchantment of a disenchanted world' through consumerism. Here, consumerism rather than Virilio's 'machine-god' becomes the dominant religious form of contemporary societies, though it offers little other than a transient stimulation of the senses and the promise of a certain amount of security, predictability and order to human life. More fundamental existential, ontological and moral questions remain unanswered. As Ritzer (1999: 217) is aware, in fact, for all the talk of 'cathedrals of consumption' and the 'enchantment' of goods and services 'the most immediate issue is how to live a more meaningful life within a society increasingly defined by consumption'.

In this respect, Lyon's (2000: 84) suggestion that consumerist patterns of consumption manifest a form of the 'Durkheimian sacred' needs to be qualified. These patterns, which can be associated with the stimulation of a range of emotional responses attached to powerful symbols, and to patterns of identification with others in relation to these symbols, clearly manifest something of the social energies and processes Durkheim (1995) associates with religion. Yet they do not offer much in the way of an engagement with the desires, struggles and limitations that characterise our mortal, embodied condition, and cannot convincingly be presented as manifestations of society's 'profoundest being'. In short, these 'cathedrals of consumption' make unconvincing 'nurseries of *meaningful life*', and the promise of 'redemption through consumption' soon wears thin (Campbell, 1987; Falk, 1994; Bauman, 2001).

This is not to say, as Stjepan Mestrovic (1997: 107) has done, that such phenomena are simply *imitations* of the 'authentically' religious processes analysed by Durkheim: his notion of a 'postemotional society' presupposes a highly implausible reconstruction of human embodiment wherein the experience of 'authentic' emotion is no longer possible, at least collectively. Rather, what such phenomena suggest is that hyper-spiritual aspects of social life emergent from human interactions reappear even in contexts that appear to be highly rationally planned and ordered, but that such contexts facilitate their rational manipulation for economic purposes. The rationally organised manipulation of sensuous experiences of the sacred is not new, of course, and is a key feature of the baroque cultures that developed in seventeenth-century Catholic societies (Mellor and Shilling, 1997: 132). None the less, the transient pleasures of consumerism are a vastly different phenomenon to the eschatological visions of Counter-Reformation Catholicism and, as Colin Campbell (1987) suggests, offer little in the way of overall guidelines about how to consume, let alone how to live and die. In fact, Bauman (2002: 182) has noted that consumerism serves to distract individuals from serious questions about human life and destiny rather than to stimulate reflections on questions of limitations and transcendence: it transforms *distraction*, which was 'once an individually contrived hideout from fate, into the socially constructed lot'. In this regard, the peculiarity of contemporary consumerism is that it strives to emancipate consumption from past instrumentality and functional bonds, which were mainly to do with survival, in favour of a new plasticity of 'needs' that can be endlessly reconstructed (Bauman, 2002: 183).

Unseaworthy society

Bauman's (2002) account of 'society under siege' not only offers a thoughtful analysis of the de-humanising distractions offered by consumerism, despite its 'religious' characteristics, but also offers clues to the appeal of that peculiar blend of *determinism* and *voluntarism* that characterises much postmodernist, post-societal and techno-scientific thought. Discussing the 'until-further-notice' character of the relationships, forms of work, patterns of belief and action, social arrangements and commitments that appear to characterise contemporary societies, he identifies a lack of trust as a key feature of our current disposition towards the world: 'Whoever chains themselves to an unseaworthy vessel risks going down with it at the next tide. By comparison, surfing seems a safer option' (Bauman, 2002: 193). Here, it is accepted that the 'next tide' (of relentless social, cultural, economic or political change) will inevitably come and that there is nothing we can do to stop it (determinism), but it is also accepted that people can teach themselves to adapt to, and make the best of, these transformations (voluntarism). Surfing, of course, although it can be done in the company of others, is an individual pursuit, so that, in so far as we can talk of a 'society' in relation to such activity it is, necessarily, an 'individualised society' (Bauman, 2001). In these circumstances, society as a *sui generis* phenomenon transcendent of individuals is simply 'an unseaworthy vessel' it would be foolish to commit ourselves to: if it has not yet sunk in the tides of change, it can only be a matter of time.

Bauman (2002: 191) suggests that such a situation contrasts starkly with Durkheim's (1972: 93–4) view of society where we 'believe that our actions have consequences which go beyond the immediate moment: that they are not completely limited to the point in time and space at which they are produced'. Now, in so far as we experience 'society', it 'makes itself present to most of us mediated by occasions which do not necessarily connect into continuous and coherent experience', so that 'society' becomes just a 'summary name' for the diverse, often disconnected phenomena of our social encounters and experiences. In fact, contrary to Durkheim's view that our lives in society give us a sense of things that outlive us as individuals, the uncomfortable fact now is that we tend to outlive particular forms of society: 'My life may be too short for comfort, but the lifespan of anything else seems disconcertingly brief by comparison' (Bauman, 2002: 192–3). Giddens's (1991a) account of the pervasiveness of threats to 'ontological security', including 'radical doubt' and a collapse into 'personal meaninglessness', also expresses a sense of the difficulties of living in such a social context.

Giddens's (1990, 1991a) account of the chronically 'reflexive society' of 'high' or 'late' modernity and Ulrich Beck's (1992) depiction of contemporary 'risk society' share many similar features with Bauman's analysis, though they focus in more detail on how this transient, 'until-further-notice' aspect of contemporary societies permeates institutional as well as individual characteristics. At an institutional level, social organisations become 'disembedded' from their local contexts to emerge as 'abstract systems' that are organised across 'indefinite tracts of time-space' and are driven by expert 'knowledges' such as science and medicine (Giddens, 1991a: 18). The abstract and 'all-encompassing' nature of these systems means that they have to be reflexively maintained, but also that they encourage a further spread of reflexivity, particularly given that these systems tend to generate new risks, dilemmas and fears as well as promises that they can control natural and social environments (Beck, 1992: 22). At the individual level, Giddens's notion of 'confluent love' is intended to exemplify the importance of reflexivity in intimate relationships. The inherently fragile, transient character of these relationships is understood to be indicative of the broader 'until-further-notice' character of reflexively defined projects. Close personal ties, like everything else, are entered into, and maintained, only for the benefits they offer to individuals (Giddens, 1991a: 89). Here, 'love' is simply a 'codifying force' for organising the competing, reflexively determined pursuit of emotional and sexual satisfaction by the individuals involved.

This thoroughgoing institutional and individual reflexivity is associated with the 'future-oriented' character of modernity which means all beliefs, values, social practices and forms of knowledge can be altered, revised or abandoned in the light of reflexive adaptations to changed circumstances (Giddens, 1990; Beck, 1992; Luhmann, 1998). For Giddens (1990: 38), modernity and tradition are incompatible, since tradition is 'past-oriented' and vulnerable to deconstruction through reflexively applied knowledge: in fact, what appears to us as tradition in the present has often been so thoroughly reconstructed through reflexivity that it is merely 'tradition in sham clothing'. Consequently, religion, which is closely tied to tradition, also tends to become increasingly irrelevant to contemporary life. It might have some value for some individuals grappling with existential problems, but this value is arrived at through a reflexive reconstruction of religion in the light of contemporary needs and circumstances (Giddens, 1990: 109). Religious fundamentalism, for example, is merely one of a number of 'lifestyle decisions' (Giddens, 1991a: 143).

Although Giddens (1991a: 179) notes the arguments of Rieff (1966), who argued that therapy had come to replace religion as the dominant form of social control in modern societies, his own understanding of religion is essentially psychoanalytic, and built on the views of Freud (1962) and Erikson (1965), for whom religion offered an infantile protection from the harsh realities of life (Giddens, 1990: 104). In fact, Giddens (1991a: 195) offers an essentially Freudian reading of 'premodern' life as a world of coherent fantasies that protected people from life's unpredictability. This is why, for Giddens, despite all the 'radical doubt' and reflexively induced meaninglessness, living in modernity is ultimately a liberating experience full of all sorts of potentialities and opportunities as well as risks. While Bauman, who has a far more sceptical view of the 'therapeutic' dimensions of contemporary societies, worries about an 'individualised society' where people surf across social and cultural changes with little sense of their moral proximity to others, Giddens (1991a: 211) suggests that such phenomena are the latest stages in the post-Enlightenment liberation of individuals from traditional constraints, and is happy to present them in terms of the development of 'emancipatory politics'.

It is in this context that Giddens's (1990: 64) suggestion that sociologists have placed far too much emphasis on 'society' makes sense: he rejects the concern with a 'bounded system' because he is more concerned with the fluid dynamics through which patterns of social life can be reconstructed. In contrast to much postmodernist theory, however, this does not result in a nihilistic social constructionism because his psychoanalytic influences encourage him to see such constructions as potentially liberating. Thus, he suggests that 'The more we reflexively "make ourselves" as persons, the more the very category of what a "person" or "human being" is comes to the fore' (Giddens, 1991a: 217). Indeed, he believes that through such a pattern of reflexive construction we can recover 'moral/existential problems' sequestrated in earlier periods of modernity, and can reconnect with Heidegger's 'question of Being' concerning how existence itself should be grasped and 'lived' (Giddens, 1991a: 224).

A significant problem with Giddens's notion of 'being', however, is that he operates with a mind/body dualism which means that people are *essentially* minds for most of their lives, organising self-narratives and broader patterns of world construction through reflexive patterns of cognition, while embodiment in a broader sense only tends to become significant when there is a breakdown of these reflexive attempts at meaning construction (Shilling and Mellor, 1996). This cognitive orientation allows him to reinforce Winnicott's (1965) psychological view of childhood as a state of 'going-on being' rather than 'being', meaning that a sense of being has to be *socially constructed* with the help of a child's 'caretakers' (Giddens, 1991a: 39). If this is so, however, then it is difficult to see how the more we reflexively 'make ourselves' the more likely we are to reconnect with 'being' in any real sense. On the contrary, all we can 'connect with' is a more or less satisfying social construction of 'being', with 'ontological security' rather than any real, ontological grounds of human being. It also follows from this that the 'reality' of society is always doubtful too: society is only a construction that, in premodern contexts at least, provided comforting fictions to shield people from existential difficulties. This makes sense of his essentially contractual understanding of social relationships: as in the case of 'confluent love', we form relationships and make psychological investments in other people in so far as they help us to construct a meaningful and satisfying narrative about ourselves and the world. Just as there is no hyper-spiritual aspect to love, so too there is no hyper-spiritual aspect to social life in general.

For Bauman (2002: 53), however, there are 'transcendental conditions of human togetherness', and the problematisation of these in contemporary societies is a real problem, rather than a liberating source of 'emancipatory politics', because, without them, notions such as justice cannot mean anything and the inherent moral capacities of individuals are not allowed to develop and to be expressed. The reflexive, transient and future-oriented character of contemporary life anaesthetises people's moral impulses and responsibilities, and encourages people to avoid taking responsibility for their behaviour (Bauman and Tester, 2001). The moral consequences of our choices and actions seem to disappear into a game of solitaire that can be evaluated as narcissistic and inherently anti-social (Bauman, 1993: 178–9). In fact, the amoral subjects that have come to populate the contemporary era are exemplified by Bauman's typologies of contemporary individuals: the 'vagabond' and the 'tourist' are concerned with their own interests and possess little grasp of the notions of moral proximity and moral responsibility (Bauman, 1993: 142; see Shilling and Mellor, 2001: 194). For Bauman (2002: 42), the images of 'closeness, proximity, togetherness, a degree of intimacy and mutual engagement' that surrounded sociological uses of society not only now look archaic, but also point towards things we cannot believe in because they are no longer embedded in our daily lives.

For Bauman, debates about the disappearance of 'society' cannot be reduced to arguments about sociological terminology: there are moral issues at stake. None the less, his position, articulated with a significant amount of regret, is simply that the world has *changed*, and that sociology must therefore change too, which means abandoning notions of society that may have had real referents in the past but no longer do so. This stress on the need to think carefully about the appropriateness of sociological theories for making sense of contemporary changes is also made by Touraine (1989: 5), who argues that sociological interpretations of social life must change along with the realities they are trying to grasp. Contrary to some post-societal theorists, however, Bauman finds little to celebrate in the 'death of society' that appears to have followed the 'death of God', and even offers us a (faint) hope in its resurrection in the lives and works of men and women who are able to resist the de-humanisation of the present time (Bauman, 2002: 51; see Arendt, 1995).

The mantra of 'no salvation by society' that Bauman (2001: 5) identifies as a key sign of contemporary 'individualised' society testifies to the power of this pattern of dehumanisation. In fact, his analysis of a post-societal form of 'liquid modernity' rests on recognition of the pervasiveness of a crude utilitarianism that, combined with the cultural relativism of postmodernism, serves to impoverish human aspirations and undermine the possibility of human solidarity (Bauman, 2002). Nevertheless, the positive endorsement of this utilitarianism, rather than its critique, underpins another influential post-societal perspective, which seeks to reduce social life to a series of 'markets'.

Market society

Contrary to various arguments suggesting that the notion of society is outmoded, the market-oriented post-societal perspective suggests that it has never referred to anything real anyway. This is not because this view endorses postmodernist relativism or technological determinism, or even that it endorses a view of modern reflexivity that makes social life uniquely problematic, but because it grounds all social phenomena very firmly in a robust view of self-interested, 'rational' individuals.[3] Drawing on the utilitarian tradition of philosophy and economics, rational choice theory urges the subordination of the notion of *homo sociologicus*, which emphasises the influence of society upon individuals, to the notion of *homo economicus*, which views individuals as having the innate power to make 'rational' decisions about what best serves their self-interests, and the ability to act accordingly. In Durkheim's time, opposition to *homo economicus* was integral to the project of establishing sociology, yet rational choice theory offers an 'economic approach to human behaviour' with philosophical roots in the work of Thomas Hobbes, Adam Smith and Jeremy Bentham, and is particularly hostile to the Durkheimian focus on the transpersonal dimensions of social life. George Homans, for example, argues that the 'social system' is a myth, that 'structures' never do anything, and that sociology's unit of analysis should be the actions of individuals engaged in processes of 'preference maximising exchange'. Social contexts and structures, values, beliefs, habits, emotions, and religious choices are all explained as products of rational, individual, 'utility maximisation'. Social order is simply the *aggregation* of the actions of rational individuals (Coleman, 1990; Abell, 1991; Bohman, 1991; Scott, 1995: 86; Iannaccone, 1997).

In some cases, this focus on the determining power of rational choices is so strong that even basic biological limits to human life are swept away. Gary Becker (1986: 116), for example, suggests that nearly all deaths can be understood as 'suicides', in the sense that death results from individuals making choices about actions that fail to ensure their longevity. This is not simply where a particular choice (for example, to smoke) results in a particular cause of death (for example, lung cancer), but is a rule that can be applied universally: even if I reach a hundred years before I die, my death can be 'explained' as a result of rational choices not to do things (for example, eat well, take exercise) and to do other things (eat too much/too little, take too much/not enough exercise). While Becker is content to reduce such matters of life and death to utility maximisation, Stark and Bainbridge (1987) extend this logic to life after death too. Viewing individuals as 'information-processors' who identify problems and seek to solve them, they note that many rewards (such as immortality) are apparently beyond reach. Religious beliefs in life after death, however, can act as 'compensators' for such elusive rewards, and therefore offer a potentially sound investment. Iannaccone's (1997) view that investing in a religion is not, in essence, any different to investing in a new house or car follows the same logic. He suggests, furthermore, that 'religious consumers and religious producers form a *religious market*', and that religious producers (for example, the Churches) necessarily 'abandon inefficient modes of production and unpopular products in favour of more attractive and profitable alternatives' (Iannaccone, 1997: 27).

As Polanyi (2001) and, more recently, Archer (2000) have suggested, the rational choice picture of people as self-oriented utility maximisers owing nothing to society rests on a particularly impoverished notion of what it is to be a human. While individuals appear to have a great deal of power, and a strong sense of their own self-interest, they are stripped of many of the emotional, moral and imaginative aspects of what it is to be human, they are deemed incapable of acting in a genuinely altruist way, and, since they appear to emerge from the womb with all their preferences and rational faculties fully formed, are apparently devoid of the capacity to develop. The 'market model' of religion offered by rational choice theory expresses this reduction of human potentiality particularly clearly: in suggesting that I might become a member of a church because I make a rational choice to 'invest' in its 'product' with the 'calculation' that, at some point (even if after death), I can anticipate a 'profit', it not only rules out the possibility of an encounter with something transcendent that might transform my desires and expectations, but also, in making economic calculation the keystone of the universe, offers an astonishingly impoverished view of the human lot. In this perspective, when we all eventually commit 'suicide', as Becker would have it, anyone trying to assess what kind of life we actually lived can only look at our cost–benefit balance sheets and hope we can show a profit.

Rethinking society

Although the 'market society' theorists appear to offer a robust challenge to the social constructionism central to notions of the 'hyper-real society', they actually display similar weaknesses in terms of a failure to offer a balanced account of the embodied capacities of humans and the emergence of collective social forms. In rational choice theory, there is a very strong emphasis on the inherent nature of individual human beings, conceptualised as a capacity for selecting courses of action that maximise self-interest (Becker, 1986; Coleman, 1990). Yet, this not only necessitates the disappearance of society into the realm of 'aggregation effects' and 'markets' (Abell, 1996), but also robs humanity of anything other than the ability to act 'rationally' in relation to self-interest. Erotic, psychological and moral motivations are excluded from analysis (Olson, 1965: 61), while phenomena such as altruism are explained as self-interest in disguise (Shilling and Mellor, 2001: 177). Consequently, although rational choice theory has produced some influential studies of religion, its reductive view of humans, and replacement of societies with markets, means that the 'religion' it envisages has no connection with a societal hyper-spirituality, and, therefore, has nothing to do with any collective engagement with the possibilities of transcendence inherent within the contingencies of life, only the self-interested attempt to maximise 'benefits' and minimise 'costs'.

On the other hand, the idea that individual identities and, indeed, reality in general are constructed by society, which has achieved a great deal of consensus in sociology, appears to offer a very strong emphasis on the importance of society. Ironically, however, this not only allows the disappearance of 'real human beings' in a flurry of social constructionism, but also robs 'society' of any real substance. If society is everything, then it is nothing in particular. This explains how it is that Urry (2000: 201–2) can see 'humanity' and 'nature' as social constructions, yet also deny any reality to 'society' (see also Strathern, 1998). It also accounts for the emergence, and sociological appeal, of postmodernist forms of philosophy. In this regard,

Baudrillard's (1983) vision of the 'end of the social', where all reality vanishes into the arbitrary significations of 'hyper-reality', is not a radical critique of this sociological consensus but its logical outcome. As with rational choice theory, furthermore, the apparent resurgence in interest in religious matters actually robs religion of any real social or human significance: playing around with religious myths and stories can express a creative response to indeterminate pluralism, but, since it cannot be grounded in anything real, religion, like humanity and society, becomes lost in the 'simulacra' of the present.

Such imbalanced accounts of humans and social realities, where one or both effectively disappear from social analysis, are also evident in the fascination with inhuman/human 'hybrids' in sociological rejections of the 'archaic society' and critiques of 'techno-society'. In offering social theories centred on machines it is hardly surprising that society is increasingly deemed to have no reality, because humans increasingly do not either. Virilio's depiction of the religion of the 'machine-god' that dominates techno-society is instructive in this regard: religion, which is emergent from the embodied, collective encounter with human contingency and potentiality, becomes the vehicle for the technological obliteration of the human. Here the reason for the apocalyptic tone of Virilio's writings becomes clear: techno-religion is actually the *anti-religion*; the 'machine-god' is the *Anti-Christ*, which is why he believes we must now choose between the two and agnosticism is impossible. Like many accounts of the 'information society', however, this overestimates the power of technology, and underestimates the powers and potentialities of human beings. It fails to appreciate how humans can 'domesticate' technological products, rather than being colonised by them, and that using email is no more likely to reconstruct our humanity than using a telephone or posting a letter. It is difficult, furthermore, to imagine humans abandoning the sensual pleasures of real, embodied sex for the digitised fantasies of cyber-sex, or the warmth of face-to-face contact for a social life comprised entirely of Internet newsgroups and chatrooms.

Sociological visions of the 'unseaworthy society' being abandoned by high modern 'surfers' tend to give 'reflexivity' the same sort of world reconstructing power that Virilio associates with technology. Here, though, it is not so much that humans are powerless in the face of changes out of their control (though this is one feature of Giddens's thought), but that humans are peculiarly disembodied creatures reflexively constructing and deconstructing relationships, beliefs, commitments and 'life strategies' in a sort of psychoanalytic rewriting of the cost–benefit calculations of rational choice theory as a therapeutic pattern of self-construction in a world of risk and instability. Religion, not surprisingly, is largely absent here, because it is associated with a 'premodern' collective constraint upon reflexivity and therefore upon human 'emancipation'. As Bauman suggests, however, this emancipation involves the anaesthetisation of moral sensibilities and the promotion of a utilitarian individualism that fails to acknowledge, let alone seeks to build on, any embodied basis for human togetherness or the moral duty of care towards others. Not only is there no hyper-spirituality, there is no spirituality at the level of the individual either: identities, beliefs, meanings, morality and commitments are always 'until-further-notice' reflexive constructions.

This anaesthetisation of moral sensibilities is also a key feature of sociological accounts of the 'consumptive society'. Here, highly rationalised social institutions exist alongside non-rational humans whose embodied predispositions towards an emotional and symbolic enchantment of reality can be manipulated for utilitarian purposes. The 'religion' of consumerism thus expresses a kind of hyper-spirituality, but one that does not develop into a serious engagement with human potentialities and limitations, promising only 'redemption through consumption' in the morally barren confines of 'McSociety'. Thus, society, humanity and religion remain significant, but all operate on the basis of a questionable ontology. As with visions of 'market society', a corrosive utilitarianism underpins the whole human and social process and, like the reflexive 'surfers' of high modernity, we can see it as an 'unseaworthy' model of society if some notion of 'meaningful life' is our goal.

In short, the various conceptualisations of humanity and society considered in this chapter have a number of different characteristics, and some of them, if not others, point to real problems confronting people in contemporary societies, and to significant difficulties in developing a satisfactory understanding of society. Overall, however, it can be argued that they do not add up to a damning critique of the value of the notion of society because some basic ontological issues concerning humanity and social life are not addressed satisfactorily or, in some cases, not addressed at all. Indeed, although nearly all of them make something of the 'complexity' of contemporary societies, they also tend to opt for various forms of reductionism that, through their simplification of social and historical processes, make possible some grand, if dubious, claims about radical social, cultural and technological transformations of the contemporary world. In order to take a further step towards a more satisfactory understanding of societal complexity, however, the issue of scientific notions of complexity, raised in relation to Urry (2000, 2003), can be commented on further.

I have already noted that Urry's work draws creatively from notions of complexity developed in the natural sciences, but prefers to focus on notions of indeterminate outcomes and 'overall disorder' found within this literature. In this respect, Urry is following a trend noted by Hayles (1990: 176), Williams and May (1996: 160) and Byrne (1998: 5), who have highlighted how social and cultural theorists, particularly those of a postmodernist orientation, tend to adopt chaos and complexity theories in order to focus on chaos as *disorder*, rather than, as it is for scientists, a *precursor of order*. In this latter sense, complexity is understood to be 'a domain between deterministic order and randomness', not the completely unpredictable contingency favoured by postmodernism (Byrne,

1998: 16; see Waldrop, 1992). The sociological implications of these divergent uses of complexity theories obviously vary considerably, but the argument of writers such as Byrne is that the postmodernist use of complexity theory is contrary to its true implications. Further to this, clarifying the true implications of scientific notions of complexity can help illuminate problems in the postmodernist position.

There is a growing interest in the potential usefulness of developments in the natural sciences for making sense of society. Zohar and Marshall (1994), for example, introduced the notion of the 'quantum society' in order to help illuminate how developments in physics can help us make sense of societies as 'emergent wholes'. What interested them was the notion of 'quantum reality' as a complex interweaving of 'particles' and 'waves' that, by analogy, allows us to see individuals as particles and social forces as waves washing over time and space (Zohar and Marshall, 1994: 326; Urry, 2000: 122). As potentially beguiling as such language is, however, it is only really useful if it helps resolve genuine theoretical problems regarding social life, rather than simply offering a new set of metaphors for social theorists to play with. Indeed, some uses of complexity theories, which assert that a new 'axial age' is upon us, look as overblown and speculative as the more creative forms of postmodernism (see Gillette, 2002). Reed and Harvey (1992: 359) and Byrne (1998: 39), however, see a real potentiality in chaos and complexity theories because they allow us to appreciate that nature and society are ontologically open and historically constituted, in some respects indeterminate but also amenable to rational explanation. Building upon these views, it is possible to emphasise four key aspects of complexity theory that need to be taken seriously in contemporary social theory.

First, complexity theory directs our attention towards *ontology*: it helps remind social theorists that, regardless of how we theorise about the world and the particular types of language we use, the question of being cannot be converted into the problem of meaning because social life has to be understood with regard to broader temporal, biological, physical and evolutionary factors (Bergmann, 1981: 17; Adam, 1990: 43). Second, though, this does not mean that society can be reduced into biological factors, for example, since complexity theory reinforces the realist emphasis on *emergence*. It thereby allows us to see that social realities are non-reducible, emergent phenomena, respecting 'the autonomous logic of sociological theory' (Byrne, 1998: 47). Third, contrary to the 'social systems' theories of writers such as Parsons, which have too strong a focus on the 'problem of order', complexity theory can encourage sociologists to recognise the *contingency* of all emergent phenomena, and, therefore, to explore the ambiguity of social phenomena with regard to problems of order and disorder (Harvey and Reed, 1994: 390; see also Durkheim, 1995: 412–13). Fourth, however, scientific notions of complexity can help remind us that engagements with contingency have to be placed within a holistic context: contrary to post-structuralist and postmodernist rejections of all notions of totality as culturally imperialistic, we simply cannot understand social life if its broader context is ignored (Hayles, 1991: 16–17). Indeed, viewed in relation to Capra's (1982) emphasis on reality as 'interconnected wholeness' (see Adam, 1990: 59), extreme forms of social constructionism look highly problematic: they offer an anthropocentric reduction of the complexity of reality into patterns of social and cultural phenomena whose nature and origins they have difficulty accounting for.

Contrary to postmodernist appropriations of complexity theories then, these scientific developments may indeed stress the difficulties of understanding the world, and clearly overturn some of the major assumptions of modern science such as Newtonian concepts of time, but they remain focused on grasping the *intelligibility of the world* as a mind-independent, ontologically stratified totality (Byrne, 1998: 159). This focus is consistent with the form of social realism outlined in the previous chapter: the arguments introduced there concerning human beings, society as a *sui generis* reality characterised by a substratum of hyper-spirituality, and the power of emergent religious forms to exercise causal power over people, can help contribute to a vision of society that interacts creatively with new visions of an ontologically stratified universe developed in the natural sciences. Indeed, in its concern with ontology, emergence, contingency and holism, the scientific understanding of complexity can complement the notion of a 'complex society' found in the work of Durkheim, Gurvitch and Polanyi and help in the refutation of those social theories that endorse the extremes of various forms of reductionism or relativistic arguments about indeterminate plurality. Gurvitch's realist focus on a 'complex, fluid, emergent social reality', for example, captures much of the essence of what Byrne sees as the potentialities of complexity theories for the social sciences (see Korenbaum, 1964). In seeking to develop this social realist argument further, however, an exploration of the concept of 'contingency' is crucial, since this is a term often adopted by those theorists who, mistaking relativity for relativism, seek to prioritise difference above totality, disorder rather than order, epistemology rather than ontology. As I shall argue in the following chapter, a proper understanding of contingency necessitates a thorough engagement with ontology, and, consequently, recognition of the embodied basis of emergent social realities.

Notes

1. Stehr and Grundmann (2001) have expressed some scepticism about the 'authority of complexity' in classical forms of sociological theory, arguing that this has inhibited the development and application of social scientific knowledge, since a full grasp of complexity is ultimately impossible. In contrast, they argue that, rather than seeking to offer faithful representations of social reality in all its complexity, sociologists should follow the example of Keynes, who worked with a simplified model of social relationships that proved to be of considerable practical utility. While these arguments raise important issues, however, they can also endorse a reductionist approach that, in the interests of practical utility, distorts representations of social reality to reflect pre-existing assumptions on the part of the analyst. For Polanyi

(2001), this is the principal error of those liberal philosophers who reduce human relationships to market forces.

2. The partiality of Castells's engagement with social reality is such that Abell and Reyniers (2000: 749) have accused him of offering a 'morass of banalities and truisms' that brings social theory into disrepute.

3. This view has a long history inextricably entwined within the development of modern notions of the 'market society' (Polanyi, 2001), but Margaret Thatcher's declaration that 'There is no such thing as society. There are individual men and women and there are families', is a key representation of this individualist post-societal view. As Strathern (1998: 65) expresses it, Thatcher emphasised that 'society' is not a concrete thing after all, but an abstraction, a piece of rhetoric. Thatcher's reduction of society to empty rhetoric was met with much protest, initially, mainly regarding the implications of her views for the maintenance of health and welfare provision by the state. None the less, the development of 'rational choice' forms of social theory has reinforced her individualist, sceptical attitude to society, and encouraged the adoption of the notion of 'markets' as the context within which individuals make choices about their actions.

3

Contingent Society

The principal aim of the previous chapter was to offer an initial critique of post-societal arguments, and related accounts of the fragmentation and problematisation of society, in relation to the core arguments of the social realist position introduced in Chapter 1. While this critique is developed throughout the rest of the book, all the following chapters, beginning with this one, also have a more constructive focus in the sense that they are all concerned with the clarification and elaboration of key aspects of society that need to be taken seriously in contemporary social theory. An important starting point in this respect is the need to develop a proper understanding of the fact that society is a *contingent* reality. Here, as David Byrne (1998: 40) has suggested, Stephen J. Gould's account of some of the key implications of chaos/complexity theory is a valuable starting point. In his book *Wonderful Life*, Gould (1991: 283) draws an analogy between evolutionary and historical patterns of contingency, and suggests that all studies of history must acknowledge the central principle of contingency; that is, historical analysis cannot ignore the fact that the 'uneraseable and determining signature of history' is the pattern whereby emergent forms depend upon antecedent states. In this view, the notion of 'contingency' implies a rejection of simplistic notions of determinism, but does not suggest randomness or indeterminacy. Rather, it directs our attention to the fact that things happen to have a particular pattern, order or character because of their contingent relation to antecedent phenomena (Torrance, 1998: vii). Applied to the emergence of society, this notion of contingency can help illuminate the need for social theory to pay attention to antecedent factors since, as Archer (1995, 2000) has emphasised, society is not a self-subsistent reality, but one that is dependent for its emergence upon the human beings who constitute it. It is for this reason that any assessment of the nature of human social life in its various forms, including those of contemporary Western societies, must grapple with general problems concerning humanity's embodied being-in-the-world and the ontological characteristics we can identify with it. Society is, ultimately, contingent upon the embodied beings constitutive of it, even though human being itself has a thoroughly contingent character.

In this regard, the arguments developed in this chapter emphasise the importance of developing an embodied understanding of society, and seek to demonstrate that the hyper-spiritual forces that are a key feature of social life are emergent phenomena contingent upon, but irreducible to, human individuals who possess particular potentialities and powers. None the less, as a phenomenon emergent from hyper-spirituality, religion illuminates further dimensions of contingency that are crucial to understanding how we make sense of the complexity of social reality. In particular, the fact that religion expresses a collective engagement with the 'open-ended' possibilities of transcendence emergent from embodied human life allows it to develop cosmological visions of the universe that can have an immense impact upon humanity's social relationships and self-understandings. Thus, the theologically realist interpretation of the ontological stratification of the universe as a signal of the contingency of all creation, including humanity and society, upon God (Soskice, 1987; Torrance, 1998), helps us to understand how religion comes to have such a powerful social influence: the recognition of the contingency of the human condition that all of us, perhaps, in one way or another, are conscious of, is characteristically intensified in religious thought and practice, but also placed in a broader cosmological context that means contingency and the ultimate meaningfulness of our lives are not incompatible. Weber's (1965) vision of religion as *theodicy* is comprehensible in these terms, though Durkheim's exploration of the embodied basis of society offers a more productive foundation upon which to illuminate the emergent character of theodicies.

The arguments of this chapter are developed through a critical discussion of a broad range of theorists but they are focused specifically upon the social theories of Turner and Rojek (2001), Archer (1995, 2000), Durkheim (1995) and Bataille (1987, 1991), all of which offer illuminating accounts of the embodied basis of society, although the visions of embodiment they propose leave variable degrees of room for the societal hyper-spirituality and its emergent religious forms that are key concerns of this book. Bringing them into dialogue, I suggest, offers a fruitful way forward for developing a social realist account of the contingent relationship between embodiment, society, hyper-spirituality and religion. Initially, however, it is useful to distinguish between the social *construction* and the social *constitution* of reality as a way of establishing the central significance of embodiment for an account of societal hyper-spirituality, since some accounts of the embodied energies within society, such as Bataille's focus on the 'excessive' character of social forces, have been adopted by postmodern theorists in a manner alien to their true character.

Constituted society

I have already discussed how social constructionism, which gives society the power to define reality, as well as all forms of identity, meaning and value, ultimately results in the dissipation of society itself into arbitrary patterns of discourses, significations and 'simulacra'. None the less, the appeal of constructionism for social theorists is not difficult to grasp because it touches upon a real phenomenon; that is, it illuminates the social and cultural specificity and contingency of much that we think, believe and experience. We can all recognise, for example, that if we had been born into another society or another time then the values we hold dear, the ways in which we conceive of ourselves and the world, as well as the basic organisation of our material needs and wants could all have been vastly different. It is easy to see, then, how the recognition of such contingency could lead to the view that all beliefs, ideas, meanings, values and even reality itself are simply social constructions. In this regard, James Beckford's (2003) adoption of a 'modest' form of social constructionism, while rejecting the more extreme claims of 'radical constructionists', offers a pragmatic and, to some extent, justifiable theoretical approach: his analysis of religion and society is situated within the recognition that meanings are always constructed through human interactions. Yet this approach, which for him is merely an 'analytical strategy', involves bracketing out basic ontological questions about the real characteristics of human beings, and how religions and societies are emergent from these (Beckford, 2003: 4). This means that Beckford cannot draw a line between 'radical' and 'modest' social constructionism except by pointing to the fact of the materiality of the universe, a fact that suggests only very basic constraints on otherwise limitless human constructions. Here, for example, the human body is seen primarily as a physical site for social constructions rather than a source or medium for emergent social and cultural forms (Beckford, 2003: 208).

It is possible, however, to see the body as something that testifies to the contingency of humans as mortal creatures born into a particular place and time, and yet as something that grounds this contingency in something more substantial than mere materiality. However important language is to the development of distinctively human experience, for example, our linguistic capacities and potentialities, and the development of these in socially and culturally specific ways, have to be placed within an embodied context that predisposes us to 'make sense' of the world in specific ways (Howes, 1991). As Archer (2000: 111) notes, 'physiological embodiment does not sit well with social constructionism … social constructions may be placed upon it, but the body is stubbornly resistant to being dissolved into the discursive'. This is so not only because we have what Archer calls a 'learning body', adapting to natural and social environments even before we have acquired language, but also because physical responses related to pleasure, pain, desire and need continue throughout our lives to challenge the constructionist overemphasis on language. In fact, even though our highly developed ability to reflect, discourse and theorise about ourselves and the world surely manifests things distinctive to humans, our embodiment means that we share certain fundamental characteristics with other animals.[1]

This is not to say that society and culture can be reduced to biological factors because, as Mauss's (1950) study of 'body techniques' and Hertz's (1960) study of the cross-cultural pre-eminence of the right hand demonstrate, the ways in which embodied capacities and potentialities are developed (or not) is thoroughly contingent upon specifically social processes. Hertz's study is particularly worth considering in this respect. His argument is that, despite the physical resemblance of left and right hands, in nearly all societies they are treated with an astonishing inequality: 'To the right hand go honours, flattering designations, prerogatives … the left hand, on the contrary, is despised and reduced to the role of a humble auxiliary' (Hertz,

1960: 89). Hertz analyses this right/left polarity in relation to Durkheim's sacred/profane dualism, noting the spread of taboos surrounding left-handedness, and the 'positive cult' surrounding right-handedness evident in a range of religious forms. Thus, the association of the right side with the gods and the left side with evil in Maori religion is mirrored by Christian depictions of the Last Judgement, where Christ's raised right hand directs the saved to heaven, while his lowered left hand directs the damned to their abode in Hell (Hertz, 1960: 100–1). Furthermore, Hertz notes that, even today, it is the *right* hands that are joined in marriage, that are used to greet each other, and that are the only ones allowed to come into contact with food in many cultures (Hertz, 1960: 106–7).

What Hertz is *not* doing is arguing that the distinction between right and left hands is either socially constructed or biologically determined. What he argues is that most humans appear to have an embodied predisposition, related to brain functions, towards right-handedness: it is upon the basis of this predisposition that social forces serve to sacralise all that is 'right' and denigrate all that is 'left'. Many musicians, of course, can retrain the left hand out of it its socially reinforced relative 'uselessness', and Hertz argues that societies as a whole could do this. Nevertheless, the embodied predisposition itself cannot be socially deconstructed, which explains why left-handed people living in societies that have striven to coerce them into right-handedness continue to have a preference for the left. In short, even though the vast array of practices, beliefs, ideas and values attributed to right and left are clearly distinctively social phenomena, the distinction between right and left is not socially constructed: it is socially *constituted* through the societal engagement with real embodied human predispositions.

This focus on patterns of social constitution rather than social construction allows humans to have some sort of access to, and connection with, a *real world* independent of the particular social and cultural forms placed upon it. In this regard, the fact that all human beings are mortal is particularly significant. The observation that those influenced by postmodern ideas are often particularly uncomfortable with the fact of human mortality, or even in complete denial about it, tells us a lot about the limits of social constructionism (Bauman, 1992b). The social and cultural arrangements surrounding death may vary dramatically, of course, and many of these offer promises or hopes of some kind of immortality, but the facts of ageing and death are incontrovertible consequences of birth, and forms of social theory that cannot take these into account can hardly be satisfactory. In contrast, it can be noted that religions as diverse as Buddhism and Christianity make the reflection upon these facts absolutely central to their systems of belief and practice. Death not only draws attention to the embodied limitations and contingency of individual human lives, however, but also to those of society.

Although Durkheim (1995: 271) suggests that belief in the immortality of the soul reflects a sense of the perpetuity of society in contrast to the unavoidable deaths of individuals, he also notes that all deaths 'enfeeble' society, robbing it of vitality, and thereby necessitating mourning rituals to reinforce and revitalise common feelings (Durkheim, 1995: 404–5); a pattern also discussed by Hertz (1960: 77) in his essay on ritual practices surrounding death. It can be said, indeed, that just as embodiment is the medium through which the social constitution of beliefs, practices, meanings, values and identities is developed, so too society itself is a phenomenon constituted through the medium of human embodiment. This is not to say that it has no reality, as social constructionists would suggest, only that it has no reality apart from the embodied human beings who constitute it: it is a *contingent* reality. It is in this sense that the body must, necessarily, be central to social theory. None the less, having emphasised this, it is clear that the particular ways in which it is possible to conceptualise the characteristics and consequences of this embodiment can vary considerably, resulting in many different accounts of society (Shilling, 2003). The recent work of Turner and Rojek (2001) on this subject, however, offers a challenging vision of embodiment centred on an 'ontology of frailty'.

Frail society

Turner and Rojek's reassessment of the sociological project is centred on a concern with the foundational significance of embodiment in the constitution of human society. In a direct challenge to forms of sociology influenced by postmodernist and post-structuralist philosophies ('decorative sociology'), which effectively dissolve social and political struggles into a philosophical and moral relativism that makes notions such as 'human rights' groundless and arbitrary, they argue for an embodied social theory able to grapple with the sensuality, frailty and interconnectedness of human being-in-the-world. The value of their study is evident in their critiques of social and cultural theories that fail to engage satisfactorily with human embodiment, and their sensitive account of how issues pertaining to embodiment permeate various intimate, fraternal and public dimensions of social life. However, their stated aim of retaining 'society' at the centre of the sociological project is, to some extent, compromised by the philosophical sources they draw upon in their conceptualisation of human embodiment, since these, in arguing for an 'ontology of frailty', tend to promote a somewhat 'frail' image of society.

These philosophical sources include British social contract theory, particularly Hobbes, and a German philosophical tradition that includes Heidegger, Marx, Weber, Feuerbach, and the philosophical anthropology of writers such as Gehlen. Following Hobbes, Turner and Rojek (2001: 215–16) argue that life is 'nasty, brutish and short', though they soften this with the Feuerbachian view that the sensuous embodiment of humans ensures that the engagement with reality is, in some respects, pleasurable. This Hobbesian position is also supplemented by the German philosophical tradition's concern with the vulnerability, anxiety and frailty inherent to the human condition. Gehlen's (1988) argument that humans are 'not yet finished animals', whose societies furnish them with cultural systems that 'complete their unfinished ontological characteristics', is understood to be in accord with Hobbes's conception of humanity's inherent ontological insecurity (Turner and Rojek, 2001: 32). This notion of an inherent tendency towards ontological insecurity, also evident in the social theory of Giddens (1991a), is central to the embodied sociology of Turner and Rojek: humanity's embodied 'ontological frailty' is manifest in biological (disease, ageing, death), psychological (fear, anxiety) and social forms (providing humans with the meanings, values and identities they inherently lack). As compelling as this vision of human embodiment is, in some respects, however, there are two major problems with it that need to be addressed.

First, for all the talk of humanity's sensual being-in-the-world, it tends to endorse a rather cognitivist view of humans as existentialist philosophers perpetually on the brink of a catastrophic collapse into meaninglessness. Berger's (1990) vision of society providing a 'nomos' of meaning that shields humans from the essentially 'anomic' reality of their 'biological unfinishedness' is built on the same German philosophical foundations, and offers a similarly anxiety-ridden vision of human embodiment. While it is important to acknowledge, sociologically, the mortality of humanity and the inherent vulnerability of human systems of knowledge and meaning, it is not at all clear that most people go about their daily lives with any great sense of their inherent ontological frailty. In fact, as Durkheim (1995: 268) suggests, the widespread belief in notions of some sort of 'soul' connected to human embodiment (often *immortal* in character) is a powerful testimony to the way in which society incarnates a sense of meaning and value within individuals, and makes their individual identities seem anything but frail and arbitrary.

A second problem with this vision of embodiment is that it goes beyond notions of contingency and conceptualises humanity's social experience in terms of a *deficiency*: the notion of ontological frailty as an inherent characteristic of our being-in-the-world not only suggests that individuals cannot escape the anxieties attendant upon their frailties, but also that society cannot, ultimately, add to, or subtract from, them in a substantive way. Society can offer patterns of organisation that take these common frailties into account and, ideally, provide collective arrangements for the protection and care of others but, in the end, society offers little more than that. For example, when Turner and Rojek (2001: 123) offer their somewhat bleak view of health as a temporary respite from an inevitable condition of disability, they start from a position asserting *biological* frailty and move, from there, to emphasise the precariousness of societal environments that either exacerbate the problems attendant upon bodily limits or partially mitigate them: there is no possibility of their transcendence or, even, their transformation. In short, their ontology of frailty constrains the possibilities whereby society might make a real difference to the human experience of embodiment: all society can do, at best, is to make life a little less 'nasty, brutish and short'.

While not sinking into the pessimism of Rom Harré (1979), whose view of human social life emphasises its futility, ugliness, pain, folly and under-current of resentment, Turner and Rojek's sociology, reflecting its depend-ence upon Hobbesian contract theory and German philosophical anthropology, none the less tends towards a view of humans that interprets contingency exclusively in terms of frailty and vulnerability, with the result that society, a contingent development of the embodied capacities of humans, also appears to be a somewhat frail phenomenon. Indeed, for Turner (1991: x), a satisfactory sociological engagement with social com-plexity has, ultimately, to grasp the fact that the 'open-ended', 'contingent' nature of human life results in an existential uncertainty that underpins all social institutions, including religious ones. In contrast, Archer's (2000) account of embodiment emphasises not ontological frailty, but an ontology of human robustness, while her vision of society emphasises not its defi-ciencies (though she is aware of its limitations) but its emergent properties and powers.

Emergent society

Like Turner and Rojek, Archer (2000: 18) stresses the unavoidability of 'our embodied accommodation to the mercy of nature', but also sees in the organic constitution of human beings a capacity for reflexivity, self-con-sciousness and moral discernment that allows people to be much more cre-ative and adaptable than an ontology of frailty allows. This is reinforced by her emphasis on the primacy of *practice* in relation to 'that prime human power, our self-consciousness' (Archer, 2000: 8). For her, people are not existentialists grappling cognitively with the arbitrary fictions of language and culture that serve to shield us from life's inherent brutality; on the con-trary, human reflexivity is exercised and developed through practical activ-ity in the world. Against the Cartesian separation of mind from practical experience, she argues that it is only through practice that thought and knowledge can develop. None the less, contrary to the 'anthropocentric' assumption that our knowledge, because it is embodied, simply *creates* the world, she emphasises that human limitations relating to the experience of reality do not exhaust all that the world is. In fact, the creative, adaptable powers that distinguish humans from other animals (though they too are engaged in practical activity) are only able to develop because of our ongo-ing attempts to survive and flourish in a world that transcends our fallible capacities to impose meanings on it (Archer, 2000: 145).

It is on this embodied basis that Archer argues that 'human interaction constitutes the transcendental conditions of human development', meaning that all humans, from different times and different socio-cultural circum-stances, share a common, practical orientation to the world through which distinctively human properties and powers are reflexively constituted (Archer, 2000: 17). The development of society is made possible by these 'transcendental conditions', but once in existence it has, like humanity, *sui generis* properties and powers since it entails emergent structural and cultural characteristics. Thus, for example, society cannot *construct*, through normative labelling, the emotional energies and capacities associated with phenomena such as shame, remorse, pride or envy, but these become 'socially *constituted* properties which are emergent from the interrelationship between a subject's concerns and a society's normativity' (Archer, 2000: 215). It is through such interrelationships that humans become 'social beings'.

For Archer, however, the processes through which individuals become 'social beings' are not simply abstract phenomena of interest only to professional sociologists, but realities confronted every day by each human being, and involving questions about freedom, autonomy, power and constraint (Archer, 1995: 1). In other words, we cannot escape 'the vexatious fact of society' in our daily lives, as well as in academic analyses of problems relating to structure and agency, freedom and responsibility, liberation and oppression. For Archer, society is a 'vexatious' phenomenon because it is inherently ambivalent. Social reality is not self-subsistent but of human constitution, yet it eludes individual and collective efforts to transform it in accordance with our ideals and projects, and often changes in ways that no one wants. Furthermore, it constrains our actions even when we are reflexively aware of our role in constituting society through our own activity (Archer, 1995: 1–2). This ambivalence means that the essential characteristics of society cannot be captured adequately through analogies with mechanics, language or cybernetic systems: society does not have fixed parts, an orderly syntax or a pre-programmed set of goals and functions (Archer, 1995: 166). Societies pre-exist people and, in that sense at least, are not reducible to them, but they are nevertheless made up of people, with all their complexities and ambiguities, and are therefore shaped by human beings, albeit in unpredictable and often unintentional ways.

For Archer, then, society is a contingent phenomenon because it is an emergent reality, but she is also interested in the fact that this emergent reality thereby imposes contingent constraints upon individuals: it is this 'double' contingency that gives social life its unpredictable and 'vexatious' character. Alongside her vision of society as an emergent phenomenon, however, she is also interested in the fact that people are not simply the embodied *ground* out of which society emerges, but are also creatures who continue to develop contingent, emergent powers and properties of their own, such as self-consciousness and the development of an evaluative orientation in terms of our interactions with natural and social realities (Archer, 2000: 316). It is this attentiveness to the 'internal conversation' inherent to individual human beings that causes her to reject Durkheim's vision of society as one that attributes it with too many powers and properties, even though she is fully attentive to the fact that social reality has *sui generis* characteristics (Archer, 2000: 19). Nonetheless, contrary to Archer's doubts, key thinkers in the Durkheimian tradition have seen these *sui generis* characteristics as phenomena that nurture and expand embodied human potentialities rather than deplete or curtail them.

In contrast to Turner and Rojek's ontology of frailty – and offering a much stronger view of society's emergent properties than Archer – Durkheim (1995), Mauss (1969) and Bataille (1991) envisage embodied being-in-the-world not in terms of an ontological deficiency or a robust practical orientation, but in terms of an *excess* of energies, emotions and forces. Rather than deploying a language of frailty, these writers focus more explicitly on contingency, in the sense that human embodiment entails a radical dependence on others, but go on from there to examine the exchanges of social energies that continually mould, sustain and transform individual identities. Durkheim (1995: 213), for example, talks of the 'stimulating action of society' as an embodied experience affecting nearly every instant of our lives. This not only contrasts sharply with a Hobbesian view of life as 'nasty, brutish and short', since it suggests a plenitude of vitality and energy endemic to social experience, but it also challenges the ontology of frailty offered by Turner and Rojek in the sense that society is not simply a collective ordering of lives marked by existential anxieties and biological limits, but a dynamic, vital phenomenon that arises from, and yet can transform, the experience and knowledge of human embodiment in all its contingency.

This concern with the emergent properties and powers of society is close to Archer's view, as is Durkheim's focus on the primacy of practical activity 'enacted and experienced concretely by real people in real time and in real places' (Rawls, 2001: 63). For Durkheim, however, the emergent properties of society possess an inherent vitality that exceeds the reflexive patterns of interrelations discussed by Archer. She identifies the 'transcendental conditions of human development' in the common, interactive and practical orientation to the world characteristic of all humans (Archer, 2000: 17), and Durkheim would clearly assent to this. He would add, however, that the *sui generis* characteristics of society introduce further 'transcendental conditions of human development' that arise from, and yet exceed, the embodied characteristics of individuals. However, his account of these develops from a very particular vision of the relationships between individuals and societies that has been subject to a great deal of criticism.

Dynamic society

For many writers, the analytical distinction between 'the individual' and 'society' central to such arguments has become highly problematic. Zafirovski (2000), for example, has questioned sociology's division into 'individualist' and 'holist' forms. In another more far-reaching critique, however, Strathern (1998: 63) notes how twentieth-century social theories have swung between the pendulum of 'individual' and 'society'; her view is that, in now rejecting 'society', we can reject 'the individual' too and free ourselves from this unproductive polarisation. For her, this Durkheimian dichotomy has become a liability, because 'social relations are intrinsic to human existence, not extrinsic' (Strathern, 1998: 66; see also Lemert, 1995:

38). In other words, pre-social individuals cannot be set against a social reality distinct from them, but of which they are members. Theory should be centred on 'sociality', not on 'society' or 'the individual'. Urry also expresses scepticism about the individual being/social being duality. He suggests that sociological debates concerning the relative merits of individualism or holism are unhelpful because they cannot account for the complex mobilities and intersections of contemporary 'regions, networks and flows' (Urry, 2000: 15). Like Strathern, he rejects both 'society' and 'the individual', though he focuses on 'sociation' rather than 'sociality' to express the fluid, mobile forms of interaction and identification characteristic of contemporary persons (Urry, 2000: 142). While it can be noted that these terms are, none the less, derivations of 'society', the appeal of terms such as 'sociality' or 'sociation' is held to rest on their suggestion of something more interactive than 'society'. According to Toren (1998: 74), who also wants to abandon 'society', these terms are more 'dynamic', and do not imply a 'system', distinct from individuals who are then 'socialised'.[2]

Archer, however, offers a more subtle critique of Durkheim's arguments. Her acceptance of the authenticity of the daily experience of ordinary people, who are conscious of themselves as individuals with an awareness of, and responsibility for, their own actions, yet who are unavoidably social beings subject to all sorts of possibilities and constraints, means that neither the 'vexatious fact of society' nor the reality of individuals can be argued away by social theorists. She notes, however, that sociologists have tended to emphasise the importance of one element of this duality against the other: methodological individualists have collapsed 'society' into 'individuals', while collectivists have emphasised the all-embracing power of society to the point where individuals are simply 'indeterminate material' waiting to be given shape and substance by social forces. For her, Durkheim is the embodiment of this collectivist 'downwards conflation' (Archer, 1995: 2–3). In the light of this critique, it can be argued that the postmodernist deconstruction of humanity actually has its roots in Durkheim's reduction of individuals to epiphenomenal aspects of societal dynamics (Archer, 2000: 19).

Contrary to this argument, however, it can be noted that Durkheim (1995: 275) stressed that his concern with social forces did not deny the importance of 'the individual factor', and that 'there can be no social life unless distinct individuals are associated with it; and the more numerous and different from one another they are, the richer it is'. Furthermore, he denies that individual psychological life begins only with societies: what he is concerned with is the greater development of human psychological life in comparison to animals, and throughout human history, as an embodied predisposition towards sociability produces ever more complex forms of social life that act back upon individuals, transforming their experiences of themselves and the world. The greater the development of this sociability, in fact, the richer and more diverse individual experiences, representations and choices become (Durkheim, 1984: 284–5). In addition, and contrary to the 'static' image of society Strathern, Urry and Toren associate with Durkheim, his notion of humanity's *homo duplex* character articulates a sense of the embodied predisposition towards a form of existence (society) that transcends us as individuals yet whose existence is dependent on individuals in a continuing dynamic process. As Moscovici (1993: 20) notes, it is Durkheim's argument that 'society springs from within us, as passions arising from each of us which are knit together by countless acts on countless occasions. Being associated with one another and being carried along together in this way, we feel ourselves different, and appear so.' In this view, 'the individual' and 'society' are neither identifiable with each other nor are they rigidly dichotomous realities. The 'spirituality' of individuals and the 'hyper-spirituality' of society have their own integrity, yet society is dependent on the individuals who constitute it even though society transcends and transforms them.

Here it is worth noting that Bataille's and Caillois's (1988) development of this Durkheimian theme emphasises the dynamism of this relationship: society is a 'compound being' in the sense that it is greater than the individuals of which it is composed, yet the individual is the embodiment of society. As Richardson (1994: 27) notes, Bataille's views were not only a development of Durkheim's thought but also were similar to those of the surrealist Mabille: differentiation between the 'individual' and 'society' is important theoretically and methodologically, because it helps us comprehend the dynamism of human relations, but, ultimately, there is no conflict between them. For Bataille, the individual *is* the *social being* (Richardson, 1994: 29; see Mabille, 1977). In Durkheim's case, at least, this is not meant to imply that individuals are reducible to society, any more than society is reducible to individuals, only that individuality is an inherently social phenomenon. It is in his account of the centrality of the sacred to social life, however, that Durkheim develops his vision of the inherently social aspects of human identities in a way that helps illuminate how attempts to grapple with the contingency of society must necessarily engage with the religious dimensions of human relationships.

Sacred society

This notion of a hyper-spirituality specific to society endows social life with an inescapably religious dimension. Human interaction does not simply broaden our horizons beyond our own immediate perceptions and desires, but transforms them under the influence of an energy peculiar to collective life: to be part of society is to experience that self-transcendence which Durkheim understands to be the essential feature of religion, and which he identifies as the experience of the sacred. It is the religious dimension of Durkheim's work that has, however, attracted most controversy. It has been suggested, for example, that his concern with the 'religious' character of social forces had such an intoxicating effect on him that he was led to deify society, treating it as a *deus ex machina* with 'powers and qualities as mysterious and baffling as any assigned to the gods by the religions of this world'

(Ginsberg, 1956: 51, 242; see Evans-Pritchard, 1956: 313; Lukes, 1973: 21, 35). For Touraine (1989, 1995), this deification of society reflects the only partially secularised character of classical sociology: 'society' filled the God-shaped hole left by the demise of Christianity, substituting social order for divine order.

It is clearly the case that the early development of sociology was marked by an experience of, and concerns about, the apparent secularisation of Western societies, and that medieval visions of a human social order infused with divine grace and eschatological hope were replaced by notions of society as a secular milieu within which humans' social capacities were shaped and expressed in historically variable forms (Shilling and Mellor, 2001: 5). With regard to Durkheim, however, in illuminating the enduring, religious dimensions of society he was not simply filling a God-shaped hole with the 'problem of order'. Touraine (1995: 352) follows Parsons in interpreting Durkheim's notion of society as the normative integration of individuals into social order. This, however, is a misinterpretation of Durkheim's views, which are focused on problems of contingency as much as a problem of order.

The underlying purpose behind Durkheim's association of society with the circulation of 'religious' forces is not the elucidation of the functional requirements of social order, but the attempt to illuminate those dynamic, always contingent, processes through which individuals become 'social beings'. As Poggi (2000: 85) has noted, for Durkheim, society is '*not* a substance existing in space', but should be 'conceived as a process, as a set of events, of activities. It should be thought of as a flow of energy rather than as a stock of objects.' This dynamism is particularly evident in relation to the polarity between sacred and profane, which Durkheim identifies as the distinguishing feature of religious thought and practice. In his view, the inherent hyper-spirituality of collective life means that society *always* has religious features, but the division of the world into two domains, sacred and profane, expresses human attempts to represent their experience of this spirituality in terms of beliefs, myths, legends and dogmas (Durkheim, 1995: 34). The origins of these representations, however, are in the embodied experience of powerful emotions and energies arsing from human relationships.

Durkheim's account of the origins of the sacred in the *contagious* emotional energies of 'effervescent' gatherings, which are then periodically revitalised through ritual activity, expresses his dynamic and embodied conception of society. The sacred is acquired by contagion, and is transmitted contagiously, as intense, emotional energies circulate within social life (Durkheim, 1995: 328). For Durkheim (1995: 352), such processes 'set collectivity in motion', bringing individuals together, and forging a sense of collective purpose and identity. The sacred, as a symbolic representation of these processes, therefore expresses something elementary and universal about the embodied basis of the constitution, development and maintenance of societies, though Durkheim also stresses the contingency of the sacred and of society, in terms of emotional energies and conceptual factors. First of all, social forces tend to lose their energy over time, and need to be replenished if society is not to fall into a pattern of decay (Durkheim, 1995: 342). Second, the *idea of society* must be kept alive in individual minds, through the support of the beliefs, traditions and aspirations of the collectivity; otherwise society will die (Durkheim, 1995: 351). As Poggi (2000: 88) notes, this sense of contingency appears to be particularly acute in some of Durkheim's reflections on modern society. Considering the 'moral mediocrity', de-Christianisation and loss of collective vitality characteristic of modernity, he expresses a sense of the fragile nature of modern society, but none the less suggests that periods of 'creative effervescence' will again occur (Durkheim, 1995: 429). He discusses the French Revolution as one such example (Durkheim, 1995: 430), and Tiryakian (1995) has also discussed the 'Velvet Revolutions' of 1989 in the same terms, but this effervescence need not apply to societal forms as large as nation-states, as Collins (1988) has noted. Rather, it can occur within a number of different social forms.

The attempts of Bataille and Caillois (1988: 77) to establish a 'sacred sociology' in the Collège de Sociologie, centred on 'the entire communifying movement of society', reflects this sense of the continuing significance of patterns of creative effervescence. As Caillois (1988a: 10) expresses it, this form of sociology was concerned to redress the neglect of 'an entire side of modern collective life, its most serious aspect, its deep strata'. Taking its lead from Durkheim's study of religion, the Collège strove to reveal 'the elementary phenomena of attraction and repulsion' that mark social existence (Caillois, 1988a: 11). Rather than identifying these phenomena with the nation-state, in fact, they were understood to pose a challenge, if not a threat, to nation-states. For the Collège, the 'epidemic contagion' of the sacred suggested a confrontation with the atomised, individualistic and 'de-virilised' world of modern nation-states (Bataille, 1988a).

This reading of Durkheim's concept of the sacred draws attention to the misleading nature of those claims that Durkheim 'deifies' society. The simple formula often attributed to him – 'God' is society, therefore society is 'God' – is a simplification. For him, the sacred may, in some social contexts, be symbolically represented in the form of an all-powerful deity, but the reality is that the sacred is a representation of the dynamic, contagious and often ambiguous processes through which individuals become 'social beings'; processes that are central to the social constitution and embodied experience of human social life but have a contingent relationship to particular social institutions and structures (Durkheim, 1995: 420). His claim that a 'society is to its members what a god is to its faithful' tends to blur this distinction between social forces and social structures, but what he is trying to express is the idea that society (like a god) can foster feelings of respect, dependence, moral obligation and restraint (Durkheim, 1995: 208). However, his emphasis on the *ambiguity* of the sacred, which is volatile, potentially destructive, productive of 'dysphoria' as well as euphoria, and can divide as well as unite people, not only shows the impossibility of associating his account of religion and society with a simple normative reinforcement of social order, but also suggests an ambiguity at the heart of society itself (Durkheim, 1995: 417). Social energies may be the stimulus for heightened moral sensibilities, self-sacrifice and even heroism, but they can also provoke barbarism, violence, oppression and fanaticism (Durkheim, 1995: 213). Society, then, for all its God-like features, remains a complex, ambiguous phenomenon within Durkheim's sociology. This ambiguity surrounding society can be illuminated further through an examination of Bataille's reworking of Durkheim's notion of the sacred.

Homogeneous/heterogeneous society

As Richardson (1994: 34) has noted, for Bataille the sacred is the 'fundamental element that makes possible the unity and continuance of society'. In contrast to some of Durkheim's followers, however, Bataille is also very much interested in Durkheim's emphasis on the fact that the sacred can only be understood fully in relation to the 'profane'. This understanding works both ways. Bataille's view is that modern assumptions about the 'profane' nature of society are inherently contradictory: there can be no such thing since, as the 'profane' is defined in opposition to the 'sacred', the idea of a 'profane society' negates itself (Richardson, 1994: 49). For Bataille, however, although the sacred is the unifying aspect of society, it is a unification that takes place at the margins of normal existence, where different realities meet in a religious mediation of excess energies emergent from human embodiment (Richardson, 1994: 34). Thus, the sacred has a paradoxical character, since it is at the heart of society, yet it is encountered at society's margins. This, for Bataille, constitutes the 'tragedy' of modern life.

This 'tragic' dimension of Bataille's thought has often been misinterpreted, especially by those writers who claim him for post-structuralism or postmodernism. As Richardson (1994: 5) has demonstrated, those who interpret Bataille in this way tend to read him via Baudrillard (1993), Derrida (1998) and Foucault (1998). While all these writers have done much to spread Bataille's influence in contemporary social and cultural theory, they have focused on the influence of de Sade and Nietzsche and tended to ignore the influence of Durkheim, while also seeking to co-opt him for their own ends rather than engage fully with his theory. Baudrillard, for example, dispenses with the moral dimension of Bataille's work, and his desire for a renewal of sacred forms of solidarity, focusing heavily on negativity and utilising Bataille to reinforce his own conception of the 'end of the social' (Richardson, 1994: 5). Similarly, Foucault uses Bataille to reinforce his own reduction of 'society' (and the 'individual') to a discursive concept, which is completely against the grain of Bataille's arguments, and develops Bataille's notion of 'transgression' while ignoring its inextricably close relationship to 'taboo' (Richardson, 1994: 7). Thus, although Noyes (2000) begins his discussion of Bataille by castigating those who fail to read his work properly, he nevertheless seeks to claim Bataille for post-structuralism and follows Foucault in presenting Bataille as the prophet of transgression and unbridled negativity.

Bataille can only be claimed retrospectively (and somewhat anachronistically) for postmodernism in the sense that his criticisms of modern societies were consistent and profound. None the less, these criticisms are not based, in Foucault's terms, on an anti-humanist, philosophical refusal of 'totality', since Bataille's whole project is centred on the clarification and pursuit of a sense of wholeness (Richardson, 1994: 7–8), but on his belief that modernity systematically stifles the sacred basis of society, and thereby deprives us of the means to realise our full human potential. Rather than being a prophet of negativity, Bataille's (1991) sociology is ultimately rooted in a Durkheimian concern with the embodied 'effervescence of life' from which all else springs, and the challenge this offers to those utilitarian and individualist accounts of social life that reduce society to the contractual arrangements of individuals. Where he goes further than Durkheim in this is in his confrontation with a problem Durkheim tended to set aside: how can the sacred (and, therefore, society) become revitalised again in a world where 'God is dead', utility is prized above value, and our lives seem more atomised and meaningless than ever before? His attempts to answer this question mark his distinctive contribution to the attempt to make sense of society as a contingent, inherently religious phenomenon.

For Bataille, human life is characterised by a series of fundamental antagonisms between life and death, meaning and meaninglessness, possibility and impossibility, necessity and contingency. His consciousness of these antagonisms informs his vision of society, which is defined by a tension between a 'negative' deconstructive impulse to question all meaning, value and knowledge, and a 'positive' commitment to the idea of society as the creative force through which humanity realises its deepest, most profound levels of being. His philosophical sources for this vision of society tended to reinforce the negative dimensions of his thought, while his sociological influences provide its more positive dimensions. Contrary to many post-structuralist and postmodernist readings of his work, it is the creative tension between these two poles that must be kept in mind when assessing his arguments (see Besnier, 1995; Hegarty, 2000). Taken together, these different elements of Bataille's work direct our attention to the fundamental sociological significance of the circulation of those social forces and energies that can be identified as the hyper-spiritual dimensions of society, even though this significance is often obscured by the utilitarian concerns of modern societies or ignored by social and cultural theorists who take the ostensible secularisation of the modern world at face value. For Bataille, in fact, this 'secularisation' has to be reinterpreted as the 'homogenisation' of society relative to the 'heterogeneity' of a society with a strong sense of the sacred/profane polarity.

The concept of 'heterogeneity' is a significant part of Durkheim's account of the sacred. He emphasises that the relationship between sacred and profane is one of absolute heterogeneity (Durkheim, 1995: 36). As Hegarty (2000: 29) suggests, Bataille takes this concept of heterogeneity further by re-conceptualising the sacred/profane relationship as 'heterogeneous' when it is 'strongly polarised' and 'homogeneous' when it is 'weakly polarised'.[3] As modernity becomes an increasingly homogeneous society, the collective effervescence stimulated by heterogeneous activity becomes less common, leading to a devitalised society (Richardson, 1994: 35). A truly vital society, on the other hand, embraces the heterogeneity that threatens its order and stability and, in doing so, realises the true nature of those forces that bring it into existence in the first place: repulsion becomes attraction, and society is renewed (Bataille, 1988b, 1988c). The heterogeneity of sacred and profane can therefore be associated with contingent processes of social creation *and* dissolution (Caillois, 1950).

Given that heterogeneity can only be understood in relation to sacred *and* profane, it is clear that heterogeneity cannot be associated with the sacred alone. Returning to Durkheim, Bataille's source for the concept of heterogeneity, Hegarty (2000: 29) suggests that this heterogeneity is evident in Durkheim's account of the sacred itself in terms of the 'pure' and 'impure' forms that have socially benevolent or malevolent manifestations. Contrary to this view, however, it is clear that these forms are not heterogeneous since they are simply various manifestations of the 'ambiguity' of the sacred, rather than radically different phenomena (Durkheim, 1995: 412). Similarly, for Bataille, the sacred itself cannot be associated with heterogeneity. Noyes (2000: 134–5), under the influence of postmodernist philosophy, removes Bataille's concept of heterogeneity from its social context as the encounter with a strong sacred/profane polarity, and interprets it as a kind of general valorisation of the notion of 'difference' (in the manner of Derrida), but this is not what Bataille's work is really about.

For Bataille, what the sacred represents is not 'difference' but, on the contrary, *undifferentiated continuity*. He argues that this continuity is evident in the condition of animals: 'every animal is *in the world like water in water*' (Bataille, 1992: 19, emphasis in original). This, however, is completely foreign to the experience of humans. In contrast to the animal world's 'immanence and immediacy', human life has a form of self-consciousness that turns other beings and other phenomena into 'things' that are separate from ourselves, thereby breaking the undifferentiated continuity (Bataille, 1992: 23–4). This tendency to objectify phenomena developed with the use of tools, but is stimulated still further by language, which reinforces the subject–object polarity (Bataille, 1992: 27, 31). The sense of the sacred amongst humans is not, therefore, simply identifiable with the immanence of the animal world precisely because humans are so remote from it. Like Durkheim, Bataille emphasises that, for humans, the sacred is *ambiguous*, in that it is a source of attraction to us in its promise of recovered intimacy and continuity, but also a danger in the sense that it threatens the profane world of consciousness, difference and utility that is distinctively human (Bataille, 1992: 36). Thus, to encounter the sacred is to encounter heterogeneity not because the sacred itself represents heterogeneity (it represents undifferentiated continuity), but because the confrontation between sacred and profane is so extreme.

In this context, the purpose of religion is to express the human yearning for a return to undifferentiated continuity, and to provide the means through which an experience of this becomes possible. The ritual function of sacrifice, for example, is to draw a victim from the profane 'world of utility' and destroy that victim as a 'thing' by returning it to the 'intimacy' of sacred continuity (Bataille, 1992: 43). This destruction threatens established social orders but, simultaneously, reveals the 'invisible brilliance' of life that is not a 'thing' and thereby confronts individuals with a world beyond their own narrow experiences, goals and desires (Bataille, 1992: 47). This tension between destruction and brilliant creativity is also evident in the festival. Here, a 'prodigious effervescence' is let loose, confronting the world of utility and production with 'the contagious movement of a purely glorious consumption' (Bataille, 1992: 52–3). The festival, as a 'fusion of human life', attempts to mediate the 'constant problem' of being human, which is the fact that surrendering completely to immanence would rob us of our humanity and return us to an animal state, while the world of utility denies our humanity by reducing us to things (Bataille, 1992: 53–4). For Bataille, the festival is not a complete return to immanence, which would involve a return to the world of animals, but a structured reconciliation with the sacred expressed in the intense heat of a communal intimacy which serves to reinforce a spirit of community (Bataille, 1992: 56).

None the less, if religion reflects a desire, and, to some extent, offers the means, for a return to a lost continuity and intimacy, then it can also reflect the degree to which humanity has become 'discontinuous'. The theological concept of a 'supreme being', for example, ostensibly reflects a sense of the unification of all phenomena in the will of a Creator God, but, for Bataille, it reflects discontinuity in the sense that God becomes a 'thing', separate from others (Bataille, 1992: 33). The Protestant conception of a God entirely transcendent of His own creation, which henceforth operates entirely according to instrumental criteria, is an extreme example of this discontinuity (Bataille, 1992: 89). Consequently, while religion is vitally important in terms of the development of humanity and society, certain religious forms can also be an obstacle to this development. This is the context in which to assess Bataille's apparent hostility to Christianity. What he objects to is that Christianity is not, in his terms, religious enough (Bataille, 1987: 32; Richardson, 1994: 115). What he admires in Christianity is its hope of 'finally reducing this world of selfish discontinuity to the realm of continuity afire with love' (Bataille, 1987: 118). He believes, however, that Christianity has compromised with the world too much. This is so not only because of its positing of a supreme being, and a whole system of sacred 'things' which serve to reinforce subject/object divisions, but in its prolongation of individual existence even into the realms of heaven and hell after death (Bataille, 1987: 120). For Bataille, the purpose of religion is not to ensure the eternal life of the individual, but to offer a means through which individuality is relativised in relation to the undifferentiated continuity of the sacred.

Thus, what Bataille, building on Durkheim, is attempting to do is broaden our conceptions of social and human realities to grapple with the potentialities endemic within humanity's embodied being-in-the-world and the constraints upon humans in modern societies. Here, the 'surplus' or 'excess' inherent within the realm of the social is understood in dynamic, inter-relational terms, though this is contrasted with a society that (mis)understands itself in utilitarian conceptions that deny the reality of hyper-spiritual forces. In this view, if modern societies are 'frail' it is not, as Turner and Rojek (2001) indicate, because of the inherent limits of society in relation to the ontological constraints of humanity, but because of their failure to embrace the full scope of human possibility. For Durkheim and, to some extent for Archer, however, this failure is signalled by the modern neglect of those religious forms that engage productively with these human potentialities emergent within social reality, while, for Bataille, the notion of the 'sacred' becomes quite separate from existing religious forms. This separation compromises the extent to which Bataille can help us comprehend the contemporary social power of religious forms such as Christianity.

Enchanted society

Bataille's manifest antipathy to Christianity is full of ambiguity: he was a passionate convert to Catholicism in his youth, and his later loss of faith rages throughout his writings in a way that suggests his acceptance of the 'death of God' is quite different to the ironic nihilism of later postmodernist writings. Bataille's understanding of Christianity as a *refusal* of the sacred (Hegarty, 2000: 91), however, indicates a marked divergence from Durkheim, who introduced the notion of the sacred as a way of understanding religions, not as a way of judging them. Consequently, while Bataille helps illuminate the contingency of humanity's embodied being-in-the-world and the contingency of society upon the circulation of energies arising from its hyper-spiritual substratum, he is not really able to offer much in the way of a constructive account of how a religion such as Christianity can come to have such a powerful social influence, or how such forms might add to our comprehension of the nature of human and societal contingency. These failings are also evident in other forms of social theory, even when they do not adopt a simplistic notion of secularisation.

Turner and Rojek's (2001) account of religion, for example, is full of ambiguity regarding its social and sociological significance. Locating their account of the sacred in Durkheim's emphasis on the effervescent energies that bind individuals into communities, and acknowledging Bataille's development of this into a theory of the surplus energies of the 'general economy' (Turner and Rojek, 2001: 130, 217), they none the less associate the essence of religion with something outside society, namely 'the unmediated inner experiences which are the foundation of all spirituality', and thereby rob it of any elementary social or sociological significance (Turner and Rojek, 2001: 131). Perhaps reflecting Turner's (1991: 10–11) considerable debt to Weber's sociological approach, this view of religion tends to accord, theologically, with some Protestant traditions of Christian religiosity, though it does not sit well with the Catholic idea that salvation is mediated through the church. Certainly, it cannot easily be yoked to a Durkheimian view of the fundamentally social nature of religion. These different sociological positions also imply different conceptions of human embodiment. In contrast to Durkheim, Weber's work is characterised by a deep scepticism about the possibilities of reconciling the rational and emotional capacities of humans, as well as a keen sense of the tensions between charismatic religiosity, a quality of individuals, and the societal patterns of rationalisation that rob it of its power (see Shilling and Mellor, 2001: 73).

Furthermore, although the Durkheimian tradition sees religion as a fundamental feature of all societies (because it is inextricably a part of the social energies that create society), Turner and Rojek (2001: 218) emphasise that 'the metaphors of human religion are now largely obsolete'. Contrary to this, however, and aside from broader questions about the contemporary power of religions such as Christianity and Islam within and beyond Europe, they draw attention to writers such as Kristeva (1986), who have drawn extensively on Christian theological themes to develop new ways of thinking in contemporary cultural theory. Furthermore, they also connect their own ontology of frailty to Christian thinking by asking 'What best expresses metaphorically the nexus between frailty, precariousness and interconnectedness? One answer would be the crucified Christ, the Lamb of God, who gave his body that we might have eternal life' (Turner and Rojek, 2001: 217). In short, the ontology of frailty central to their vision of embodiment, because it limits what society can add to individuals, leaves little room for an account of religion which locates it at the heart of societal dynamics, even though they are partially persuaded by its expressive power that this should be so.

In contrast to Turner and Rojek, Lemert (1999: 249) offers an unambiguous statement of the significance of religion in relation to embodiment and society. His argument that human beings in society are creatures limited by the fact of their dependence on community, while each community is limited by its context-specific relation to others, offers not an 'ontology of frailty', but an ontology of contingency. In this view, religion is not simply an *expression* of human contingency but the *means* through which it is encountered socially. Contrasting the utopian dreams of liberal hope with the religious metaphor of 'heaven', for example, Lemert (1999: 261) suggests that while the former simply conveys human aspirations, the latter tempers hope with the chastening reality of common contingencies attendant upon human embodiment. Although Lemert suggests that Durkheim does not go far enough in stressing the full implications of this contingency, Poggi (2000: 85) recognises that he does, in fact, stress that not only individuals but also 'society is a contingent reality'. This is why Durkheim's sociology of religion culminates in a sociology of knowledge: humanity's religious characteristics not only illuminate the true characteristics of embodied being in society, including the collective forms of consciousness through which meaning, identity and knowledge are constituted, but also signal the potentialities and limitations of human life in a universal chain of interdependencies (Durkheim, 1995: 432).

Archer's (2000) account of religion is, in many respects, quite close to Durkheim's, despite her critique of his 'downwards conflation'. Like Durkheim, she emphasises that religion arises on the basis of practice, arguing that religious knowledge entails a 'feel for' the sacred rather than a prepositional knowledge about it, an exercise of spiritual 'know how' rather than a cognitive acceptance of abstract principles. This challenges the Enlightenment's *logocentric* view of human beings, in cutting through the distinction between reason and emotions: as she expresses it, 'unless we are already affective beings, then no amount of knowledge could move us to anything' (Archer, 2000: 185). This echoes Durkheim's (1995) critique of post-Enlightenment views of religion centred on beliefs and ideas, rather than action and the emotional dispositions of humans.

Following this line of thought, religion is 'a codification of practice, and thus there is no such thing as a non-liturgical religion' (Archer, 2000: 184). This codification gives rise to developments in art, music, architecture, artefacts and other cultural forms, while the institutionalisation of a 'church' is usually connected to the development of a 'priesthood' to act as custodians of codified practice (Archer, 2000: 185). Not only do these developments impact back upon practical activity, elaborating new forms of embodied relations and new bodily practices, however, but the essence of religion also remains fully embodied. Discussing the (Catholic) Christian tradition, for example, Archer (2000: 186) notes that the practice of Christian life as an embodied commitment of the whole person 'is distorted if fragmented into a cognitive-propositional "grammar of assent" and a modern decalogue of prescribed behaviour'. Rather, the real centre of Christian life is in the bodily disciplines of prayer, pilgrimage and contemplation and, especially, in the corporeal reception of the Body of Christ in the Eucharist. Archer's arguments here not only accord with those of Durkheim, but a whole tradition of theological, philosophical and historical accounts of Christian practice (see Mellor and Shilling, 1997).

None the less, Archer's (1995: 38) argument that Durkheim is guilty of 'bundling personal properties (thoughts, convictions, feelings) into collectivities ... and thus representing them as predicates of the social' indicates her desire to grant individuals a greater autonomy than she believes he allows, and thereby seems to distinguish her view of religion from his quite sharply. She criticises his attempt 'to discover the causes leading to the rise of religious sentiment in humanity' by noting that the conclusion is pre-judged: the only causes entertained are social, so it is no surprise that religious sentiments turn out to have social causes (Archer, 1995: 291). Against this, she asserts the importance of allowing for the possibility of 'authentic personal experience' which, rather than simply arising on the basis of social causes, facilitates an individual's ability to filter the social practices that are sought or shunned, and which thereby makes a significant difference to their 'chosen way of being in the social world' (Archer, 1995: 292). For Archer, in fact, this possibility expresses the 'enchantment of being human': human embodiment predisposes individuals towards a 'fundamentally evaluative' engagement with the world, stimulating an 'inner conversation' constitutive of our 'concrete singularity' (Archer, 2000: 318–19).

Essentially, Archer's argument is that practical activity, through which religion arises, is not *identifiable* with the social, even though it is unavoidably intertwined with the social for much of our lives, because it is a feature of human embodiment that has pre-social origins. Consequently, it is possible for individuals to have an authentic religious experience (for example, some sort of encounter with God) that does not have social causes, even if that experience is, in other respects, thoroughly social (for example, participating in rituals, reflecting theologically on the nature of God, trying to live as God wishes etc.). On the other hand, of course, Durkheim appears to offer an atheistic and rationalistic identification of the 'reality' of religion *entirely* with social forces, contrary to the beliefs of those who actually practise religions (Lukes, 1973: 461). Furthermore, although he says that the reasons the faithful accept in justifying their rites and myths 'may' be, rather than 'are', mistaken, he none the less suggests that in Christian theology we find a God 'constructed entirely out of human elements' (Durkheim, 1995: 2, 64).

While Durkheim's personal atheism is well documented, and his reduction of God to a symbolic representation of society is well established, however, it is less clear that his *theory* of religion does not allow (with some development) for the possibility of the sort of 'inner conversation' discussed by Archer or, even, the possibility of religion expressing something real in a transcendental sense. Like Archer, he emphasises a *natural* reality out of which society is an emergent phenomenon (Durkheim, 1995: 17). Like Archer, his *homo duplex* view of humans emphasises the *pre-social* embodied capacities and potentialities of individuals, and he stresses that the power of the religious ideas we encounter in society 'cannot add anything to our natural vitality', but 'can only release the emotive forces that are already within us' (Durkheim, 1995: 419). Thus, he stresses that, rather than individuals being constituted entirely by collective forces, there are purely individual as well as collective states of consciousness within us, and that the former constitute the basis of our individual personalities (Durkheim, 1984: 61). For Durkheim, in fact, the idea that individuals are simply 'tools' of the *conscience collective* is incompatible with the notion of individual freedom he held dear (Stedman Jones, 2001: 7). Consequently, he arguably presupposes the kind of 'inner conversation' Archer discusses, since without it individuals have no reality at all. In short, it can be suggested that Durkheim is not guilty of 'bundling personal properties (thoughts, convictions, feelings) into collectivities', since he acknowledges their location within the individual: what he emphasises, as does Archer, is the power of society to constitute these properties which are emergent from the interrelationship between individuals and social forces (Archer, 1995: 38; 2000: 215). Nevertheless, something Archer's work does draw our attention to, indirectly, is Durkheim's failure to take *belief* seriously enough, a failure which means it is necessary to move beyond his account of religion in certain respects.

Believing society

As Susan Stedman Jones (2001: 70) has argued, for Durkheim certain elements of human knowledge and experience are irreducible to particular forms of society and culture, and can be understood to be characteristic of humans in general and precede social codifications of experience. As she suggests, the necessary embedding of consciousness, even if it is collectively shared, in human agents with these capacities ensures that representation becomes possible in the first place, as well as ensuring that reality, even if collectively constituted, cannot simply be identified with representations (Stedman Jones, 2001: 70–1). Consequently, as Jones (1999: 81) suggests, Durkheim may have argued that the plasticity of human nature was greater than many suspect, but he also asserted that it 'cannot become just anything at all'. Here, the human capacity to *believe* is particularly significant: while the specific contents of belief systems may be socially constituted, this constitution process would not be possible without an analytically prior capacity to believe that is an innate aspect of human embodiment. Thus, he does not suggest that the *capacity* to believe is socially constituted, only that the *nature* of beliefs is shaped by social relationships (Durkheim, 1995: 34).

For Durkheim, then, it is clear that there is an embodied basis for belief, in the sense that beliefs are propositional attitudes that play causal roles in generating actions, and that humans have an innate capacity for adopting such attitudes (Lacy, 1998: 477). He does not take specific sets of beliefs seriously, however, in the sense that they refer to anything real other than the social forces they represent 'symbolically', and he tends to see practical activities as being far more important than beliefs in terms of generating and maintaining particular types of religion and social order (Rawls, 2001). It is this view of belief that has encouraged writers such as Smith (1978) and Ruel (2002) to argue that studying religions in relation to their beliefs reflects a Christian bias, since it is only in this context that belief has such a central significance. As Ruel (2002: 109–10) elaborates, in contrast to the 'monumental peculiarity' of the Christian concern with belief, Judaism is centred on the *Torah*, law, rather than belief, just as Islam is centred on the law of the *shar'ia*, while Buddhism is centred on *dharma*, and does not even have a word for 'belief'. Contrary to this view, however, no one with any detailed knowledge of these religious forms could deny the immense importance of belief: Buddhist notions of rebirth and karma clearly depend upon belief (see Harvey, 1990), for example, while Jewish and Islamic notions of religious law make no sense at all without a corresponding belief in God (see Nasr, 1988). In fact, with regard to Islam, as Ruel (2002: 109) himself notes, submission to God (*islam*) can be identified with having belief (*iman*), while a 'Muslim' is defined as a 'believer' (*mu'min*).

Where Ruel is on stronger ground is in noting the peculiarities that have marked the history of Christian belief, particularly with regard to the emergence, with Luther, of an existentialist focus on the subjective appropriation of belief through an intense struggle (Ruel, 2002: 107). In this regard, it can be noted that some forms of Protestant and Catholic Christianity can express divergent forms of theological anthropology: it is clear, for example, that a Protestant tendency to stress the foundational significance of revelation in relation to an individual's 'faith', mysteriously given by God, is quite different from the Catholic emphasis on revelation as building on a general, innate human ability to gain some real understanding of God and the world. Even so, as Trigg (1998: 175–82) has argued, without some allowance for 'natural theology', grounded in the embodied capacities of humans, Protestant claims concerning revelation and the universality of Christian truth could not make any sense, and on this basis it is possible to appreciate the immense sociological significance that religious beliefs can have.

If we view religion as a collective engagement with the 'open-ended' possibilities of transcendence emergent from the contingencies, potentialities and limitations of embodied human life, then the particular sets of beliefs societies develop do not have an entirely accidental, relativistic character making them unworthy of study in their own right. Weber (1965) appreciated this point, and clearly appears to take the comparative study of particular belief systems far more seriously than Durkheim did, though he also tended to adopt a form of psychological reductionism. Thus, he argued that there is an 'inner compulsion' in humans 'to understand the world as a meaningful cosmos', and analysed religions principally as *theodicies*, contextualising life's challenges and sufferings within a meaningful totality (Weber, 1965: 117; Morris, 1987: 73). Berger's (1990: 53) account of the role of theodicies in protecting a sense of meaningful order 'against the threat of its destruction by the anomic forces endemic to the human condition' develops this aspect of Weber's thought, and illuminates the philosophical anthropology underpinning this approach to the study of religion and society. In both cases, as in the case of the recent work of Turner and Rojek, there is an 'ontology of frailty' that sees meaninglessness and chaos, rather than contingency, as characteristic of humanity and society. The role of religious beliefs is to conceal the chaos, and thereby make social life bearable. Indeed, Berger (1990: 26), following Eliade (1959), transforms Durkheim's distinction between sacred and profane into a distinction between the sacred and chaos, and argues that religious beliefs about the cosmos falsify, conceal and alienate people from their real experience of life to protect them from the threats of chaos and death that would otherwise paralyse all social action (see also Berger, 1990: 86–7).

Although this Weberian tradition appears to take religious beliefs seriously, then, it only does so up to a point. In the end, religious beliefs are reduced into psychological compulsions and ontological deficits: religious beliefs are social constructions motivated by psychological needs that artificially invest the world with a meaning it does not have, and which always remain vulnerable to chaos they attempt to keep at bay. In contrast, Michel de Certeau's analyses of society and culture in relation to a passion for *believing*, apparent in human experience at its deepest and most ordinary levels, is not psychologically reductionist and focuses on an ontologically grounded surplus of human potentiality, rather than some sort of deficit (de Certeau and Domenach, 1974; de Certeau, 1984, 1987). Indeed, just as Bataille posits an excess of social energies within the hyper-spiritual substratum of society, so too de Certeau is concerned with an excess of meaning that escapes culture but which humans try to grasp through the beliefs that shape our day-to-day experiences of the world (Moingt, 1996: 481). For him, if the (post)modern world now teeters on the brink of a collapse into meaninglessness it is not because of the frailty of belief but because of an *effusion* of belief: there are too many things to believe, and the real nature of society and the world can become lost in this effusiveness (de Certeau, 1984: 179). None the less, in his more optimistic writings de Certeau also grapples with the persistence of forms of belief that express something real about humanity, society and the world since, although their emergence comes through the relationships of human society and history, they are not social constructions but social encounters with religious forces that reveal the contingency of human life in a more profound sense than that implied by an 'ontology of frailty'. In this sense, de Certeau's writings also connect with a broader tradition of thinking about the inherent potentialities of social life, including those of von Balthasar (1982).

In criticising positivism for its naïve empiricism and emphasising the common basis of theology and philosophy in an attitude of wonder before the contingency of being, von Balthasar (1982: 65) reflects sentiments that are pervasive amongst diverse strands of modern philosophy. Discussing Wittgenstein, for example, Kerr (1986: 140) has noted his view that philosophy must begin with *wonder*, and his consequent attempt to encourage the abandonment of a widely disseminated 'antipathy to bodilyness' evident in, amongst other things, a failure to take seriously the embodied interactions, relations and dynamics that mark the day-to-day lives of people. Irigaray (1984) has also sought to reassert the importance of an attitude of 'wonder', in her case as the basis for an ethics of sexual difference tied to an engagement with human embodiment. These evocations of wonder express a desire to avoid reductionist analyses of social life, and suggest the value of an engagement with the transcendent and open-ended nature of human and social phenomena. As such, they return us to the issues of contingency introduced at the beginning of this chapter.

Wonderful society

This chapter began with reference to Gould's (1991) *Wonderful Life*, which is a critique of reductionist visions of science, and an argument for the importance of grappling with the notion of contingency in our attempts to make sense of history. The notions of wonder evoked by writers as diverse as von Balthasar (1982), Wittgenstein (see Kerr, 1986) and Irigaray (1984) articulate a similar sense of the value of a non-reductionist view of society, as does Williams's (2000) recent attempt to reassert the value of Bossy's (1985) notion of the 'social miracle'. In this respect, if reality can be understood as an open-ended series of emergent strata, collective engagements with transcendence should not be reduced into lower level phenomena, even if they have their social origins in the hyper-spiritual dimensions of social life. With regard to these dimensions, and in contrast to Archer's (2000) association of the 'enchantment of being human' with individual qualities, Durkheim's account of a hyper-spirituality specific to society helps to make sense of the 'social miracle' since it recognises a transcendent, 'enchanted' dimension to humans at a collective level. In this regard it is fair to say, perhaps, that Archer's (2000) sociological vision of human embodiment, while rightly acknowledging the properties and powers inherent to individuals, none the less tends to invest them with a self-sufficiency that Durkheim helps challenge. That is to say, for her, society is unavoidable and in some respects desirable, but there is not the sense of the powerful forces of 'attraction and repulsion' to others that Durkheim illuminates and that those following in his wake, such as Bataille, have sought to develop.

While it is the Durkheimian view that allows us to appreciate an inherently religious dimension to human being-in-the-world at a *societal* level, however, it is only by embracing the idea that downwards reductionism is theoretically unacceptable that the real social significance of religion, as a causal power affecting people's views, choices and actions, can be appreciated. Rightly, Durkheim (1995: 2) recognised the absurdity of claims that religions were based on errors and falsehoods, since their social power and influence over huge numbers of societies across vast tracts of time testifies to their expression of something true. However, his reduction of this truth to social forces is analogous to the reductionism he critiques. Consequently, Durkheim's (1995: 351) argument that God is *purely* a 'symbolic expression' of society cannot be accepted, since it reduces emergent theological phenomena into social forces, and thereby precludes the possibility that individuals can also have what Archer calls an 'authentic' encounter with transcendental reality. In this respect, sociological attempts to 'bracket out' theological questions are no longer either desirable or necessary (see Berger, 1990). In fact, a sociological acceptance of the possibility of religious claims on reality need not compromise the ambition of its project, even if it must temper this with some humility. In short, religion may be emergent from society but it is not reducible to it: this helps us to make sense of society as much as it helps us to make sense of religion.

A sociological location of religion within an embodied vision of ontologically open, emergent strata also helps illuminate weaknesses within those theories of religion that overemphasise the significance of culture. Here, Talal Asad's (2002) anthropological argument about the Christocentric character of much academic study of religion is of note. Asad would concur with Bossy (1985) that the Reformation has had a major impact upon modern conceptions of religion; he goes further, however, and claims that the whole idea of a general theory of religion has a specific Christian history, often replicating Protestant ideas about the essence of religion. There are two major dimensions to this argument, which concern the distinction between religion and other social elements, and claims about how religions relate to reality. First, Asad (2002: 115) criticises Dumont (1971) for acknowledging that religion was inseparable from social and political factors in medieval society but nevertheless suggesting that religion is *analytically* identifiable in this context. He believes that this makes it possible to say that the essence of religion today is the same as it was then, encouraging the idea that religion is a trans-cultural and trans-historical phenomenon, while also creating significant problems in terms of understanding Islam, where 'religion' and 'politics' are not demarcated in the modern, Western way. None the less, this misunderstands Dumont's argument, which is precisely that religion is *not* the same today as in the Middle Ages, and serves merely to reinforce Asad's (2002: 116) own, very modern, belief that what constitutes 'religion' are historically specific 'discursive processes'. In fact, Asad's (2002: 129) Foucauldian deconstruction of religion into 'a particular history of knowledge and power' looks more like cultural imperialism than Dumont's attempt to get to grips with religious diversity within the context of a broader account of religious phenomena, and fails to address why a general theory of discourse and power is okay, but a theory of religion is not.

Second, however, Asad (2002: 123) also criticises Geertz (1973) for implicitly adopting a modern 'theological' viewpoint in associating religion primarily with beliefs and practices that must '*affirm something about the fundamental nature of reality*'. In this regard, Asad's (2002: 125) reference to Harré's (1981) social constructionist view that all beliefs are simply mental states confined to particular social contexts reveals a lack of sympathy with the idea that there is any possibility of an access to reality through religion. Furthermore, it is hard to think of a religion that does not make some sort of claim about reality: it can be noted that Theravada Buddhism, for example, which is firmly anti-theological in the sense that it acknowledges no God, nevertheless makes very explicit claims about the fundamental nature of reality (Gombrich, 1980). Again, it might be said that there is something more culturally imperialistic about reading the world's religions through the lens of post-structuralist philosophy than taking them seriously as different expressions of the human attempt to grapple with reality.

Further to this, however, Weberian visions of reality analysed within the strictures of an 'ontology of frailty', where religion offers fictitious, if vitally necessary, universes of meaning to stave off the reality of chaos, can also be called into question. Berger and Luckmann (1966: 211) may conclude their account of *The Social Construction of Reality* with the suggestion that sociology 'reawakens our wonder at this astonishing phenomenon' of society, but their vision of the 'unfinishedness' of humans, like that offered more recently by Turner and Rojek (2001), is not fully alive to the potentialities, powers and transcendent phenomena that circulate within society, and that are emergent from the embodied being-in-the-world of humans. In contrast, writers such as Durkheim, Bataille and de Certeau, though in many respects very different, all help illuminate a 'surplus', 'excess' or 'effusion' that is at the heart of social life and should be at the centre of sociological study. Here, human and societal contingency do not signal relativism, constructionism or chaos, but the complex, dynamic and patterned processes through which a social world without self-subsistence nevertheless offers a medium through which reality, meaning and some grasp of truth become possible. Further to this, however, it is precisely such contingency that allows for the emergence of an obligatory character within many aspects of social life, even though this character might appear to be under threat in a world apparently marked by processes of de-traditionalisation, secularisation and the systematic elimination of genuine religious consciousness (Virilio and Lotringer, 1997: 124; Gane, 2003: 166). None the less, the clarification and discussion of key aspects of society as a *necessary* reality is the focus of the next chapter.

Notes

1. Studies of 'chimp carnivals', for example, have noted that the 'collective effervescence' Durkheim (1995) associates with human assemblies is also evident in the 'social excitement' that occurs when apes from different areas gather together where food is in abundance (Reynolds, 1967; Allen, 1998: 158).

2. As Freitag (2002: 175, 177) has suggested, what this 'slippage in vocabulary' does is conceal the fact that 'the social is first apprehended as the societal', thereby obscuring the ontological reality of society and promoting a crisis of representation amongst sociologists.

3. As Richardson (1994: 35) points out, however, as well as being rooted in Durkheim's concept of the sacred/profane polarity, Bataille's concepts of homogeneity and heterogeneity can be understood to build on Tönnies's distinction between *gesellschaft* (the 'homogeneous' society of organisation, law and cohesion) and *gemeinschaft* (the 'heterogeneous' society of cooperation, custom and ritual expression).

4
Necessary Society

Throughout the history of thought, the notion of *contingence* has regularly been contrasted with that of *necessity* (Torrance, 1998: 85). As with 'sacred' and 'profane' or 'public' and 'private', however, these notions are not simply opposites, but depend upon and express a close interrelationship. This is particularly evident with regard to society. In the previous chapter, the contingency of society was examined in terms of its dependence upon the embodied human beings who constitute it, seeking to develop the idea that society is an emergent phenomenon in an ontologically open and stratified world. Although society can, in this sense, be seen as 'contingent', in this chapter I shall, nevertheless, attempt to establish the idea that one of society's key characteristics as an emergent phenomenon is its power to impose itself as an unavoidable reality. In other words, my argument is that society's contingent origins do not result in its appearance as an accidental, arbitrary or random human development but as an obligatory, unavoidable and necessary reality. This is not simply so in the sense that individuals find it necessary, for example, to speak particular languages or use certain currencies (Durkheim, 1982a: 51), but also in the sense that even governments, for all their immense economic, legal and political powers, often have to acknowledge and submit to societal demands, even where these appear to contradict or undermine their manifest policies and ideological commitments (Polanyi, 2001). In developing this argument, however, some influential accounts of contemporary social and cultural life need to be challenged.

Offering arguments that are representative of a broad swathe of contemporary sociological opinion, Giddens (1991a), for example, has identified one of the key characteristics of modern societies as the fact that individuals are presented with endless choices, possibilities and decisions, since all routines, habits and rules are open to reflexive adjustment and deconstruction. For Bauman (2002), indeed, the plurality of choices, options and decisions now open to people results in an 'individualised society', where individuals are no longer bound into tight social relationships but surf across social life in pursuit of their own, reflexively constructed projects and desires. In a similar vein, Beck (1992: 135) emphasises how identities are now 'dependent on decisions' and our biographies are 'self-produced'. In these circumstances, the very essence of modern societies appears to involve a rejection of any notion of obligation or necessity beyond the essentially utilitarian needs of the individual. As Giddens (1990, 1991a) expresses it, social obligations that do not have a reflexively constituted 'until-further-notice' character can now be pictured as 'pre-modern' phenomena. Giddens, in fact, explicitly defines modernity *against* notions of social obligation, allowing him to interpret even the most intimate of personal relationships in terms of individual choices.[1] For him, indeed, the reflexive

character of modern intimacy is essentially the same as that which characterises global capitalism and modern systems of knowledge: everything is
'disembedded', open to revision and reconstruction, and radically discontinuous with all that went before it.

While Giddens (1994, 1998) distinguishes the social and political implications of his arguments from the 'free market' theorists of neo-classical
economics, they have much in common. Giddens's (1998: 66) vision of the
reflexive construction of social and political orders through, and with
respect for, individual interests and choices, for example, rests on the sort of
individualistic, utilitarian and nominalist view of society that would not be
out of place in rational choice theory. In broad terms, in fact, his notion of
'dialogical democracy' arguably implies a reflexively constituted lifestyle
market more than a society (see Giddens, 1991a: 231; 1994; 252-3). Even
within this type of sociological analysis, however, there is a contradiction,
which is picked up by Beck (1992: 116) who notes that, even if other societal obligations tend to disappear, the one thing that will not go away is *the
obligation to choose*: in one sense, 'anything goes', since choices open up and
constraints become the objects of reflexive scrutiny, but, on the other hand,
not making choices 'is tending to become impossible'. At the very least, this
suggests that obligation is not entirely a thing of the past, even if the plurality of choices and options available to modern persons might lead them
to believe that this is the case. Beyond that, however, Beck's comments not
only raise questions about other obligations that might still be significant in
contemporary societies, but also raise more fundamental questions about
the necessary character of society in a more general sense.

In order to make sense of this necessary dimension of society, the contemporary reluctance to acknowledge an emergent, *sui generis* aspect to
social relationships that imposes various obligations upon individuals looks
highly questionable. With regard to sexual relationships, for example,
Giddens does not allow that the hyper-spiritual dynamics of the couple
might make infidelity something more significant than the breaking of a
reflexively constituted contract, resulting in the sort of 'righteous anger' and
violence discussed by Randall Collins (1988: 121; see Dobash and Dobash,
1979). Here, the 'cult of the dyad' imposes sacred obligations upon the individuals concerned, not agenda items for a reflexively constituted relationship committee. With regard to societies in general, it is also clear that
Giddens's lack of attention to obligation is unsatisfactory for similar reasons.
Day-to-day rules governing social encounters considered by Goffman
(1969), the social constraints upon economic forces and activities that
recurrently frustrate free market philosophies (Polanyi, 2001), the persistence of taboos on things such as paedophilia, and the continuing social value
attached to the sacrifices offered by military and civilian personnel in times
of war or terrorist attacks, all indicate that participation in social life entails
an encounter with various forms of obligation which we ignore at our peril.
Even in 'reflexive modernity', people who ignore everyday social rules face
ostracism; paedophiles are objects of such contempt they are not even safe

from attack in prison, while, in military and certain civilian contexts, at least a certain amount of 'bravery' is obligatory, and accusations of 'cowardice' still carry a very significant sting. Furthermore, as Stiglitz (2001: xii) has suggested, it is hardly surprising that the contemporary British and American devotion to the idea of 'free market' economics, which denies any *sui generis* aspects of society, has wreaked havoc in Russia, East Asia and other places where Western economists have encouraged experiments with unusually pure forms of free market theory, since social realities are much more complex than such economic models allow.

If developing an understanding of society with greater sensitivity to this complexity goes against the grain not only of neo-classical economics but also of some current views within sociology, however, it is of note that there is a strong counter-trend against such views in the history of sociology. As Caillé (1986) has suggested, within sociology there has long been a willingness to question the presuppositions of economists and to engage with the anti-utilitarianism that developed out of Western Christianity (see Richman, 2003: 30). In this regard, Caillé's organisation 'M.A.U.S.S.' (*Mouvement Anti-Utilitariste dans les Sciences Sociales*), not only draws its inspiration from Marcel Mauss's (1969) anti-utilitarian account of gift exchange, but also from the work of Durkheim, Bataille and Karl Polanyi, all of whom sought to place modern views of society, economics and religion in a broader historical and anthropological perspective. This broader perspective, which drew upon studies of 'primitive' or 'archaic' societies, served to demonstrate the partiality, reductionism and insufficiency of economic models of human beings and their vision of society as marketplace for pleasure-maximising individualists (Kurasawa, 2003: 20). Indeed, while Polanyi's (2001: 47) critique of market societies was titled *The Great Transformation*, like Durkheim, Mauss and Bataille, his sensitivity to the specific characteristics of modern societies did not lead him to adopt a 'discontinuist' view of history in the manner of writers such as Giddens, but to recognise the fact that differences between societies and peoples have often been 'vastly exaggerated', especially by economists. Indeed, what characterises the work of all these writers is the recognition that society, though emergent from human relationships, is a necessary and unavoidable reality grounded in human embodiment, and that many of the dangers facing the modern world stem from a failure to acknowledge this fact.

Consequently, in developing an account of some of the necessary dimensions of society, the works of these writers are particularly important. The first part of this chapter is focused on the analysis of taboo, which, despite the postmodern concern with transgression, can be considered as a central manifestation of the impact of society as a *sui generis* reality upon individuals, in the sense that taboos express some of the obligatory aspects of hyper-spiritual dynamics. While there is a great deal of ambiguity about the nature and social implications of taboo in the anthropological and sociological literature devoted to its study, its capacity to challenge a purely utilitarian or contractarian view of social relationships is striking. Following this, Mauss's

(1969) account of gift exchange is considered as a key study of how patterns of reciprocal obligation come to circulate within various types of society, while Bataille's (1991) development of Mauss's arguments in his own account of the 'general' and the 'restricted' economy is discussed as a direct challenge to those postmodern theorists who seek to co-opt Bataille for their own ends. What both Mauss and Bataille demonstrate is that the economy is always embedded in society, an idea that is also the cornerstone of Polanyi's (2001) contribution to the study of modern economic systems. Consequently, the rest of the chapter examines Polanyi's thoroughgoing critique of the market model of humanity and society, which, though originally published in 1944, illuminates tendencies towards an economically driven dehumanisation of social realities which are particularly relevant to the contemporary era of globalisation.

Forbidding society

As Radcliffe-Brown (1952) has noted, the term 'taboo' is derived from the Polynesian term *tapu*, meaning 'forbidden', though the concept has a number of associations, including prohibition, sacredness, uncleanness and contagion (Morris, 1987: 130). Radcliffe-Brown's emphasis upon the emotional foundation of taboo is developed on a Durkheimian basis, and, for him, taboos express 'social' rather than 'natural' dangers. In a similar vein, Steiner (1956: 20–1) has suggested that 'taboo deals with the sociology of danger', in the sense that it is concerned with restrictive behaviour in dangerous situations, with the protection of individuals in danger, or with the protection of society from dangerous forces or persons. In the French sociological tradition, in particular, these dangers were often understood in terms of 'contagion' or 'infection'. In the work of Lévy-Bruhl (1926), for instance, the concept of contagion expresses the social character of danger, and thus the necessity of a collective response to a threat to the social body (Steiner, 1956: 114). Beyond this tradition, however, others have also understood taboo as a response to a perceived threat of contagion. Freud's (1950: 21) understanding of taboo also emphasises its connection to danger, noting how certain prohibitions are perceived to be necessary 'because certain persons and things are charged with a dangerous power, which can be transferred through contact with them, almost like an infection'.

It has been recognised that taboos continue to be of immense social significance in (post)modern societies. Robert Hughes's (1994) critique of the phenomenon of 'political correctness' discusses how a discourse of liberal permissiveness coexists with a whole series of prohibitions, many related to speech, covering issues such as race, gender and sexuality in contemporary American society; an insight also evident in the work of Bloom (1987) and Hunter (1991). Aside from such distinctively late modern taboos, however, prohibitions of a more long-standing nature continue to be significant, such as the incest taboo. James B. Twitchell (1987), in a study of the incest taboo in modern culture, explores the challenging of this taboo in a wide range of

Romantic literature, but also observes its continuing strength; a strength he connects to the women's movement and to contemporary notions of 'child abuse'. As well as connecting taboo to ritual, however, many studies of taboo also link it with patterns of inclusion and exclusion that define and reinforce the boundaries of community.

Christie Davies's (1982) study of sexual taboos and social boundaries makes this linkage explicit, suggesting that the strong taboos that exist against homosexuality, bestiality and transvestism in the West are the result of attempts to establish and defend strong ethnic, religious or institutional boundaries. These boundaries, which can be both internal and external, and cover male/female and human/animal polarities, are the means through which a community establishes a distinct identity for itself (Davies, 1982: 1032). The resurgence of conflicts surrounding the construction of such boundaries in advanced modern societies would therefore suggest that the analysis of the development of taboos should remain an important socio-logical concern. Nevertheless, an awareness of the complexity of modern societies has led many writers to focus upon the role of taboos in more 'primitive' social forms in order to illuminate enduring features of all human societies, or to propose evolutionary schemas that contextualise changes in patterns of prohibitions within broader arguments about the developing complexities of human societies.

Although the association of non-white, non-Western races with 'primitive' forms of society and culture has now, itself, become taboo, theories and analytical studies of 'primitive' society have a long history in sociology and anthropology (see Evans-Pritchard, 1965). Durkheim's (1995) and Lévi-Strauss's (1969) theories of taboo, for example, along with the evolutionary dimension of the theories of Freud (1950), Bukert (1983) and Girard (1995) in relation to taboo, are all examples of this. Beyond these, however, evolutionary conceptions continue to shape certain types of theorising about society. Yehudi Cohen (1978), for example, has suggested that the more complex a society is, the less likely it is that the incest taboo will apply to relatives beyond the immediate family. This accords with Parsons's adoption of a broadly evolutionary understanding of the development of societies (see Robertson, 1991), and his argument that there are two types of incest rule, one related to the immediate family and one to that of broader kinship groups (Parsons, 1954: 108). Cohen's argument is that the latter type of rule is disappearing as societies become more complex. Similarly, White (1948: 432) has argued that in complex societies tribal bonds have been replaced by the power of the state, so that the incest taboo becomes severely weakened in comparison with 'primitive' societies; a view reinforced by Leavitt's (1989) cross-cultural analysis of the disappearance of the incest taboo. More broadly, however, there are also arguments about the embodied potentialities of humans, especially in relation to their capacity for sociality, that underpin such evolutionary models.

Leslie White (1948: 423), for example, has developed Edward B. Tylor's (1888) emphasis on the essentially cooperative nature of human communities, and it is in this context that he places the incest taboo: the taboo exists as an example of humans cooperating in order to ensure the survival of the group (Leavitt, 1989: 117). Jonathan H. Turner (1996), however, has offered a radically different view of humanity and sociality. Putting forward what he calls a 'Darwinian–Durkheimian' analysis of the evolution of emotions, he challenges the widely held sociological assumption that humans are inherently social beings. Drawing on Maryanski's (1987, 1992, 1993, 1994) analysis of the social behaviour of apes, and the implications of this for how 'human nature' is conceptualised, Turner (1996: 24) argues that the emotional capacities of humans in relation to sociality only developed very slowly, and had to counter a genetic disposition towards a less social, if not anti-social, attitude. Turner (1996: 1) distinguishes his analysis, however, from those of rational choice theorists who see humans as 'ego-centered-resource-maximizers' (Coleman, 1990; see also Hechter, 1987) and sociobiological theorists of 'selfishness' as 'the underlying genic pressure behind sociality' (see Lopreato, 1984; Van den Berghe, 1981). Turner (1996: 24–5) adopts Durkheim's concept of the *homo duplex*, arguing that humans have embodied predispositions towards sociality (collective life), but anti-social (individual) dimensions also. What Turner is proposing, then, is taking Durkheim's basically ahistorical concept of the *homo duplex* and historicising it within an argument about the slow evolution of human society.

The tension between conceiving of 'primitive' human societies as basically *simpler* forms of enduring, universal patterns of sociality, or as significantly *different* forms of social life in a broad evolutionary schema, has run throughout much sociology and anthropology. It can be found, for example, in Durkheim's (1995) sometimes ambiguous use of the term 'primitive' in order to illuminate the origins of religion: he concentrates on 'primitive' religion because it is a 'simpler' manifestation of universal characteristics (Durkheim, 1995: 6), but also incorporates evolutionary assumptions into his argument (Durkheim, 1995: 236). This ambiguity is reflected in the differing interpretations of those anthropologists influenced by Durkheim. Lévy-Bruhl (1926), for example, associates primitive society with an emotionality and mysticism he believes to be entirely alien to modern societies. Lévi-Strauss (1996: 251), however, has taken a different view, and has criticised Lévy-Bruhl's arguments. Viewed in this context, Turner's (1996) attempt to place Durkheim's concept of the *homo duplex* in an evolutionary framework, in order to describe how human sociality, and therefore human *society*, became possible, has much in common with earlier sociological theories of taboo. Basically, however, these theories are attempts to account for recurrent patterns of social inclusion, order and security, while simultaneously recognising elementary patterns of exclusion, disorder and danger. Without endorsing an evolutionary framework, it is possible to see in them an attempt to grapple with some of the most elementary social processes that bind individuals into societies through the imposition of obligations.

Inclusive/exclusive society

For Durkheim (1995: 304), the phenomenon of the 'taboo' can best be understood as a form of prohibition that, together with others, constitutes a 'negative cult' regulating contact with the sacred. Prohibitions can have the purpose of separating one form of the sacred from another, but are more extensively characterised by the purpose of separating all that is sacred from the profane. The negative cult thus serves as 'the precondition of access to the positive cult' (Durkheim, 1995: 313). Durkheim notes that the 'primary taboos' are characteristically prohibitions of contact, covering not only touching, but also looking, speaking, hearing and tasting (Durkheim, 1995: 308–9). The negative cult is therefore often composed of rules governing what people are allowed to see or not see, what they can or cannot say or hear, and others governing when they can or cannot eat, the types of food allowed to particular social groups, and all sorts of other regulations governing labour, washing, nakedness and sexual relations. Taboo is, therefore, a thoroughly embodied phenomenon.

Hertz's (1960) analysis of the widespread prohibitions governing the use of the left hand develops from this basis, noting how certain objects and beings are 'impregnated' with sacred or profane characteristics. The purpose of taboos is to prohibit any contact or confusion of beings and things belonging to each category, provoking emotions of fear and aversion in order to preserve social order (Hertz, 1960: 7). Prohibitions arise from the emotions evoked by the sacred and, despite the fact that certain magical or supernatural consequences are sometimes understood to flow from the breaking of taboos, they are essentially collective, human phenomena involving, at the very least, blame and public disapproval (Durkheim, 1995: 304–5). This collective character does not imply, however, that such rules apply equally to all sections of a society. For example, certain ritual functionaries, such as priests, are commonly understood to have a special authority regarding the sacred and can interact with sacred objects in a manner prohibited for others, whose contact with the sacred is mediated through such priests. In broader terms, however, embodied differences between men and women can be, and often are, taken up and elaborated upon within the negative cult, investing these differences with a sacred or profane character and thus providing a religious basis for the authority of one gender over another. It is such processes that help us comprehend the difficulties women face in seeking to overcome their oppression and marginalisation in so many societies: in the vast majority of societies the negative cult has provided the principal means through which women have been subordinated to men; a subordination evident in the greater number of prohibitions directed towards women. As Hertz (1960: 9) expresses it, 'In general, man is sacred, woman is profane'.

Discussing the Maori, Hertz (1960: 12) notes how left/right polarities are not only associated with the sacred and the profane, but also with men and women. The right side, which is the male side, is associated with the sacred, goodness, creativity, strength and life. The left, the female side, is associated with the profane, maleficent powers, weakness and death. Such polarities both express and stimulate men's fear of women, and consign them to an inferior social status: if all that is good is associated with men, then women must be seen as sources of danger. Many of the prohibitions concerning women in some societies, however, relate specifically to aspects of female embodiment. The Hebrew Bible, for example, rules that a woman is 'unclean' for seven days and must 'not touch anything consecrated nor go to the sanctuary' during her monthly periods. After giving birth to a boy she is also 'unclean' for seven days, though her blood will not be 'purified' for another thirty-three days; after giving birth to a girl she is unclean for fourteen days, and her blood 'purified' after sixty-six days (Leviticus, 12: 1–8). While a woman is in a state of 'menstrual pollution' she makes 'unclean' anything she touches, and anyone who touches anything she has touched must wash their clothes and their body and will be unclean until the evening. Furthermore, 'If a man goes so far as to sleep with her, he will contract her menstrual pollution and will be unclean for seven days' (Leviticus, 15: 24).

As Davies (1982: 1034–5) observes, these taboos on certain kinds of contact between men and women are part of a broader insistence on the separation of categories; a separation that establishes and reinforces the identity of the Jewish community over and against the other cultures that surround them. Such prohibitions are evident in a variety of cultural contexts too. Durkheim gives numerous examples in Native American and Australian Aboriginal religions where men are associated with pollution, and thus denied contact with the sacred, only if they are 'uninitiated', but where women are denied such contact permanently, purely on the basis of their gender (Durkheim, 1995: 125, 132, 137, 138, 288, 308, 395). For Durkheim, the separation of categories, such as 'men' and 'women', can be related back to the fundamental opposition between sacred and profane. It is the category of the sacred that provides the symbolic focus for order in the face of what would otherwise be what Davies (1982: 1035) calls 'utter confusion' (see Berger, 1990). Mike Gane suggests that 'what is universal is the application of the sacred/profane dichotomy to human blood and sexual practices, and sexual relations are deeply affected by this tendency' (Gane, 1983a: 248). Blood becomes identified with the sacred forces unifying a group, and thus the subject of taboos repulsing any contact with it. Since women naturally bleed, a 'vacuum' is created between men and women since they now threaten impure contact with the sacred substance (Durkheim, 1963: 83; Gane, 1983a: 248).[2]

In this context, prohibitions can exclude women from the fundamental constitution of society itself, since the negative cult is the precondition for the positive cult through which society symbolically represents itself to itself through its conceptualisation of the sacred (Durkheim, 1995: 138, 313). In other words, women are excluded, or at least marginalised, with regard to human social order on the basis of their embodiment.[3] The constitution of social order therefore becomes dependent, to some extent, upon the regulation of women, especially the regulation of women's bodies. The sacred may symbolically represent all that a society values, and may bind individuals into collective patterns of meaning and identity, but it is also simultaneously exclusionary as well as inclusionary. The sacred/profane dichotomy that makes society possible is also, therefore, the basis upon which obligatory social differences, divisions and polarities are constructed. Here, Durkheim's (1995: 404) observation that women frequently fulfil the ritual function of the 'scapegoat', anticipating Girard's (1995) similar argument, is notable: women are, in a sense, 'insiders' who are also 'outsiders' and can become objects of real, as well as symbolic, violence that aims to channel away destructive energies and thus preserve the cohesiveness of (male) societies.

Such arguments have been criticised by feminist thinkers for reinforcing the idea that society and culture belong to males. In her study of sacrifice, religion and paternity, for example, Nancy Jay (1992) expresses concern that the ritual construction of (male) society, and sociological theories of it, rest on the attribution of certain universal biological characteristics to men and women, while ignoring the embodied relationships men have with their mothers 'before' they enter any world of social relations (Jay, 1992: 133). Looking back to Thomas Hobbes, for example, she notes his view of the 'state of nature' as a violent war of all against all where life is 'solitary, poor, nasty, brutish and short' (Hobbes, 1957: 143). She observes that in this view the relationship between mother and child counts for nothing as it is merely 'natural', not 'social': 'Society is the rational creation of adult males, who alone contribute to it' (Jay, 1992: 129). Thus, looking at Bukert's (1983) theory of the hunt, she interprets his 'intraspecific violence' as just another version of Hobbes's war of all against all, and sees Girard's (1995) account of sacrifice as making similar assumptions about how gender relations are shaped by a biologically given male violence (Jay, 1992: 132–3). Jay (1992: xxiii) sees in Girard's work, as well as a vast range of other literatures on sacrifice, a close association of sacrifice with the construction of gender dichotomies and the social marginalisation of women. Focusing upon the embodied basis of these rituals, in fact, she goes so far as to see 'sacrifice as a remedy for having been born of woman'.

None the less, while Jay's criticisms of implicitly Hobbesian views of 'nature' and the biologically determinist conceptions of men and women that flow from them are illuminating, it is not simply the case that sociological theories of the ritual construction of society are necessarily complicit in the subordination of women. On the contrary, such theories can help illuminate the social processes through which such subordination takes on its obligatory character. As Rawls (2001) emphasises, a key aspect of Durkheim's study of religion and society is the emphasis upon enacted social practices: in his account of taboo he is illuminating the ritual mechanisms through which the relationships between men and women become integrated into a sacrificial economy. Rituals channel the hyper-spiritual dynamics of the group towards particular systems of symbolic classification through enacted practices: the denigration or subordination of women (as of any other oppressed or marginalized group) is manifest in actions, and can only be changed through actions (see Rawls, 2000). In fact, contrary to Jay's view of the ordination of women into the Church representing their incorporation into a male sacrificial order, such patterns of ordination invariably transform that order, in time, since the order is an emergent outcome of social action.

One conclusion that could be drawn in the light of these arguments is that directing attention towards the sacrificial structure underpinning social relationships can help illuminate how patterns of inclusion and exclusion become obligatory, and thereby offer an opportunity to work towards their transformation. None the less, a more radical conclusion is often drawn by writers such as Jay, namely that the entire network of sacrifice, taboo and obligation that appears to have an enduring significance for the development of society should be deconstructed and rejected. In Jay's case this is because of what she perceives to be the inherently 'patriarchal' character of this network, even though many feminist attempts to conceptualise elementary social processes tend to come back to patterns of inclusion/exclusion reflected through taboos (Shilling and Mellor, 2001: 126). More broadly, however, a widespread cultural interest in *transgression* rather than taboo has raised questions concerning the nature of contemporary societies and, in the case of some theorists at least, has tended to endorse the idea that more or less any form of social obligation is fragile, undesirable or even impossible. Here, the significance of Bataille's work is much disputed.

Transgressing society

Toffler's (1970) notion of the 'throwaway society' made a link between the throwing away of produced goods and the throwing away of values, rules and received ways of acting and being (Harvey, 1989: 286). Hawkes's (1996) account of the emergence of the 'permissive society' makes a further link between these processes and the reduction of sex to a consumer product (or, rather, an increasingly diverse range of products) to be dreamt about, pursued, acquired and discarded. Noting Bauman's (1989: 165) vision of a culture where 'for every human problem there is a solution waiting somewhere in the shop', Hawkes (1996: 115) observes that the promise of liberation, choice and self-development ushered in by this consumerisation of sex actually concealed an oppressive obligation to submit human desires to capitalist regulation. Like many cultural critics, however, Hawkes's (1996: 126) response to these empty promises is not to question the logic of the 'permissive society' *per se*, but to argue for its radical extension, eulogising the 'disruptive possibility' of sexual pleasure freed from all social regulation, taboos and any procreative association. For those contemporary writers who share such 'disruptive' desires, the radical claims of Bataille's sociology/philosophy seem to anticipate and legitimate the unrelenting assault upon the societal taboos, rules and moral codes that seek to regulate human desire. In short, Bataille has been embraced as the postmodern era's 'prophet of transgression' (Noyes, 2000).

While the ambiguities of Bataille's work mean that there is some justification for interpreting his project in these terms, such readings also simplify his arguments a great deal. In this respect, it is especially worth noting that the adoption of Bataille by post-structuralists and postmodernists tends to ignore the influence of Durkheim and emphasise the influence of Nietzsche and de Sade. Foucault (1998: 25), for example, emphasises the importance of the concept of 'transgression' in Bataille's work, which he defines as 'profanation in a world which no longer recognises any positive meaning in the sacred'. In some respects, however, Foucault's understanding is entirely alien to Bataille, since the profane cannot mean anything at all apart from the sacred. In fact, for Bataille, where profanation is pursued without reference to a need to revitalise the sacred it tends to encourage patterns of individualism that weaken society further. In fact, Caillois (1988b: 35), Bataille's early collaborator, notes that 'the greatest individualists', such as de Sade and Nietzsche, were actually 'weak men' precisely because they cut themselves off from the social and its substratum in the sacred. Similarly, Bataille (1988a: 20) emphasises the inescapable weakness of the 'isolated individual', and suggests that Nietzsche's will to power condemns the individual to madness unless it is connected to collective energies. Consequently, people should 'concentrate not on profaning but making sacred' (Caillois, 1988b: 36). Indeed, contrary to Noyes's (2000: 95) claim that 'for Bataille transgression is an impulse that is irreducible to religion', the reverse is true: transgression is only meaningful with reference to the sacred. For him, just as the profane is only meaningful in relation to the sacred, transgression cannot be considered apart from taboo.

For Bataille, taboo and transgression have a dichotomous but mutually enriching relationship that mirrors that of the sacred and the profane: 'the profane world is the world of taboos. The sacred world depends upon limited acts of transgression' (Bataille, 1987: 67–8). Here, his argument essentially restates Durkheim's (1995: 414) view that all contact with the sacred implies a kind of sacrilege, which is why contact is often simultaneously sanctifying and polluting. It also endorses Caillois's (1950: 227) account of the violence and excesses of feast days, an apparent profaning of what is sacred, as an effervescent revitalisation of the sacred itself. For Bataille, then, the sacred cannot simply be associated with order: it orders but it also destroys, confusing the categories and distinctions created by profane life (Hollier, 1998: 65). For Bataille (1987: 68), taboos bind humans together through fear, but also through a compelling fascination for the sacred object. It is this tension between fear and desire that is the essence of social life. The categories, distinctions and boundaries of normal social life are always vulnerable to a disruptive encounter with 'heterogeneous' elements. As Habermas (1998: 168) comments, Bataille applied the concept of the heterogeneous to social groups, the outcast and the marginalised, who suggest the presence of elements beyond the boundaries of normal social life and thus become the objects of taboo: prostitutes, untouchables, the insane, the bohemian. These groups become objects of fear, but also fascination and even desire, because they suggest a world of intoxication, excess and the transcendence of day-to-day rules and boundaries. The logic of this, contrary to Hegarty's (2000: 33) association of taboo with homogeneity and transgression with heterogeneity, is that a state of heterogeneity is one of transgression *and* taboo, since it is characterised by a strong sacred/profane polarity, in contrast to the dominance of utilitarian concerns and 'weak' forms of religion in a state of homogeneity.

In the light of this account of Bataille, it is clear that, rather than hailing him as a postmodern 'prophet of transgression', he can be acknowledged as a writer who offers a damning critique of the 'anything goes' mentality of a consumerist society that imagines obligation, sacrifice and taboo to be things of the past. Essentially, his argument is that an interest in transgression without recognition of the importance of taboo condemns individuals either to a de-humanised existence in a 'world of utility', such as one where all value and meaning are reduced to market forces, or, in extreme cases, to a state of madness such as the one that engulfed Nietzsche. Contrary to Foucault's interpretation of his project, for Bataille the urgent necessity for modern societies is the revitalisation of the sacred, not the profaning of everything, since the sacred represents those hyper-spiritual social energies which underpin societies yet also threaten their tendencies to reduce human potentiality to utilitarian considerations. Following Durkheim, the 'heterogeneous' society Bataille desires is therefore a society with a strong sense of the sacred/profane polarity, and of the sacrificial and obligatory actions that lead us from an individualistic focus on self-interest into an encounter with the inter-relational wholeness of life.

In the course of his critique of Durkheim's influence upon sociology's focus on society as an object of study, Urry (2000: 26-7) contrasts what he believes to be Durkheim's concern with a 'fixed and immutable' structure lurking beneath the flux of social life with Derrida's (1987: 27) focus on *différance*, which implies a dynamism incompatible with the concept of structure. For Bataille, whose core arguments are very much dependent on Durkheim, however, it is a close attentiveness to the dynamic circulations of social energies that illuminates the reality of a structure beneath the manifest, observable features of society. In so far as a society respects this structure, and the heterogeneous reality emergent from it, then human potentialities and powers can flourish: if this underlying structure, and its sacrificial logic, are ignored, then societies will become de-humanising and vulnerable to decay and corruption. It is the latter set of processes that can be identified in those consumerist societies that have 'grown far more comfortable with the unreal than the real' (Ritzer, 1999: 180), however much they might play around with religious dynamics in a superficial way. For Bataille, at least, these processes could also be associated with a relativistic valorisation of *différance* for its own sake, since this implies the lack of any grounding in a substratum of collective social energies. It is only in Bataille's (1988a) image of himself as the 'sorcerer's apprentice', perhaps, unleashing forces over which he has little understanding and control, that he might be said to exemplify the spirit of 'postmodern' times. What he helps illuminate, however, are the dangers facing those contemporary societies where individuals imagine themselves to exist in a world without limits, and where everything can be the object of choice, reinvention and market forces. In this respect, his work has much in common with Virilio's account of the contemporary valorisation of transgression.

As Virilio (2002: 10) suggests, many of the dangers facing humans in the twenty-first century inevitably follow from the fantasy that humanity can actually live in a world without limits. He notes that, in contemporary Western societies, our cultural heroes are often those who spectacularly flout 'any prohibition', from the scientists who intervene into the conception of life itself through to the serial killers and gangsters who become 'charismatic' objects of fascination for newspapers, books, films and television (Virilio, 2002: 23–4). Although he argues that the only prohibition is now the 'prohibition to prohibit' (Virilio, 2002: 25), however, he also draws attention to a paradox at the heart of contemporary society. He notes, for example, that the portrait of the child murderer Myra Hindley in the *Sensation* exhibition at the London Royal Academy appeared in the same year that the British government passed the Sex Offenders Act, aimed at curbing paedophilia and the industrialisation of the sex trade (Virilio, 2002: 75). Virilio does not develop any thoughts on this paradox, since it becomes lost in his relentless interrogation of a world that has completely lost its moral, religious and human bearings. It is nevertheless significant, perhaps, because it indicates a society that is losing, rather than has lost, its connection to an identifiable moral and religious substratum.

The cultural fascination with taboo-breakers noted by Virilio is a real enough phenomenon, but the limits of the 'anything goes' interpretation of contemporary societies are indicated very clearly by the fact that we are not yet ready to accept phenomena such as paedophilia as 'lifestyle choices'. On the contrary, certain taboos remain fiercely powerful, even if some in the art world and the media appear to exploit the iconography of evil for utilitarian purposes. One of the reasons for this enduring power is the fact that the world we inhabit is not one of our construction, but an already existing reality, where our choices and actions are structured by a hyper-spiritual substratum that necessarily imposes certain obligations upon us. These obligations are not only evident with regard to taboos, however, but also with regard to the 'embeddedness' of economic forces and structures within society. Mauss's (1969) influential study of the social significance of gift exchange illuminates key aspects of these deeper patterns.

Obligatory society

The purpose of Mauss's *Essai sur le don* (*The Gift*)(1969) is to refute the idea that human action and social order can be explained with recourse to the notion of individuals seeking to maximise their self-interest in contractual forms of social, political and economic arrangements. He argues that, at the very foundations of human society, there are powerful social dynamics that attract us into relations with others, and he seeks to illuminate these dynamics through his analysis of patterns of gift exchange. According to Mauss, the apparently voluntary character of gift exchange disguises how it creates, nurtures and expresses allegiances between different individuals and groups. These allegiances encompass gift exchange within a complex series of rules and moral obligations. Much of the discussion of these gift exchanges, obligations and allegiances is focused on premodern societies, specifically Polynesia, Melanesia and the tribes of North West America, though Mauss also touches upon Roman law, ancient Hindu texts and practices, and modern social contexts.

An important part of the book's argument is that much classical economic theory is wrong. This theory supposes that economic activity between individuals seeking to achieve their self-interest through some form of market is universal. It is assumed that all individuals, and all societies past and present, are focused on self-interest in this way, despite the fact that particular market forms may vary. Mauss argues that this view of *economic man* is specifically modern, however, and has never existed in the past or in contemporary 'archaic' societies. The modern prioritisation of economic factors is, therefore, culturally and historically specific. This specificity is also evident, furthermore, in the modern separation of economics from other areas of life, such as the religious. It is in this context that Mauss emphasises the significance of what he calls *total social facts*. Building on Durkheim's (1982a) emphasis on sociology as the study of 'social facts', Mauss's notion of 'total social facts' centres on those phenomena that encompass a range of religious, economic, political and psychological factors within a society. As Gofman (1998: 65) suggests, Mauss had a general interest in notions of totality, talking of the 'total human being', the 'totality of the body of society' and 'total prestations', as well as 'total social facts'. He rejected the idea that human phenomena could be divided into distinct categories. In this regard, he developed Durkheim's *homo duplex* conception of humans to offer his own view of *l'homme total*, encompassing sociological, psychological and biological aspects of humans within one inter-relational whole.

The 'total' approach to human phenomena involves interpreting each phenomenon in relation to others within a society, investigating interdependencies and interconnections (see also Gurvitch, 1964, 1971). This approach is an epistemological and methodological strategy on Mauss's part, but he also credits total social facts within an ontological reality distinct from other social facts (Gofman, 1998: 67). Total social facts are those social facts that penetrate an entire society, concentrating its hyper-spiritual energies, and channelling them into particular symbolic, ritual and conceptual patterns. The *gift*, in 'archaic' societies, is Mauss's best-known example of a total social fact. The systems of 'total prestations' he focuses on not only involve the exchange of wealth or goods, but also courtesies, entertainments, ritual, military assistance, women, children, dances and feasts (Mauss, 1969: 11–12). Some of the examples he discusses concern the *potlatch*, which is the gift of an effervescent gathering, feast, or festival. The potlatch is, simultaneously, wildly celebratory and a solemn tribal gathering. On these occasions, wealth is consumed, destroyed or simply given away, hierarchies are challenged and reconstructed, marriages, initiations and shamanic séances occur, and religious cults centred around gods and totems perform rituals. For Mauss, rituals of giving, and the obligations that flow from them, permeate the entire proceedings.

He argues that the essence of potlatch is the *obligation to give*. A chief must give a potlatch for himself, his son, his son-in-law or daughter, and for the dead. He has to demonstrate his good fortune and great wealth by expending it (Mauss, 1969: 37). There is an obligation to invite others outside the family or clan, and only the invited can attend. Neglecting to invite someone invariably has fateful results (Mauss, 1969: 60). In European folklore, the myth of the bad fairy or witch not invited to a wedding or a baptism, with a resulting curse, as in the Sleeping Beauty myth, has the same character and origins as the obligations surrounding the potlatch. There is also an *obligation to receive*, however, and an invitation cannot be refused without loss of honour (Mauss, 1969: 39). Following this, there is also an *obligation to repay*. As with all gifts, the potlatch must be returned, ideally with interest. If this cannot be done, a person risks losses of honour and social status (Mauss, 1969: 40).

In these examples, Mauss is addressing patterns of gift-giving in 'archaic' societies but, as he often points out, such activities endure even within modern Western societies, where 'Much of our everyday morality is concerned with the question of obligation and spontaneity in the gift' (Mauss, 1969: 63). A wedding, for example, which involves a vast expenditure of wealth (traditionally by the bride's father), has many elements of the potlatch about it. It is both a celebratory and a solemn occasion, involving a feast as well as a ritualised public (and traditionally religious) enactment of vows. The list of invitations to the wedding often has an obligatory character, involving two families and an opportunity for reconciliation in relation to inter-familial or intra-familial conflicts, or the opportunity for one family to assert itself over another through its generous expenditure. Attendance, if asked, is also obligatory, at least with regard to the close family. Furthermore, the vast expenditure of wealth by the bride's father is, ideally, matched or exceeded by the flow of gifts to the bride and groom. The customary practice of putting on a public display of gifts at the wedding reception also offers an opportunity for those in attendance to exhibit their generosity, or risk shame, by having their offering available for all to see.

In all of these exchanges, as Mauss implies, there is often a competitive element even though this cannot be reduced into an individualistic attempt to maximise self-interest. This is evident with regard to the ritual exchange of Christmas presents. Just as a tribal chief lavishes his wealth on a potlatch in a grand expenditure that reinforces his social status, so too people often spend vast amounts of money on presents they can ill afford. This might look like a lavish expression of generosity, but it also signals the kind of social status and affluence the gift-givers aspire to. It also places an obligation on the recipients of gifts to be equally lavish in return: an expensive present cannot be repaid with an inexpensive one without social awkwardness, loss of face, or conflict. For similar reasons, a thoughtful, carefully chosen gift demands something similar in return: an inability, or refusal, to 'repay' appropriately can cause hurt, offence and damage to social relationships. Patterns of gift exchange, then, involve rituals of obligation, even thought they might *appear* to be voluntary and gratuitous. It is in this way that they build up patterns of solidarity between people. A gift made or received binds the people concerned into a pattern that cannot easily be broken. This is why, as Mauss points out, a common way of seeking to control enemies in tribal societies is to bestow gifts upon them: once someone accepts a gift they are indebted until they repay it. More positively, within friendships the exchange of gifts is not simply an expression of solidarity, but a means for its creation: in bestowing gifts upon friends, and happily receiving them, we are establishing enduring patterns of solidarity that tie us to each other beyond our immediate actions, feelings and circumstances. It is also worth noting that mythical gift-bearers, such as Father Christmas and the Christ Child, ensure that children too are integrated into the cycle of reciprocity that encompasses adults (Berking, 1999: 15).

The inseparable connection between gifts and solidarity is expressed in what Mauss refers to as 'the confusion between the person and the thing'. Amongst the many examples of this confusion noted by Mauss is the persistence in China, even today, of 'mourning licences' where the person who sells property retains the right to 'weep over it' for the rest of his life (Mauss, 1969: 62). Specifically in relation to gifts, however, he notes several examples in Hindu texts where people become so confused with their property that the gift of any part of it creates a bond that is almost unbreakable, and yet invokes dire consequences for those who do not respect the bond and attendant obligations appropriately (Mauss, 1969: 56–7). It is important to note that this confusion is not some sort of 'commodity fetishism' in a consumerist sense, however, since the thing given is transformed in the emergent 'electricity' of social relationships. In fact, the basis of the confusion of person and thing is that a gift from someone is, in a sense, a gift *of* that person. This continues to be apparent in contemporary Western societies: the gift of a thing from a loved one, for example, which may have no significant monetary worth or 'market value' might be invaluable to the recipient because of the association of that thing with the beloved. All the emotions, memories and thoughts aroused by the beloved become condensed around that thing, and the possession of it remains immensely significant, to the point where the loss of it might be unbearable.

The 'confusion' between the person and the thing is especially complex, however, when the things exchanged are *words*. Language, as a system of symbolic representations through which communication takes place, often has a highly ritualised character. This is evident not only in formal contexts, where particular patterns of words, ways of speaking, and attendant gestures and bodily dispositions are often expected, if not demanded, but also in the informal encounters that characterise our day-to-day interactions. Words exchanged upon meeting or leaving friends and acquaintances, for example, tend to follow established patterns that are simply taken for granted, though we have to socialise children into recognising and conforming to them (Goffman, 1969). In fact, these patterns vary across time and between cultures, but they are always there, even where, as in late modern Western cultures, there is a strong valuation of the *personal authenticity* of communication rather than highly ritualised patterns of earlier forms of Western society.

In this regard, Sennett (1977) has discussed the shift in Western societies from a public life characterised by thoroughly ritualised social encounters to one where an 'ideology of intimacy' dominates. This ideology places a great emphasis on the *authenticity* of social relationships, and our communications are meant to reflect our 'inner psychological concerns' rather than our grasp of a society's ritual dynamics. None the less, and despite Sennett's anxieties about the destruction of the social following from the spread of this concern with psychological authenticity, it is clear that this ideology tends to obscure, rather than simply undermine, the degree to which social relationships can be highly ritualised. David Moss's (2001) study of the phenomenon of *pentimento* in Italy, referring to the collaboration of former Mafia members with the judicial system, is instructive in this regard.

Moss (2001: 301) analyses the confessions of former Mafiosi as gift exchanges, involving the exchange of words in return for reduced sentences, financial aid and police protection, and notes that critics of these judicial arrangements have denounced the 'dangerous confusion of legal, religious and moral considerations' they appear to involve. It is precisely such 'confusion', of course, that characterises Mauss's notion of total social facts, as Moss notes, but he illuminates how such gift exchanges stimulate potentially endless chains of other exchanges so that confessions not only lead to other confessions, but have implications for the value of other confessions, for the future operation of judicial processes, for religious and moral questions concerning repentance and absolution, and for questions about the authority of the state (Moss, 2001: 304–5; see Godelier, 1999: 69–70). Furthermore, in offering a 'potlach of former comrades and weapons', the Mafiosi informers had to take care not to appear to be acting purely in terms of their self-interest as this would devalue the nature of their gifts, so their information took on characteristics of the Catholic confessional and the appearance of authentic contrition for past sins (Moss, 2001: 309, 318). In these cases, at least, it is possible to see a confusion of the two things Sennett (1977) believes to be separate, since the *pentimento* phenomenon involves an obligation to convey personal authenticity within what are clearly highly ritualised exchanges. Furthermore, although these exchanges are apparently of a very specific sort, given Italy's particular problems with the Mafia, they do have a broader significance. This is so not simply because various other types of lawbreakers, from petty criminals to religious terrorists, are often participants in similar exchanges, but because the gifts of the former Mafiosi involve *information*.

From Bell's (1980) announcement of a new 'axial principle' of modern societies with the rise of information technology through to Virilio's (2000) notion of the 'information bomb', it has become conventional to see information exchange as destructive of society and social relationships. As Moss (2001: 303) observes, however, the *pentimento* phenomenon not only turns information into a commodity that can be exchanged, but also turns it into something that forges new forms of solidarity, integrating criminals (and their interrogators) into new patterns of social relationship through rites of reconciliation. These rites of reconciliation, however, are evident in many Western societies, where confessions, apologies and expressions of remorse have come to be a significant feature of public life; they are evident, for example, in relation to injustices towards minorities, the legacies of the Holocaust, and the ostensibly 'therapeutic' gloss given to confessional rituals enacted on certain television talk shows (Moss, 2001: 329; see Schwan, 1998).[4]

As in the case of other forms of consumerist appropriations of social dynamics for utilitarian ends, the highly commercialised and 'mediatised' pattern of much contemporary gift exchange points towards a deeper obligatory structure in the substratum of society, though without engaging with it fully. None the less, the potent social forces unleashed by gift exchanges can 'electrify' social relationships and impose significant obligations, even in crassly commercialised festivals such as Christmas. What Mauss was trying to get to grips with are the obligations, compulsions and rituals that order social life. The dynamic, exuberant effervescence that Durkheim associates with the origins of sacred symbols is, in Mauss's analysis, translated into a vision of society based on expenditure, consumption and obligation, rather than an economistic vision of humans saving, producing and interacting on the basis of self-interest. Mauss's insights in this regard become central to Bataille's attempt to rewrite what we understand as 'economics'.

Accursed society

In *The Accursed Share* (1991) Bataille uses Durkheim's (1995) analysis of the sacred and Mauss's (1969) work on gift exchange to develop a theory of a 'restricted' and 'general' economy. The 'restricted' economy is the conventional subject matter of classical economics and much contemporary philosophy, politics and social theory. Based upon the concept of scarcity, and

the accumulation of precious resources, this notion of economy is repre-
hensible to Bataille because it ignores the fact that economic activity cannot
be explained by economic facts or activity alone, and because it therefore
'surrenders the possibilities inherent within society to immediately perceived necessities that are often illusory' (Richardson, 1994: 68). In contrast,
the notion of a 'general' economy is focused on 'excess' rather than scarcity,
and 'expenditure' rather than production: in this understanding of 'economy', 'a human sacrifice, the construction of a church or the gift of a jewel'
are as significant as the production and sale of economic goods (Bataille,
1991: 9). The 'excess' referred to here is the surplus of social energy that
characterises human life and which must, necessarily, be expended in some
form. Contrary to classical economics, then, Bataille emphasises not the utilitarian pursuit of self-interest but a collective impulse towards 'useless'
expenditure, manifest in the gratuitous, prodigal gifts of wealth and energy
characteristic of all societies other than modern ones. The 'restricted' economy is important in that it helps produce the surplus wealth (the 'accursed
share') that is uselessly expended, but if this broader context for productive
activity is ignored, then a society becomes oppressive to its members and
alienated from its own essential being (Richardson, 1994: 73).

The modern tendency towards such a pattern of alienation is evident
with regard to 'leisure'. For Bataille, leisure is important because it offers an
opportunity for 'useless' expenditure, regardless of material, economic or
productive factors. In so far as capitalism 'allows' time for leisure, however,
this is largely related to the need to give people sufficient rest so that they
can work as efficiently and productively as possible the rest of the time
(Richardson, 1994: 72). This is 'perverse' in the sense that leisure (part of
the 'general economy') is defined, negatively, in relation to the 'restricted'
economy, rather than the other way around. The increasing commodification of leisure in modern societies, where a 'market' mentality tends to
shape people's experiences of cultural, sporting and aesthetic activities,
makes this situation worse.

Featherstone (1991: 96) has noted that leisure is now part of a market
where people consume particular types of experiences in specifically created centres, such as 'theme parks', and tend to associate such patterns of
consumption with 'lifestyle' choices. With respect to such transformations,
Featherstone (1991: 22) uses Bataille to highlight how they can be interpreted as excesses of energy translated into contemporary patterns of consumerism. Thus, the sports stadia, theme parks and shopping centres of
contemporary societies allow individuals to expend the 'accursed share' produced by the 'over-production' of capitalism. A similar interpretation of
such phenomena is also offered by Botting and Wilson (1998: 18), when
they talk of capitalism's ongoing evolution into a more 'Bataillean universe'.
This use of Bataille, however, would clearly have appalled him. For him, capitalism was a perverse alienation of society from its own being precisely
because it reduced what is human to the condition of commodities (Bataille,
1991: 129). The kind of shift from a 'production' to a 'consumption' orien-

tated economy described by Featherstone is not a shift from a 'restricted' to a 'general' economy, but the colonisation of things that properly belong to the general economy by patterns of commodification. Thus, leisure becomes a market we 'buy into', figuratively and, increasingly, literally, and part of a broader series of market-sensitive choices through which we construct identities on the basis of the commodities we consume. In Bataille's terms, the development of modern patterns of consumerism can be seen as a de-humanising phenomenon, and evidence of a 'sick society'. He argues that what is essential to a society, and what modern society tends to marginalise, is the encounter with something that 'causes one to tremble with fear and delight' (Bataille, 1991: 129). This has nothing to do with the consumerist pleasures of shopping, nor even the experience of 'white-water rafting' at an outdoor activities centre. What Bataille is talking about is the *sacred*.

In his account of Brahmanical notions of sacrifice, the Indologist Sylvain Lévi described the sacred as 'electricity', a view that contributed to Hubert and Mauss's (1964) focus on the socially embodied nature of sacrifice as a form of action manifesting the 'deep-seated energy' of the sacred (Mauss, 1900: 353; Strenski, 1998: 122). Below such ritualised forms of sacrifice, however, in the substratum of society itself, is a deeper sacrificial structure. Contrary to utilitarian and individualist notions of society as the aggregate outcome of individual choices and actions, Durkheim (1973: 163) argues that it is because 'society has its own nature' that there is always some degree of conflict between individual interests and the demands placed upon us by society. This is so not simply in Archer's (1995) sense that the society we have to live in is not necessarily the society we want, but also in the sense that individual interests often have to be forsaken for the greater good of society as a whole. As Durkheim (1973: 163) expresses it, 'society cannot be formed or maintained without our being required to make perpetual and costly sacrifices'. In short, society 'obliges us to surpass ourselves' to our real cost, a fact evident in the daily acts of generosity, empathy and heroism that mark many people's lives, but also, in a somewhat corrupted form, in societies where it seems that 'anything goes'. This helps us to understand, for example, how it is that in Beck's account of reflexive individuals endlessly reconstructing their biographies, relationships and orientations to the world, there is an undercurrent of pain, fear of failure and sacrifice in the face of what are supposed to be individual freedoms but often turn out to be oppressive and de-humanising (Beck, 1992: 135–6). Understood in this light, the highly ritualised patterns of consumer culture do not reactivate the sacred, but parody it: the 'electricity' of the sacred does not animate the desire to shop, hyper-spirituality is not manifest as 'hyperconsumption', and redemption promised through the sacrifice of all meaning and value in the glittering vacuity of global capitalism's 'cathedrals of consumption' turns out to be empty (Ritzer, 1999).

On the basis of Bataille's (1991) notions of the 'general' and the 'restricted' economy, it is possible to interpret modern consumerism as the attempted colonisation of the general economy by the utilitarian concerns that belong to the restricted economy. In short, it could be said that hyper-spiritual forces are being manipulated for monetary purposes. If these hyper-spiritual forces manifest the real substratum of society, however, or, in Bataille's terms, if the restricted economy is ultimately dependent on the general economy, then below the sacrificial demands of consumer culture there will be deeper patterns of obligation and sacrifice with much greater significance than the money economy, and with a social power that will always elude utilitarian attempts to control it. Mayfair Mei-hui Yang's (2000) study of the Wenzhou region of south-eastern China, where patterns of ritual expenditure have been revitalised alongside the emergence of new capitalist developments, testifies to the importance of the 'general economy'. With regard to Western societies, however, what Bataille's analysis suggests is that consumerist impulses towards the elimination of all obligations except the obligation to choose, while immensely powerful, must ultimately meet the resistance of those hyper-spiritual dynamics that confront self-interests with social and moral obligations. Karl Polanyi's (2001) magisterial analysis of the dehumanising fictions, misconceptions and moral dangers of the market mentality emphasises this point in a particularly comprehensive and challenging manner.

Economic society

It has been noted that 'Polanyi exposes the *myth* of the free market: there was never a truly free, self-regulating market system' (Stiglitz, 2001: xiii). Furthermore, he not only argues that this system has never existed, but that it *cannot* exist without destroying humanity and the earth's natural resources (Block, 2001: xxiv). What he examines, therefore, is the *attempt* to impose a particular kind of economic vision upon human beings, and the disastrous social and moral consequences that have flowed from this. His arguments have a moral dimension, since he illuminates how all societies other than modern ones have attributed a sacred dimension to nature and human life, but, through a detailed economic and historical analysis, he also demonstrates how the inevitable and persistent interventions of states into the running of economies expose the aim of disembedding the economy from society as a utopian, anti-realist project (Block, 2001: xxv). More than that, he stresses how the notion of a free market depends upon a completely fallacious view of humanity's 'natural propensities' (Portes, 1994: 432), and that a study of 'primitive' and 'archaic' economies alongside those of modernity reveals the unavoidable fact that the economy is always embedded in society, and that religion can be just as important to the structure and function of the economy as monetary institutions (Polanyi et al., 1971: 250). In this respect, his arguments build upon views expressed by Durkheim:

> Political economy ... is an abstract and deductive science which is occupied not so much with observing reality as with constructing a more or less desirable ideal; because the man that the economists talk about, this systematic egoist, is little but an artificial man of reason. The man that we know, the

real man, is so much more complex: he belongs to a time and a country, he lives somewhere, he has a family, a country, a religious faith and political ideas. (Durkheim, 1970: 85; see Smelser and Swedberg, 1994: 11)

In this passage, Durkheim is emphasising that economic factors cannot be separated from their societal context, and cannot rest upon the fictitious concepts of humans as anti-social egoists dreamt up by modern liberal philosophers and economists. Polanyi's great contribution to the study of modern economics is his detailed examination of how this 'economistic fallacy' arose, and the dangers it represents for the present and the future of Western societies.

Polanyi (2001: 46) notes that history and ethnography furnish us with knowledge of various types of economies, most of them containing markets of various types, but argues that it is only in the modern West that the economy has come to be regulated and controlled by markets. The general rule is that the economy is deeply embedded with social relationships, especially within patterns of obligation, reciprocity, religious beliefs and actions, and an array of other forms through which societies direct human passions and desires towards non-economic ends (Polanyi, 2001: 48–9). Drawing on the works of Malinowksi (1930) and Thurnwald (1932), for example, Polanyi (2001: 49–50) notes the significance of *reciprocity* and *redistribution* in societies characterised by 'superabundant non-economic motivation for every act', so that foods, goods and services can never be separated from obligations, responsibilities and religious motivations, and the idea of exchanging, bartering or 'selling' these for economic gain makes no sense at all. Further to this, he argues that such examples reveal that, contrary to modern neo-classical economic myth, the 'individualistic savage collecting food and hunting on his own or for his family has never existed' (Polanyi, 2001: 55). It is on this basis that he takes issue with Adam Smith's view of humanity's innate 'propensity to barter, truck and exchange one thing for another', noting, however, that this notion of 'Economic Man', while a misreading of the past, 'proved more prophetic of the future' in its often dire social consequences (Polanyi, 2001: 45). Indeed, Polanyi (2001: 88) argues that, under the influence of a liberal political philosophy that viewed the liberation of individuals from society's regulation of their innately selfish propensities as a march of progress to be undertaken with 'unbounded hope', the historical development of the modern West was marked by 'limitless despair' and 'painful dislocations'. As he suggests, the traditional unity of Christian society gave way to a denial of obligations and responsibilities towards others, as 'unheard-of wealth turned out to be inseparable from unheard-of poverty', and 'a stoic determination to renounce human solidarity in the name of the greatest happiness of the greatest number gained the dignity of a secular religion' (Polanyi, 2001: 107).

This 'secular religion' of utilitarianism that heralded this renunciation of solidarity did not seek to disentangle the economy from society but, rather, to subordinate the economy to the market, with the effect that society too becomes subordinate to the market and a 'market economy' becomes synonymous with a 'market society' (Polanyi, 2001: 60). Within this market society, labour, land and money become commodities to be traded for profit. This serves to 'subordinate the substance of society itself to the laws of the market', because 'labour' actually refers to human beings, and 'land' refers to our natural surroundings and they 'are obviously *not* commodities', since they have not been 'produced for sale' (Polanyi, 2001: 75). Money is not a commodity for similar reasons: it is a symbolic token of exchange that is not produced for sale. Consequently, the commodity description of labour, land and money is not only 'entirely fictitious', but also robs human beings of their physical, psychological and moral substance (Polanyi, 2001: 76). The inevitable consequence of subjecting humans to market economics in this way is, ultimately, the annihilation of 'organic' forms of existence, and the reduction of human relationships to the principle of 'freedom of contract': 'non-contractual organisations of kinship, neighbourhood, profession and creed were to be liquidated since they claimed the allegiance of the individual and thus restrained his freedom' (Polanyi, 2001: 171). In this respect, Giddens's (1991a: 89) picture of how even intimate relationships are now socially disembedded, in the sense that they are increasingly free of traditional bonds and are subject to an essentially contractarian balancing of individual needs, can be seen to reflect broader patterns of market-oriented utilitarianism that arose with industrialisation. In each case, the liberation of the individual is the liberation from society, even if it is also notable that Polanyi's account of the de-humanising suffering of industrialised labour in early modernity is to some extent mirrored in Beck's (1992: 49) suggestion that, in today's 'risk society', one of the last remnants of real solidarity people experience is that which arises from a 'commonality of anxiety'.

Contrary to many such accounts of modernity, however, Polanyi, in emphasising the *complexity* of the contemporary world, also draws attention to the fundamental significance of forces that challenged and limited such de-humanising attacks on society. As he argues, alongside this utilitarian project aimed at deconstructing social bonds through the subjugation of economy and society to the market, there developed, from the beginning of industrialisation, 'a deep-seated movement [that] sprang into being to resist the pernicious effects of a market-controlled economy': in short, 'society protected itself' through a series of collectivist interventions into economy and society. Of particular note in this regard, is that this resurgence of society spread throughout Europe, cutting across divisions between Catholics and Protestants, Christians and atheists, Conservatives and Liberals, as 'almost exactly the same measures' were enacted 'under the most varied slogans' (Polanyi, 2001: 154). Furthermore, in a direct challenge to Marxist attempts to relate these changes to class interests, Polanyi (2001: 161) emphasises the *general* interests underpinning them, in the sense that people are not just members of a particular class, or producers and consumers, but mothers, lovers, commuters, hikers, gardeners, sportsmen and so forth. In other words, the resurgence of society, manifest in the regulations and limitations imposed upon free market economics, was the resurgence of what Durkheim had called the *real* human beings, who could not be reduced for long into the fictional egoists of classical economic theory (Durkheim, 1970: 85). This is not to say, however, that the resurgence of society was an unambiguously desirable phenomenon. Indeed, a further key connection between Polanyi and Durkheim is that both of them are sensitive to some of the ambiguities that characterise complex social realities.

It has been noted that one of the more blatant failings of rational choice theory, the current sociological incarnation of utilitarian philosophy, is its inability to account for *altruism*, which implies a constraint of self-interest by morals or values transcendent of individuals (Collins, 1993). Coleman (1990), for example, like many other rational choice theorists, talks of *apparent* altruism that can be 'unmasked' as self-interested action (Wrong, 1994: 199). Following this model, it is possible to argue, as Stark (1997) has with regard to religion in general, that all sorts of 'sacrifices' can be interpreted as rational, self-interested decisions to seek some sort of 'compensator' (for example, Heaven or Paradise) to outweigh the apparent loss incurred by the sacrifice. Intriguingly, this utilitarian pursuit of 'compensation' can include even the sacrifice of life in the case of martyrdom. One of the problems with this type of interpretation, however, like Giddens's analogous emphasis upon reflexive decision-making, is that all sorts of different types of action are reduced into one model. Clearly, there are certain actions that can be interpreted as the results of self-interested actions by individuals, but others appear to resist such interpretations very strongly. This is so, for example, not only with regard to altruistic actions that benefit others without, in any obvious way, benefiting the altruistic actor, but also with regard to certain *obligatory* forms of 'altruistic suicide' evident in a range of cultures, such as the Japanese example of *seppuku* (suicide by ritual disembowelling) and the Indian example of *suttee* (where a widow burns herself on her husband's funeral pyre) (Davies and Neal, 2000: 38; see Durkheim, 1952). Further to this, utilitarian explanations also look deficient with regard to religiously-inspired 'suicide bombings' which are not characterised by an altruistic desire to help others or, simply, by individuals enacting their own deaths. On the contrary, suicide bombers only accept their own deaths as a by-product of their desire to kill and maim others. For both Durkheim and Polanyi, such phenomena would not be explained in terms of utilitarian choices, but in terms of social forces manifest as barbarism.

A significant feature of Durkheim's account of society is the recognition of an ambiguity at its heart: social energies may be the stimulus for heightened moral sensibilities, self-sacrifice and even heroism, but they can also provoke barbarism, violence, oppression and fanaticism (Durkheim, 1995: 213, 417). Polanyi's (2001: 265) account of the resurgence of society against the dehumanising utilitarianism of the market economy expresses an analogous sense of ambiguity, in that he observes that this resurgence can be manifest in the form of a heightened sense of moral responsibility for others, but also in the fascist obliteration of freedom and morality as the individual becomes totally subsumed into society. Indeed, he argues that this ambiguity is now firmly established at the heart of the modern world, where free market economics still pushes towards the obliteration of society in the name of individual freedom, while the inevitable reassertion of society against this always threatens to turn into a fascist obliteration of freedom (Polanyi, 2001: 266). Bauman's (1993) attempt to fashion a 'postmodern ethics' in a situation characterised by individualistic consumerism on the one hand, and a resurgent, violent tribalism on the other, testifies to the contemporary relevance of Polanyi's analysis. Contrary to Bauman's general antipathy to the association of morality with the notion of society as a *sui generis* reality, however, Polanyi argues that it is with the recognition of this reality that an engagement with the morality inherent to the human condition must begin.

Free society

Bauman (1993: 231) has noted that the way in which the world economy now operates depends upon the fact that the state *cannot* effectively impose constraints upon the economy, since 'the economic assets crucial for the daily life of its population are "foreign" – or, given the removal of all constraints upon capital transfers, may turn foreign overnight, in case the local rulers naïvely deem themselves strong enough to meddle. The divorce between the political autarchy (real or imaginary) and economic autarky could not be more complete; it also seems to be irrevocable.' While Bauman (1993: 237–9) identifies an 'explosive sociality' that emerges in opposition to this disembedding of the economy, however, he fears the 'pathogenic' social and moral consequences of this resurgence of society, and pins his hopes instead on the capacities inherent to the 'autonomy of the moral self' which, in so far as they can resist contemporary attempts to 'anaesthetise' them, can offer greater chances of 'safeguarding human lives against cruelty'. Thus, while he shares Polanyi's sensitivity to the immense cruelties inflicted upon humans in the name of disembedding the economy from society, he does not relish the idea of a resurgent society either.

For Polanyi (2001: 267), however, to resist the reduction of society to the market while also counteracting the slide into fascism involves grappling with the 'moral and religious' aspects of social life, and therefore with the specifically Christian influences upon the development of Western societies. Consequently, he argues that the study of economy and society must be attentive to 'three constitutive facts in the consciousness of Western man': the first, knowledge of death, was revealed in the Old Testament; the second, knowledge of freedom, was 'revealed through the discovery of the uniqueness of the person in the teachings of Jesus as recorded in the New Testament'; and the third, knowledge of society, was revealed through the complex, disruptive and far-reaching processes associated with the emergence of modernity, and remains 'the constitutive element in modern man's consciousness' (Polanyi, 2001: 268). While the recognition of the significance of death for the social, cultural and psychological aspects of human life has been an important element of some areas of sociological theory (Berger, 1990; Bauman, 1992b), Polanyi's argument is not only that the uniqueness of the person and the reality of society are equally important, but also that the due recognition of their necessary inseparability is absolutely fundamental to the creation of just social order. For him, market economics has a strong focus on the individual, but denies society and there-fore has barbaric social and moral consequences. On the other hand, fascism recognises the reality of society, but negates the Christian discovery of the uniqueness of the individual, thereby facilitating atrocities, barbarism and contempt for the consciences of individuals. Consequently, contrary to Bauman, 'the meaning of freedom in a complex society' rests on the accept-ance of the reality of society, just as we must accept the reality of death, but it also rests, as Bauman would concur, upon the development of the courage to accept that individual moral responsibility which is the spring from which the critique of injustice and oppression flows (Polanyi, 2001: 268).

Returning to the subject of taboo, it is possible, in the light of Polanyi's arguments, to have a clearer sense of how this phenomenon is a manifesta-tion of the obligatory characteristics of society, and yet is something that can manifest itself in morally ambiguous and dangerous forms. Contrary to the (post)modern assumption that greater permissiveness leads to greater liber-ation (Hawkes, 1996), the persistence of taboos surrounding incest, for example, demonstrates the resistance of society to those forces that seek its reduction into a market for the expression of egoistic desires (Twitchell, 1987). Here it is possible to see that the 'anything goes' mentality has defi-nite societal limits. On the other hand, the critiques of taboos surrounding women offered by writers such as Jay (1992) illuminate the dangers of an acceptance of the reality of society that overrides the ability to challenge injustice and oppression. With reference to Polanyi's stress on the role of Christianity upon the evolution of Western notions of freedom, however, it is worth noting that the Christian transformation of patterns of taboo into the systems of community ethics, manifest in notions of the Seven Deadly Sins and in the Ten Commandments, tend to support rather than curtail such critiques, since they embody the idea that individual moral integrity is exercised through social responsibility towards others (Bossy, 1985; Williams, 2000). More broadly, as discussed in the last chapter, although society has the power to impose itself as an unavoidable reality, recognising its contingency upon the humans who constitute it also opens up a space for a moral critique of existing social forms.

In confronting the destructive impact upon society of a particular form of economics, then, Polanyi's intention is not to suggest that money itself is the cause of modern social problems: under the influence of Polanyi's vision Zelizer (1994), for example, has challenged the Weberian vision of money as a rationalising mechanism, arguing that money is always embedded in social relationships and cultural meanings (see Mizruchi and Stearns, 1994). The major source of many modern social problems, rather, is that this embeddedness has been obscured by disembedding philosophies. Temple and Chabal (1995) have emphasised this in their illumination of how market-oriented philosophies have distorted human values, and how, in the name of a 'free society' they have made us slaves to global economics. In this context, contrary to Mauss's account of how, in 'archaic' societies, the confusion between the person and the thing invests the thing with some of the qualities of the person, persons now simply become things. It is this tendency towards dehumanisation that explains Polanyi's (2001: 248) point about the intimate connection between fascism and market economics: they are poles apart in terms of the reality of society, but both obliterate moral responsibility and both, therefore, dehumanise people. In this respect, it is also worth noting that Virilio's (2002: 10) argument that many of the dangers facing humans in the twenty-first century inevitably follow from the fantasy that humanity can actually live in a world without limits also resonates with much of Polanyi's analysis. In both cases, it is recognised that dehumanisation begins with a 'double denial'; namely, the denial of individual and collective moral responsibilities.

Like Polanyi, however, Temple and Chabal (1995) also recognise the persistence of a social substratum that always resists such economic reductionism. Consequently, in challenging free market economics, and the liberal philosophy underpinning it, they propose that we embrace the human and environmental benefits that would flow from the extension of the reciprocity that exists within families and small communities into the states and those global relationships that are currently dominated by economic thinking. What such studies demonstrate, along with the works of Durkheim, Mauss and Bataille considered in this chapter, is that the engagement with society as a *necessary* reality is essential to any proper grasp of humanity's social, economic and cultural lot, and that a failure to do this can have some dire social and moral consequences. The issues raised by the anti-globalisation marchers and rioters who took to the streets of cities across Europe and America at the turn of the twenty-first century testify to the popular recognition of these consequences, contrary to sociological visions of contemporary youth as reflexive individualists only interested in their own lifestyle options (Stiglitz, 2001: vii).

None the less, to understand contemporary social trends and conflicts fully involves a proper engagement with the temporal processes through which Western societies have developed. Indeed, the fact that society is a thoroughly ambiguous phenomenon in much sociological theory, modern philosophy, politics and economics is no accident: the attempt to obliterate society in the name of individual freedom and the contrary reassertion of society that always threatens to turn into a totalitarian denial of freedom reflect a deep fissure in Western views of social life that has a long history. What is important to understand, however, is that this history has a specifically religious character. Durkheim, Mauss, Bataille and Polanyi all recognised that many of the key characteristics of a society, including its key conflicts, were of a religious origin, even though such arguments have been underplayed in many appropriations of their arguments. In developing the reassessment of society further, however, I suggest it is important to consider the religious origins of Western understandings of society, including many of those developed in sociology, if we are to develop a satisfactory understanding of contemporary social characteristics and conflicts.

Notes

1. Thus, his notion of 'confluent love' expresses the idea that modern relationships are entered into, and sustained, purely as the result of individuals' reflexive assessment of their needs, desires and overall life plans, and judgements about whether another person can assist in the achievement of these ends (Giddens, 1992). In this perspective, the transience of many modern relationships reflects their inherently contractarian, utilitarian character, combined with the individualistic impulse of late modern life. Contracts can be made, and broken, as we seek to pursue our own individual goals and desires. In this view, love may have emotional and sexual dimensions but these are contained within a reflexive framework centred on the utilitarian calculation of different life options. Relationships are always contractual and until-further-notice: they are not characterised by any sort of necessity, only a contingency that is rooted in lifestyle decisions rather than embodied powers and potentialities.

2. The association of women with blood has given rise to conflicting interpretations of male circumcision rituals. Bettelheim (1955), for example, has offered a psychoanalytic theory of circumcision centred on the idea that male envy of female bleeding produces this ritual of cutting and bleeding (see Douglas, 1966: 116). Beidelman's (1973) study of the Kaguru in East Africa, on the other hand, sees in these rituals not an envy of women but a desire by men to disassociate themselves from bleeding female bodies. Discussing the ritual circumcision of young men, he notes the difference in colour of the glans before and after circumcision. Before the ritual the glans is soft and moist in contrast to the brown/black colour of the rest of the body, but after circumcision, and the healing of the wound, the glans takes on the dark colour of the rest of the body. Beidelman (1973: 160) suggests that circumcision removes feminine 'wetness', but also a feminine 'redness' with its implications of blood. In Durkheim's terms, we can read this transformation of the male body as an attempt to harden up sexual differences in order to avoid the confusion or intermingling of sacred and profane.

3. Van Gennep's (1909) and Schurtz's (1902) studies of rituals of male initiation, which explore the creation of a male culture antagonistic to women (see Van Baal and Van Beek, 1985: 127), are also supportive of this view.

4. A strong account of the ability of television to act as a channel for such religious, moral and social forces is also evident in the works of Featherstone (1991), Dayan and Katz (1988), Lundby (1997) and Martín-Barbero (1997). Contrary to Mestrovic's (1997) view of televised spectacles as 'postemotional' parodies of real religious and social dynamics, Martín-Barbero (1997: 111), for example, interprets even the cult of celebrity as an emotionally charged manifestation of religious energies, rites and myths in contemporary societies.

5

Temporal Society

One of the characteristics common to many of the assessments of society, or its disappearance, considered in the previous chapters is the belief in some sort of radical, epochal transformation in Western social and cultural life. Accounts of the nature, temporal location and sociological implications of this transformation are extremely varied and often contradictory, but embrace claims about the 'death' of God, tradition, humanity, history and the social, and arguments concerning the appearance of modernity, post-modernity, radicalised modernity, the information age, hyper-reality and so forth. The persistent references to contingency, uncertainty, unpredictability and risk evident within many of these accounts reflect a sense that, in the words of Bauman (1992a: xxv), we have been ushered 'into an as-yet-unex-plored world' where all the maps and signposts from the past are now redundant. It is on this basis that sociologists can come to view classical the-orists such as Durkheim as naïve explorers of a 'lost world' (Lemert, 1995: 48), that studies of tradition, memory, history and religion come to be focused on the disappearance or deconstruction of their subject matter (Fukuyama, 1992; Heelas et al., 1996; Hervieu-Léger, 2000; Bruce, 2002), and that even some theologians and priests can come to view belief in God as a quaint relic of a more gullible era (Boulton, 1997: 9). Indeed, Touraine (1989: 5) has argued that sociological interpretations of social life must change along with the phenomena they are trying to grasp, but, since these phenomena seem to change so radically and so often, then we should not be surprised if the 'rules of sociological method' need rewriting every week.

A major problem with many of these accounts of radical, epochal change, however, is that arguments about historical change are actually used to *limit* the degree to which sociologists should take history seriously. This results in self-contradictory claims about modernity giving way to an age of postmodernity marked by the end of metanarratives such as 'history' (Lyotard, 1984), but also in sociological arguments that marshal all social and cultural phenomena into two compounds marked 'premodern' and 'modern', locating much of what is 'historical' in the former and defining modernity *against* it (Giddens, 1990, 1991a). In some recent sociological studies, this highly questionable use of 'history' is reinforced and extended by the problematisation of the notion of *time*. Harvey's (1989) notion of 'time–space compression', Augé's (1992) account of the *acceleration* of his-tory, Fukuyama's (1992) vision of the *end* of history, and various postmod-ern notions of the 'death of the past' share a common vision of the radical reconstruction of temporality ushered in by postmodernity (see Jameson, 1992: 307–11). As Lyon (2000: 122) has aptly expressed it, what such accounts express is the idea that the arrival of postmodernity or 'radicalised' modernity does not simply herald a 'time of crisis' but a 'crisis of time'.

Here, phenomena such as the instantaneous exchange of information through computers are deemed to have led to the collapse of past, present and future into the 'timeless time' or 'virtual time' of information exchange (Lyon, 2000: 121; see Castells, 1996). In short, the fragmentation of societies mirrors the fragmentation of time (de Connick, 1995).

While such arguments undoubtedly draw attention to significant contemporary changes in the social organisation of time, and the cultural meanings attached to it, they also tend to ignore what Barbara Adam (1990: 154) has referred to as broader questions concerning 'the more universal principles of time that are to be found throughout nature'. Here, the lack of an engagement with humanity's embodied being-in-the-world is crucial, not simply in the sense that bodies age, but also in relation to the fact that human beings are, in their depths, *temporal beings* who are 'practising centres of action' (Adam, 1990: 70–1). Indeed, in their critique of the 'contemporary utopian writing about the social consequences of the internet', Turner and Rojek (2001: xi) have suggested that such writing fails to account for the 'emplacement of action' that follows from human embodiment and thereby limits the expansion of virtuality beyond a certain point. Attendant upon this neglect of embodiment, however, is the further neglect of those hyper-spiritual forces emergent from embodied relations and constitutive of the 'substratum of collective life' (Durkheim, 1982a: 57). Under the influence of technological determinism or a neo-Kantian conception of self-determining, reflexive subjects able to reconstruct time and space, this inattention to a social substratum also leads to the neglect of the immense significance of Christianity in Western history, and an inability to recognise that this influence may continue into the present.

In this chapter, I shall argue that such views tend to overestimate Christianity's apparent lack of contemporary social significance because they depend upon a questionable understanding of the *temporal* dimensions of society. The 'temporal' dimensions of particular note here are not the immensely diverse experiences, codifications and transformations of time discussed by Adam (1990), but two very specific phenomena. The first of these is the broad temporal context within which societies develop: the *longue durée* of societal development. A focus on the fact that contemporary societies have to be analysed in relation to this *longue durée* can help reveal to us some significant ways in which Christianity has had a very significant influence upon contemporary social life. The second phenomenon at the heart of this chapter, however, which emerges out of this Christian influence, is the distinction between the *temporal* and the *spiritual*. This distinction, central to medieval thought, was transformed, at the time of the Protestant Reformation, into a distinction between the 'religious' and the 'secular' that came to have a major influence upon various modern philosophical and sociological visions of society, though the influence of the medieval view is also apparent in this regard, even if this has been less commented upon. Indeed, although the Protestant view of religion as essentially distinct from society became normative for many forms of sociology, for others, something close to the medieval Christian understanding continued to be significant for understanding the complex inter-relationship between religion and society.

The chapter is structured as follows. After discussing the value of a social realist account of the significance of time for how we conceptualise society, I examine how Christian history has provided Western societies with certain cultural contradictions, concerning the temporal and the spiritual, that continue into the present and still affect how we make sense of social life. Following this, I examine how these contradictions run through influential philosophical accounts of social bonds and contracts, and then explore their presence in some key sociological visions of modernity. Throughout, I shall argue that many conventional assumptions about contemporary secularity tend to confuse the way we think about things with the way things really are, and that in this respect the distinction between the temporal and the spiritual can be more analytically precise and useful than that between the secular and the religious.

Time-binding society

The importance of interpreting the temporal constitution and development of society in terms of the *longue durée* of human history can be established by looking at problems arising from theories that suggest otherwise. In a well-known argument, Berger (1990: 3), for example, says that 'Society is a dialectic phenomenon in that it is a human product, and nothing but a human product, that yet continuously acts back upon its producer.' This 'dialectical' process of world-building involves three stages: *externalisation* (the physical and mental 'outpouring of human being into the world'), *objectivation* (the appearance of 'reality' attained by the products of this activity), and *internalisation* (the 'reappropriation' of this reality within subjective consciousness) (Berger, 1990: 4). It is on the basis of this dialectical process that Berger develops his social constructionist account of religion and society. For him, externalising activity results in the construction of a 'nomos', a meaningful order, that imbues life with reality, although this is continually vulnerable to collapse because it 'hangs on the thin thread of conversation' (Berger, 1990: 17). Religion, which he defines functionally (despite his protestations to the contrary), 'guarantees' the reality of the nomos by identifying it with cosmic order: the sacred is our 'ultimate shield against anomy' ('the sacred canopy'), because it hides the constructed nature of the world with 'fictitious necessities'. The decline of religion in modern societies, whereby large areas of 'society and culture are removed from the domination of religious symbols' and religion loses its subjective 'plausibility' (Berger, 1990: 107, 128), thus involves the stimulation of broader 'anomic' processes, as the socially constructed nature of 'reality' becomes increasingly fragile. Although Berger does not say so explicitly, the logical implication of his argument is also that 'society' is in danger of collapsing in these circumstances.

As Bhaskar (1979: 33) has argued, however, people and society are *not* related 'dialectically' within one process, since, contrary to Berger's suggestion that we 'reappropriate' products of our own activity, the society that is appropriated by human beings is always *already made*: we may *reproduce* or *transform* society, but we cannot create it because it is already there. As Archer (1995: 63) suggests, the same argument can also be made against Giddens's (1984) structuration theory: to deny the notion of an emergent reality distinct from human agents not only massively overestimates the creativity of people, but also denies what is obvious to all of us, namely, that the conditions and consequences of our choices and actions are constrained by the fact of the pre-existing societies we inhabit. Consequently, contrary to Berger, we cannot simply construct meaningful realities independent of the social circumstances in which we find ourselves but, also, we cannot simply deconstruct existing ones either. With regard to religion, this means that the Christian dimensions of Western societies do not necessarily vanish in a flurry of anomic social currents, however 'implausible' Christian beliefs and practices might appear to many contemporary persons.

What Berger's analysis lacks is an adequate recognition of the importance of the temporal dimensions of society. Although he notes that society 'both precedes and survives' the individual, and that externalising activities 'persist over time', he none the less fails to see how these ideas contradict his 'dialectical' model (Berger, 1990: 3, 7). In contrast, it can be noted that, although Berger (1990: 189) derives his notion of 'nomos' from an inversion of Durkheim's (1952) concept of 'anomie', Durkheim's understanding of the importance of the temporal aspects of society is much stronger, and builds on Fustel de Coulanges's (1956: 14) argument that 'the past never completely dies for man ...take him at any epoch, and he is the product, the epitome of all earlier epochs'. For Durkheim (1977: 15), we cannot even begin to understand the present if we sever its connection to the past. Furthermore, the importance of the past is not simply *subjective*, in the sense that people, places and things that have a particular significance in terms of our individual biographies somehow 'live on' within us, but is *objective*: at the level of the individual and at that of large-scale societal forms, the present is shaped by an 'agglomeration' of actions, events, experiences and traits that occurred in the past. We may not be fully conscious of many of these, but that is because 'they are so deeply rooted within us' (Durkheim, 1977: 11; see Strenski, 2002: 116–17). As Archer's (1995: 169) account of the necessity of seeing structure and agency as analytically distinct also makes clear, the emergence of the social structures that confront us as social agents depends on the activities of previous 'generations'.

As I suggested in Chapter 2, however, Bauman (2002: 191), amongst others, has argued that Durkheim's (1972: 93–4) view of human actions having consequences that go beyond the immediate moment seems to be called into question by the diverse, apparently disconnected phenomena of contemporary social encounters and experiences. Giddens's (1990, 1991) arguments concerning the 'chronic reflexivity' of the present, which serves to undermine any real connection to the past, express a similar view, as does Hervieu-Léger's (2000) account of the deconstruction of those collective chains of memory that have shaped Western civilisation in the past. A potentially even more damning critique is offered by Urry, however. Specifically challenging Archer's temporal distinction between culture and agency, he accuses her of offering 'a Newtonian conception of time' that 'goes against the entire thrust of twentieth century science'. For him, she reduces time to a linear 'before-and-after' model that ignores the significance of multiple 'times' and the 'warping of time–space' ushered in by those global changes that make 'instantaneous' time one of the most powerful post-societal human/technological 'hybrids' (Urry, 2000: 16).

The value of Urry's analysis rests on its capacity to illuminate key characteristics of sociological analyses of time, including the social organisation of work, leisure and identity around 'clock-time', and to draw attention to some of the complexities of attempting to theorise different dimensions of temporality in a globalised world. However, his critique of Archer is questionable on two counts. First, it is not clear that Archer has a 'Newtonian concept of time' at all. The key characteristics of the post-Newtonian conception of time are its emphases on the *irreversibility* of time and on the fact that events do not simply occur in one, linear, temporal form, but that temporality is inherent within events and actions themselves (Adam, 1990; Prigogine and Stengers, 1984). As Byrne (1998) and Sayer (2000) suggest, critical realist conceptions of time are entirely consistent with these arguments developed by complexity theorists in that both agree reality is constituted by multiple causes and multiple effects in a dynamical but irreversible temporal pattern characterised by emergence. In this regard, it is important to note that, contrary to Urry's suggestion that 'before-and-after' understandings of time are now theoretically questionable, the notion of irreversible time *reinforces* such understandings.

Second, Urry does not distinguish between the specific matter of contemporary social reconstructions of time and general issues to do with the temporal dimensions of societies. Thus, he is able to integrate chaos and complexity theories with Castells's (1996) account of the transformations in time stimulated by the information society to argue that the current significance of 'instantaneous time' is evident in the importance of technological processes dependent on 'inconceivably brief instants which are wholly beyond human consciousness', the collapse of the temporal distinction between cause and effect that follows from the instantaneous character of social and technical relationships, and the spread of a general cultural experience of temporal fragmentation and short-termism (Urry, 2000: 126). These arguments resist the implications of chrono-biology and thermodynamics, which, taken together, can endorse a focus on irreversible flows of time grounded in human embodiment, and they ignore how Adam, Urry's principle source for his account of post-Newtonian notions of time, stresses

that chaos and complexity theories reinforce the need for social organisations of time to be assessed in relation to the broader natural contexts out
of which societies emerge (Adam, 1990: 154–5; Urry, 2000: 119–20).

As Bauman (1992b) has noted, in fact, one of the essential aspects of
what it is to be human is the tension between 'time-binding' minds, which
allow us to conceptualise in diverse ways human life, destiny and experience, including the various temporal dimensions of the human lot, and the
'time-bound' fact of humanity's mortal condition. Heidegger's (1962) view
of the fundamentally temporal character of human beings also took full
account of this mortality. Urry (2000: 116), again following Adam (1995:
94), notes that feminists have challenged such views as signifying an essentially 'masculine' approach that ignores the 'time-generating capacity of pro-
creation', but the recognition that all humans are embodied beings who
eventually die is an undeniable anthropological fact transcendent of gender
issues. It is a fact, furthermore, that means the human experience of time is
inherently embodied: we are 'bodies in time' in terms of our individual existence, while humanity as a single species populating different historical
periods within the *longue durée* of biological and social evolution also has a
fundamentally temporal character (Mellor and Shilling, 1997: 18; see
Braudel, 1972). Indeed, it is possible to elaborate upon Bauman's (1992b)
vision of the tension between time-binding minds and time-bound flesh by
noting that *societies* also have the capacities to 'bind time' in various ways,
but are, ultimately, *time-bound* in the sense that they are embodied phenomena *of their time* (see Gurvitch, 1963: 174; 1964; Adam, 1990: 122).
Consequently, the disembodied vision of 'instantaneous time' might make
sense of how computers operate, but cannot account satisfactorily for the
general temporal dimensions of human social life, however conscious we
become of the logistics of speed, the fragmentation of particular social
organisations of time, and the spread of short-termist values and practices in
public and private lives.

A further point to make is that, rather than revealing the redundancy of
a 'before-and-after' temporal distinction between cause and effect, such
developments are likely to illuminate its value: as Bauman's (2002) account
of contemporary society demonstrates, a key dimension of social and cultural experience is the sense that events are often completely out of our
control, rather than the idea that everything can be instantaneously reconstructed according to our current whims. This is not to say that everything
is out of our control, unless we adopt the sort of technological determinism
characteristic of some information society theorists, which would effectively
deny the possibility of human agency. Rather, it is to say that we cannot
avoid what Archer (1995: 2) calls the 'vexatious ambivalence of social reality' because humans are beings in time who exercise their agency in situations that are not of their own choosing, let alone of their own creation, even
though society is, ultimately, of human constitution. It follows from this, of
course, that sociology ignores history at its peril, since, as Auguste Comte
expressed it, the majority of actors are the dead (Archer, 1995: 148).

Time-bound society

For Durkheim (1982b: 211) 'there is no sociology worthy of the name which does not possess a historical character'. A similar view has also been expressed by Giddens (1991b: 205), who has called the social sciences 'irremediably historical'. None the less, Giddens (1990: 4) has a 'discontinuist' view of history, distinguishing sharply between modern and premodern societies in his argument that 'The modes of life brought into being by modernity have swept us away from *all* traditional types of social order, in quite unprecedented fashion.' This seriously underestimates historical continuities. It could be said, in fact, that, just as Giddens's account of agency tends to place too much emphasis on the creativity of individuals (Kilminster, 1991), so too his view of history appears to place far too much emphasis on the discontinuities ushered in by modernity. More than that, he does not give sufficient attention to the fact that the idea of 'modernity' itself has a particular history, rooted in Christian tradition. Kumar (1995: 69), indeed, has argued that 'much of what we understand as modernity is contained in the Christian philosophy of history'.

Kumar (1995: 68) notes how 'Christianity recharged the notion of time and history', infusing time with meaning through an eschatologically grounded vision of past, present and future. Contrary to Giddens's (1990: 37) vision of a future-oriented modernity defined against a past-oriented, traditional and religious premodernity, Kumar (1995: 69) notes that Christianity was, from the start, *future-oriented*. Its eschatological hopes (Christ's Second Coming and the Resurrection of the Body) were based on an event in the past (the life and death of Christ), but this was an 'unrepeatable and incomparable event' that gave time, and human history, their future-oriented direction and meaning. As de Lubac (1950: 66–7) expresses it, one feature of the uniqueness of Christianity has been its recognition that the course of history is real, being characterised by 'ontological density', and evolving towards a particular end. What distinguishes modernity, then, is not its future-orientedness, but the fact that the Christian concept of time is partially secularised, robbing it of those apocalyptic aspects which Kant referred to as Christianity's 'moral terrorism' (Kumar, 1995: 79), though even here the return of apocalyptic themes in contemporary theories of historical development suggests a limit to this secularisation (Baudrillard, 2002; Virilio, 2002; Zizek, 2002).

In the light of this view of modernity, the claim that *nation-states* , for example, can be understood as distinctively modern phenomena, radically discontinuous in relation to premodern states (Giddens, 1990: 13), is questionable. Giddens's view is consistent with that of Benedict Anderson's (1991) conceptualisation of the nation-state as a phenomenon realised through a politically validated imagination in modern societies. None the less, while certain institutional organisations and understandings of nation-states can be dated in this way, the notion of the 'nation' has a much longer

history. Hastings (1997) has drawn attention to this fact, and the very significant role of Christianity in shaping this history, while Rémond (1999:
109) has also claimed that 'In Europe, the birth of a nation often coincided
with the transition from paganism to Christianity'. This long historical link
between Christianity and the idea of a nation has biblical origins: the Bible
presented, in Israel, the model of what it meant to be a nation: 'a unity of
people, language, religion, territory and government' (Hastings, 1997: 18).
From the twelfth century onwards, bearing in mind the immense influence
of the Bible in its Vulgate and vernacular forms, the vast multitude of texts
in the Bible that used the word 'nation' served to establish a clear sense of
its meaning as relating to a people united by common language, custom,
laws and habits (Hastings, 1997: 16–7). For Hastings and Rémond, it is this
biblical understanding of nations that has a formative influence over
Western societies in the *longue durée* of their development. Building upon
this, it is possible to see that the *relative* rather than *radical* discontinuity of
modern and premodern views of the nation also has religious origins: in the
Middle Ages, the biblical legitimation of a diversity of 'nations' was balanced
by the universalism of the Catholic Church, and it was only with the
Protestant Reformation that national churches and nation-states, in their
modern form, started to emerge.

Such reflections on the religious origins of notions of the nation-state,
aside from complicating suggestions that its origins can simply be located in
the early modern period, also raise broader questions about the historical
significance of the religious dimensions of Western society. One of the most
important of these concerns how we can make sense of the influence of
Christian ideas in the *longue durée* of Western history when the past few
hundred years of this have so often been conceived in terms of a process of
secularisation. One way of attempting to deal with this is to focus on the
relationship between religion and the hyper-spiritual substratum of society.
In the first chapter of this book it was argued that religion is a phenomenon
that expresses a collective engagement with the possibilities of transcendence emergent from the hyper-spiritual dimensions of society as a *sui
generis* reality, and that this engagement allows the development of forms of
philosophy, theology and ritual mechanisms that can then have causal
power over the subsequent development of societies. A notable characteristic of Christian theology is its attentive engagement with these social
processes. Thus, historically, the highest Christian calling has been the nurturing of the 'social miracle', where salvation and social solidarity were
inseparably linked (Bossy, 1985: 57), while contemporary theology's greatest challenge can still be found in the illumination of ultimate truth through
the emergent convictions and experiences arising from 'the social sub-structure of knowledge' (Torrance, 1985: 112; Williams, 2000). Common to
these views is not only the recognition that social reality has religious
dimensions alongside others that have a different character, but also the
belief that these different dimensions are, ideally at least, interactive with
each other.

In the Middle Ages, these dimensions were conceptualised in terms of the distinction between the 'temporal' and the 'spiritual', though these were also understood to have a productively interactive relationship. The significance of this distinction is evident not only in relation to the historical development of Western beliefs, practices and institutions, but also in relation to philosophical and sociological reflections upon the nature of social reality, even when these appear to have a 'secular' character, and where the distinction is not adopted self-consciously, as in the case of Comte, who embraced it as offering a vital insight into the nature of society (Aron, 1990: 93–4; Pickering, 1997: 31–2; Serres, 1995: 453). Before examining these philosophical and sociological reflections, a further examination of specifically Christian understandings of society can help establish the significance of the temporal/spiritual distinction.

Christian society

Something akin to the distinction between the temporal and the spiritual is evident in pre-Christian as well as post-Christian thought. Indeed, although post-societal theorists tend to see 'society' as a modern construct of sociological discourse, the Western origins of the notion of society, and an engagement with what Christianity deemed its temporal and spiritual dimensions, can be traced back to Aristotle, at least. Aristotle does not simply offer an account of the manifest structure of his society, but a philosophical vision of the potentialities inherent within social dynamics. Thus, he offers a vision of *the good life* and *the good society*, which locates human action in various social domains that can nurture, sustain and organise human dispositions in such a way as to establish good habits in human relationships (Levine, 1995: 116-17). Aristotle's reflections centre on the notion of fellowship or community (*koinonia*), and the belief that human beings are distinct from animals because of our ability to tell good from evil, the just from the unjust. Society, as an embodiment of human friendship, exists not simply for utilitarian reasons but to nurture and uphold justice (Frisby and Sayer, 1986: 14). For Bauman (2002: 53–4), Aristotle illuminates 'the transcendental conditions of human togetherness' that have haunted social thought ever since: *virtue* can be a property of the individual, but *justice* necessitates a society where all the contingencies and limitations of particular forms of human co-habitation are measured against the inherent potentialities for a 'just order of shared living'. This understanding of society as a *moral*, rather than simply a sociological phenomenon, is also evident in the Christian theological understandings of social life that have had a marked effect upon the development of modern notions of society.

In the New Testament, the Greek term *koinonia* is used to refer to the early church, signalling that human society should be marked by the love and reciprocity that is characteristic of the Christian relationship with God (Torrance, 1985: 119). This Christian fellowship was manifest, sociologically, as a *communion*, where individuals were ritually incorporated into the church through the eating and drinking of Christ's body and blood in sacramental form, now commonly referred to as the Eucharist (Hastings, 2000). In this conception there is a strong sense of the capacities of individuals with regard to different aspects of human embodiment: they are endowed with cognitive faculties and the free will to choose between good and evil, but it is also recognised that it is through bodies as well as minds that Christian conversion is able to take place (Miles, 1989: 31). In medieval Catholic ritual, the powers and potentialities of human embodiment in this broad sense became intimately entwined within a strong theological and liturgical focus upon the constitution of a Christian *society*. Through the ritual incorporation of individuals into its structures, and the generation of theological representations of human life and destiny, the church promoted the idea that the fully Christian form of being is inherently social: humanity's full moral and spiritual development, as desired by God, comes through participation in the fellowship and communion embodied in the church. In Europe in the Middle Ages, where the church held a powerful influence across a vast plurality of social, geographical and cultural domains, incorporation into the communion of the church through the Eucharist was supplemented by other sacraments relating to life stages (birth, marriage, death), the nurturing of 'confraternities' offering fellowship and support, and the spread of ideas and ritual practices emphasising a 'communion of saints' uniting the living and the dead (Mellor and Shilling, 1997).

These developments, most obviously in the case of sacraments relating to life stages and in the construction of chains of interdependence between the living and the dead, recognised a distinction between the temporal (pertaining to the world) and the spiritual (pertaining to the church), but served to orient the temporal towards the eschatological. This orientation is evident in Beckwith's (1993: 66–7) account of how medieval texts, such as Nicholas Love's *Mirrour*, sought to link individual and social time with liturgical time and with the temporal sequencing of Christ's Passion, so that 'the crucifixion structures the time of everyday life'. It is often said that time in the Middle Ages was thought of in much more cyclical terms than in modern societies, often connected with the seasons (Régnier-Bohler, 1988: 380), but it was also very much tied in with patterns of human togetherness nurtured by the church, where embodied community, symbolic orders of meaning and the ritual structuring of temporal life were all understood to be interrelated (Beckwith, 1993: 53). Thus, church bells provided the rhythm for passing hours, days, nights and a broad range of other events, including births, deaths, accidents and holidays (Rémond, 1999: 68), but did so in a way that sought to connect individuals to a specifically Christian vision of the spiritual dimensions of society, and through that to connect people to God and to the unfolding drama of universal history under the sign of the Cross.

In the medieval view, then, the 'transcendental conditions of human togetherness' were expressed in explicitly theological terms: society was a human, temporal phenomenon, but was also an arena for the development of human sociality and morality that was infused with the divine grace mediated through the 'spiritual estate' of the church. Politically, this was expressed through temporal and spiritual forms of authority that came to define 'Christendom': kings and emperors exercised their temporal powers in what was regarded as a state of 'equilibrium' with the spiritual power of the Church (O'Donovan, 1999: 204). Although the legitimacy of various forms of temporal authority was accepted by the church, there was also a recognition that the spiritual dimensions of society were ultimately the most important, since the 'Kingship' of Christ far transcended that of secular rulers (O'Donovan, 1999: 205). The church itself, none the less, also had temporal and spiritual aspects: it was both a sociological reality (constituted by embodied human beings with all their faults and virtues), and a mystical reality (the Incarnate Christ continuing in sacramental form), and thereby offered a model of community life that could transform society as a whole. This, then, was how the inherent hyper-spirituality of collective life was harnessed to explicitly religious ends: the church's self-defined mission was the development of what Bossy has called the 'social miracle', the transfiguration of a familiar social universe into fellowship with God and man through 'charity', which, in this period, meant *solidarity* (Bossy, 1985: 13).

With the Protestant Reformation, however, the inherently *social* nature of the Church's self-identity, and its productive engagement with the hyper-spirituality emergent from human embodiment, was replaced by a sceptical view of the relationship between 'religion' (now defined in terms of *correct belief*) and human society, and a new stress on the importance of individual belief rather than collective ritual that rejected the traditional distinction between the temporal and the spiritual, or transformed it into a psychological rather than a sociological phenomenon (Cameron, 1991; Luther, 1995; O'Donovan, 1999). Here, in some forms of Protestantism at least, even Churches, aside from societies in a broader sense, were seen as profane associations of individuals with shared beliefs, and any attempt to sanctify them, as the Catholic Church did, was seen as, at best, misguided, and, at worst, idolatrous (Wilson, 2002).

In this regard, it is instructive to look at Bossy's (1985) account of how Protestantism's emergence affected what is meant by 'religion' and 'society'. Bossy suggests that, from 1400, the word 'religion', which had been revived from classical Latin by Christian humanists, signalled an attribute of individuals and communities centred on a worshipful attitude to God or a respect for holy things. After 1700, however, the Christian world was full of competing 'religions', marked out from each other, with clearly defined belief systems and rules of inclusion and exclusion, alongside vague, abstract notions of religion in general: 'Above their multiplicity planed a shadowy abstraction, *the* Christian Religion, and somewhere above that, in an upper region of the classifying system, religion with a capital 'R', planted in its new domain by people who did not usually feel or believe in it' (Bossy, 1985: 170). The development of what was understood by 'society' was intimately tied up with these religious changes:

> In the fifteenth century 'society' meant a state of companionship, fellow-ship or mutually recognised relation with one or more of one's fellow men ... By 1700 or shortly after, it had already come to mean mainly an objective col-lectivity, exterior to its members and delimited from other such collectivities. Above them, as above the numerous examples of religion, planed the larger abstraction Society, an entity from which most actual human contact had been evacuated ...[Religion and Society] are like the sexes according to Aristophanes, effects of the fission of a primitive whole, yearning towards one another across a great divide. The whole, for better or worse, was 'Christianity', a word which until the seventeenth century meant a body of people, and has since then, as most European languages testify, meant an 'ism' or body of beliefs. (Bossy, 1985: 171)

For Bossy, then, this transformation of 'Christianity' from a body of people to a body of beliefs was intimately tied to the process of abstraction sur-rounding the notion of 'society', following its cleavage from 'religion'. From this point on, however intently individuals may have believed in their reli-gion, the medieval consciousness of the links between Christianity and soci-ety, spirituality and temporality, tended to fade from view or, at least, become much more problematic. The so-called 'disenchantment' of the Western world associated with the Reformation does not, therefore, simply express a 'secularisation' of society in the sense that religion becomes socially (and sociologically) insignificant: what it expresses is the emergence of a new religious consciousness that uncouples the temporal from the spir-itual. This is not to say, furthermore, that Protestantism lacked an interest in society: on the contrary, some versions of Protestant Christianity, such as Calvinism, were characterised by a desire to reconstruct society in a manner that far exceeded that of the medieval Catholic Church in some respects (Taylor, 1989: 227). Nevertheless, even where such social activism was apparent, it tended to reflect a sense that society could be reconstructed by religiously minded individuals for the glory of God, rather than indicating any sense of the inherent religious potentialities of society itself. Some of the distinctive features of such Protestant views are evident in some of the the-ological, philosophical and sociological accounts of embodiment, religion and society that have had a significant impact upon modern understandings of the world.

Post-Christendom society

One of the ironies of the West's religious history is that the end of 'Christendom', where society had been envisaged in explicitly Christian terms, was nurtured not by waning religious enthusiasm but by revolution-ary religious fervour (Ozment, 1992). This Protestant 'revolution' does not signal the end of Christianity's social significance, however, but provides the religious context for the emergence of distinctively modern views of society. Here, from the start, society is a *problem*, not least because many Christians no longer saw it in Christian terms. As Bossy (1985: 154) notes, the divorce between the religious and the social was given a constitutional warrant by Martin Luther's doctrine of the two kingdoms, which 'appeared to mean that the social world was in any case the province of the Devil'. Early modern attempts to construct and make sense of the interrelationships between notions of 'political society', 'civil society' and ' human nature' arise from this divorce, and, rather than seeing society in terms of 'the transcendental conditions of human togetherness', often tend to envisage it as a necessary evil.[1] The Protestant influence upon notions of civil society can be examined further in relation to some of the basic assumptions evident in the British social contract theories of Hobbes and Locke.

In Hobbes's (1957) *Leviathan* societies are necessary in order to regulate, through contracts and the power of the state, the competitive interests of individuals that would otherwise result in a war of everyone against everyone. As Rist (2002: 53) notes, humans are understood to be endowed with little in the way of natural powers and properties, while society is necessarily coercive: Hobbes invests humans with a 'minimal rationality that will enable the subject to do an unavoidable deal in favour of despotism'. Consequently, although it has been noted that there remains a 'moral' dimension to Hobbes's vision of society, this is reduced to a coercive strategy for 'the conservation of men in multitudes' (Frisby and Sayer, 1986: 19); a strategy not dissimilar to the mixture of religious individualism and societal totalitarianism in Calvin's Geneva (Roper, 1994). In contrast, it has been suggested that Locke's Protestant ideal of the autonomous individual was 'embedded in a complex moral ecology that included family and church ... and a vigorous public sphere in which economic initiative grew with public spirit (Bellah et al., 1992: 265). It has nevertheless been suggested that full membership of Locke's 'civil society' was limited only to those capable of a 'voluntary obligation to the law of reason', identified as men of property (Frisby and Sayer, 1986: 20). This view of humans and society does not rest on the brutality inherent in Hobbes's view of human nature, but it also endorses the view that humans are, for the most part, deficient in terms of a capacity for social existence: the 'natural rights and powers' of all individuals (with regard to self-preservation and the ownership of property) are, in society, handed over to a propertied elite who govern on the basis of a rationality the masses lack (Macpherson, 1962: 256). Furthermore, rather than challenging Hobbes's view of humans with a focus on their positive qualities, Locke only emphasised that they can have benign dispositions, and that selfish dispositions can have benign social consequences (Levine, 1995: 130).

What is quite clear from a close reading of Locke's work is that belief in God is absolutely central to his view of society, since it is this that guarantees a proper commitment to moral foundations of social order, a commitment he believed to be impossible for atheists (Waldron, 2002: 225). In contrast, it has been argued that Hobbes sought to construct a 'purely secular rational ethic', even though he defined the 'laws of nature' as commands of God (Levine, 1995: 124), and that it is possible to remove the theology without substantively altering his theory (Plamenatz, 1963: 21). This does not indicate the unimportance of this theology, however, only its tendency to conceive of society in exclusively temporal terms and associate spiritual values with individuals. Just as many of the Protestant Reformers came to see ecclesial communities as purely human constructions to foster the religious commitments of individuals (Cameron, 1991: 145), so too Hobbes and Locke envisaged societies as artificial constructions to preserve individual interests. These 'interests', however, tend to reflect a diminished view of the embodied characteristics and potentialities of humans compared to the medieval view. Indeed, Hobbes's view of nature and Calvin's view of 'natural man' shared a similarly bleak view of the essential character of human beings (Hill, 1966; Chatellier, 1989; Colas, 1991). Societies, like churches in the Protestant view, needed to be constructed (only deviant forms could arise spontaneously) to promote self-interests and constrain the more depraved dimensions of humans, rather than to offer a social context where a broader range of human potentialities could flourish. For all their appearances as 'secular' theories, then, these conceptions of society clearly owe a great deal to a particular set of religious beliefs and perspectives.

A similar debt, though taking a significantly different form, is evident in relation to early modern theories of society in Germany. Here, Kant's conception of moral value lying not in nature or society but in self-determining individual subjects was influenced by Luther's (1957: 24) argument that good works do not make a good person, but that a 'person himself [must] be good before there can be any good works, and that good works follow and proceed from the good person' (Levine, 1995: 182). Thus, Kant's focus on *duty* has nothing to do with natural impulses, social rules and dynamics or the inherent qualities and consequences of particular actions, only the rational capacities of individuals to ascertain moral imperatives subjectively. While Herder focused on *sentiment* rather than *rationality* , he also endorsed a concern with 'nature-transcending and self-determining subjects' (Levine, 1995: 187–9). Similarly, Hegel's vision of society drew on both Kant and Herder, but also added a partially secularised vision of humanity's progress throughout history towards universal freedom manifested through self-made laws (Levine, 1995: 191). Marx's later 'reversal' of Hegel's idealism also retained this Judaeo-Christian eschatological vision of human destiny within his materialist account of history, though Marx's work has a focus on social dynamics and forces that distinguish him significantly from much of the German philosophical tradition.

Contrary to the philosophical emphasis on self-determining individual subjects, which he saw as an ideological legitimation of capitalism endorsed by Protestantism, Marx insisted on recognising the *collective* and *social* bases of human action. For him, humans can individuate themselves 'only in the midst of society', while the idea of individuals being able to survive economically outside society 'is as much of an absurdity as is the development

of language without individuals living together and talking to each other'
(Marx, 1973: 84). In this respect, although Marx's distinctive contribution
to philosophy rests on his elevation of class conflict to a position of unparalleled importance as a determinant of collective action, it can be noted that
he has a strong interest in the significance of collectively nurtured patterns
of social and moral consensus. This significance is evident, for example, in
his accounts of class-consciousness, solidarity, loyalty and group consciousness (Aron, 1990: 163; Marx, 1956: 489). In particular, his vision of the con-
flict-free conditions of 'primitive communism' and those that will prevail in
a future communist state, contrasted sharply with the 'alienating' individualism of capitalist societies, and exhibits a clear rejection of both Hobbesian
and Kantian conceptions of humans and their relationships to society
(Aron, 1990: 145, 171).

Supra-individual society

Early modern French theories of society, in contrast to much of the German
philosophical tradition but closer to Marx's views, tended not to focus on
self-determining human subjects but on social dynamics, forces and energies. Here, rather than Protestant influences, and despite the anti-clericalism
that has marked the history of modern France, the influence of Catholicism
is suggestive, particularly with regard to new attempts to engage with the
hyper-spiritual dynamics inherent within medieval notions of the 'social
miracle'.[2] These philosophical arguments are also, in general, attempts to
develop ostensibly 'secular' theories of society, but they reject individualism
and build on the medieval view of the collective characteristics and potentialities of social life, and the distinction between the temporal and the spiritual. Montesquieu, for example, challenged Hobbes directly on social realist
grounds, emphasising the absurdity of trying to find the origins of society in
the raw dispositions of individuals, since 'humans are always born into a
society and never encountered outside of a society' (Levine, 1995: 153). His
understanding of society is not, therefore, an abstract one, but one attentive
to the particular circumstances in which individuals encounter it. As Aron
(1991: 18–19) notes, Montesquieu was aware of 'the almost limitless diversity of morals, customs, ideas, laws and institutions' far removed from
abstract notions of a unified, 'ideal society', but attempted to find within
this diversity an intelligible order. His notion of the 'general spirit' (*esprit
général*) of a society, anticipating the Durkheimian concept of hyper-spirituality, expresses a key aspect of this attempt. This spirit was the product
of the totality of the physical, social and moral dimensions of a society
that, over time, gave a particular society its unity and originality (Aron,
1991: 46).

Building on Montesquieu's work in certain respects, but also returning to
the type of social contract theorising Montesquieu had rejected, Rousseau
(1983) developed a notion of the social contract that saw in the theories of
Hobbes and Locke a transposition of the early modern suspicions about the

anti-social characteristics of humans into an entirely fictitious 'state of nature'. None the less, he followed Hobbes in building a theory of society on his own speculations about a pre-social state of nature. In Rousseau's vision of a state of nature, however, humans were amoral and asocial. Society was not a natural development of this state, but a product of the emergence of private property and subsequent inequalities. In such circumstances, only the development of a social contract grounded in a 'general will' for the common good (*volonté générale*), a notion developed from Montesquieu's conception of the 'general spirit' (*esprit général*), could provide a basis for morals and a measure of the corrupting power of social institutions (Frisby and Sayer, 1986: 21; MacIntyre, 1967: 183–4; Levine, 1995: 155). Here, society is an inherently ambiguous phenomenon: it is either a corrupting force that unjustly curtails human freedom, or a morally enriching, collective endeavour guided by the 'general will'.

Mark Cladis (2000) has mapped out the contours of this ambiguous view of society across Rousseau's work, which offers a number of (sometimes contradictory) attempts to make sense of the relationships between individuals, society, virtues and vices. Cladis emphasises that Rousseau's accounts of society have to be placed within a French theological context that distinguished between *amour-propre* (base self-love), *amour de soi* (benign self-love) and *charité* (disinterested love) (Cladis, 2000: 225). This term *charité*, like its English equivalent of 'charity' discussed by Bossy, had originally referred to a specifically Catholic combination of love of God and solidarity with others, but came to inform broader social ideals concerning the public good and the need to transform *charité's* opposite, *amour-propre*, into something that would not weaken society (Cladis, 2000: 227). Contrary to Luther's view of humans as essentially hateful, disgraceful creatures, and Hobbes's view of humans as naturally violent, Rousseau saw *charité*, in the form of *pitié* (a compassion for the suffering of others) and *amour de soi* as a characteristic of the state of nature, while *amour-propre* was classed as a characteristic of humans in society (Cladis, 2000: 223). For Rousseau, society is potentially corrupting only in so far as it nurtures *amour-propre*; society's legitimacy rests on its cultivation of *amour de soi* and *charité*.

Thus, although Rousseau introduced a significant qualification of the idea that society is irreducible to individuals, his overall arguments were, nevertheless, consistent with the general French concern to depict society as a supra-individual phenomenon against British theorists who focused so heavily on individuals. With regard to Germany, Scheler's (1961: 166) suggestion that 'society' is simply the 'rubbish' left over from individuals and the masses, rather than a genuinely inclusive phenomenon, is by no means alien to the broader theoretical tradition. If, as I have suggested, however, it is possible to see distinctive Christian influences upon these divergent social theories, it is also possible to observe their continued presence in specifically sociological accounts of society that developed in these different contexts.

Individualised society

Talcott Parsons's (1968) argument that classical (and, indeed, contemporary) sociology converges around a Hobbesian 'problem of order' has been highly influential, but it is also highly misleading. Society is only reduced to a 'problem of order' for Hobbes because of his vision of the individuals who compose it, with their competing interests and lack of social instincts, and because of his rejection of any notion of a spiritual substratum underpinning its temporal form. For Montesquieu, on the other hand, such a reduction is absurd because society is an unavoidable reality rather than an artificial imposition upon unruly individuals motivated only by their own interests. For Kant, Hobbes's tension between nature and society is transcended completely by self-directing subjects' rational embrace of moral imperatives. Given that the philosophical positions developed by Montesquieu and Kant became so influential, respectively, for the French and German traditions of sociology that have dominated the modern social sciences, it is clear that Hobbes's significance can be overstated.

Where Parsons (1991) might well have been correct, however, is in his insistence that the individualistic social and cultural values of American society have a recognisably Protestant character (see also Robertson, 1991). In this respect it is interesting to note that, from the start, American sociology often tended to favour a strong focus on individuals and a minimalist view of society. Discussing the pioneering work of Park and Burgess (1921: 36), for example, Morrison (2001: 103) notes that they 'took the position that the only investigative reality was the individual and that society as such is a category that exists only in name, and is not itself a real object or category'. Rational choice forms of sociology, which developed primarily in the USA, push this strong view of the individual and nominalist view of society still further. It is in rational choice theory, in fact, rather than sociology in general, that the influence of Hobbes is unambiguously apparent. The 'aggregation model' of social actions offered by rational choice theories clearly returns to Hobbes's minimalist conception of society (Bohman, 1991: 148–9). Hobbes's influence is also evident in the suggestion, by Olson (1965), that coercion is necessary to encourage cooperative action, and the general emphasis this approach places on 'individual interests' above all else. Similarly, Coleman (1990) explicitly identifies his attempted reconstruction of sociology on rational choice lines with Hobbes, while Becker's (1986) stress on the importance of Bentham and Smith, who developed aspects of Hobbes's thought, underlines this continuity with early modern British social theory, particularly in terms of its economistic tendency to define all human phenomena with reference to 'markets'. In some influential quarters of the American sociology of religion this continuity is also evident, particularly with regard to the attempts of Stark, Iannaccone and Finke to analyse religion in terms of stable individual preferences for religious goods, and shifting supply-side patterns in changing markets (see Young, 1997; Mellor, 2000).

In German sociology, a Protestant influence is also apparent, though it is of a significantly different sort. Here, Kant's focus on self-determining individual subjects proved to have a decisive influence upon Simmel and Weber, both of whom tended to be sceptical about the notion of 'society' in general, but particularly with regard to any suggestion of a spiritual substratum (Levine, 1995: 211). Simmel refused to accept the reduction of society to individuals, yet saw society as an abstract 'summing-up concept' for the patterns of interaction, or 'forms of sociation', that shape human experience (Frisby and Sayer, 1986: 58–60). For him, it is only because 'an extraordinary multitude and variety of interactions' exist at any moment that a 'seemingly autonomous historical reality' has been attributed to 'society' (Simmel, 1971: 27). Simmel also rejects the view that individuals are socially determined beings. Humans, he suggests, are characterised by a distinction between pre-social impulses and individualised mental forms on the one hand, and social emotions and reciprocated mental forms on the other: they are naturally predisposed to interact, yet are partly shaped by social interaction (Shilling and Mellor, 2001: 59). For Weber, similarly, the subject matter of sociology is not 'society' but different types of social action and their meanings for individual actors (Frisby and Sayer, 1986: 68). Offering a Kantian interpretation of action, Weber (1978:4) suggests that 'Action is "social" insofar as its subjective meaning takes account of the behaviour of others, and is thereby oriented in its course.'

For both Simmel and Weber, however, society is not simply an abstract concept, but also something that, historically, has been problematised by social and cultural transformations. This sense of the historical problematisation of society is especially evident when each of them discusses religion. Simmel suggests that humans possess inherent religious needs for transcendence and completeness, and that religion therefore has an immense significance in terms of bringing subjective (interior) and objective (social) aspects of human experience into a coherent whole that makes life meaningful (Simmel, 1997: 142). Nevertheless, although it is still a 'concrete reality within the soul', religion is paralysed in modernity where the gap between subjective and objective has become too wide to traverse, creating immense existential difficulties for individuals (Simmel, 1997: 9). For Weber (1991), it is, ironically, because of ascetic Protestantism's promotion of an individualist ethic of rational mastery of the world that modern societies now deny many of the moral capacities and values that allow human beings to flourish in social contexts.

In broad terms, it could be said that the Protestant rejection of Catholic conceptions of the religious dimensions of social life provides an important context for, and influence on, the emergence of the German sociological tradition's interest in the separation of religion from society (and the development of theories of secularisation), and, more broadly, the problematic nature of society itself. The distinction between *Gemeinschaft* 'community' and *Gesellschaft* 'society' in the work of Tönnies (1957), for example, expresses a sense of the shift from a taken-for-granted social habitus shaped by tradition and religion to one that is more associational, contractual and individualistic. Also within this tradition, Berger's (1990) vision of modernity in terms of a 'sky empty of angels' not only offers a sociological analysis of the Protestant reconceptualisation of social life in profane terms, but, in a sense, reflects it: the 'sacred canopy' has been ripped up, Berger tells us, and nothing can piece it together again.

Transcendent society

Turning to French sociology, however, an ostensible repudiation of Catholic doctrines and practices does not result in methodological individualism and narratives of secularisation. On the contrary, the medieval 'social miracle', society as 'charity' or 'solidarity', tends to take on a sociological form in a number of different visions of the interrelationship between the temporal and spiritual dimensions of society. In the work of Comte, who first introduced the term 'sociology', the gradual, ongoing de-Christianisation of society is simply assumed, but he nevertheless builds religion into his very strong emphasis on society as a real phenomenon transcendent of individuals. Comte (1853: 350–2) criticised Hobbes, in fact, for his focus on individuals and his denial of the 'spiritual' dimensions of society, and sought to build on Montesquieu's concern with society as a supra-individual entity. For Comte, the 'temporal power' of society (its manifest institutional, contractual or political form) was contingent upon something greater than itself (Aron, 1991: 93–4). Comte discusses this transcendent basis of society in terms of 'spiritual power' and suggests that religion has the power to generate 'sympathetic emotions' and bind individuals into a sense of unity (Pickering, 1997: 31–2). Having made this distinction between the temporal and the spiritual, which he traces to the Catholic opposition between heavenly and earthly interests, Comte's suggestion is that the positive polity must re-establish this distinction, shorn of any supernatural referents, in a sociological 'religion of humanity'.[3]

As eccentric as Comte's ideas might now appear, they helped reinforce Durkheim's concern with the importance of religion in relation to society; a concern also evident in the writings of Montesquieu, Rousseau, Saint-Simon and others in the French tradition of social thought. Furthermore, just as Comte associated patterns of social breakdown in early modern Europe with the attacks of Luther and Calvin on the 'organic fusion' of religion and society in the medieval period (Nisbet, 1993: 228–9), so too Durkheim (1952: 170) identified Protestantism with a weakening of the common beliefs and practices that bind individuals into society. He poured scorn, however, on 'Comte's attempt to organise a religion using old historical memories, artificially revived', and emphasised instead that new religious forms would inevitably arise of their own accord (Durkheim, 1995: 429). His sense of the inevitability of these new religious forms emerging underlines his general view that religion is an 'eternal' feature of social life, and that the history of societies is always, therefore, in some sense, the history of religions. In consequence, he was prepared to accept that many of the beliefs and practices that had most meaning and value for him were of Christian and Jewish origin, despite his avowed atheism and his conviction that these religions were dying (Pickering, 1993: 53).

Comte's arguments also informed Durkheim's view of society as a reality transcendent of individuals. For Durkheim (1974c), it was Comte who had given sociology 'a concrete reality to know' and who, though he saw society as real, recognised it could not exist apart from individuals. Durkheim criticised Comte, however, for focusing on 'Society' rather than 'societies', and for using the words 'humanity' and 'society' interchangeably (see Lukes, 1973: 82). In other words, he found Comte's notion of society too abstract, and too prone to conflate different aspects of human experience into one overarching narrative. Durkheim's attempt to be more precise, and more attentive to the complexity of human societies, is indicated in his reassessment of Rousseau's work, which he had earlier dismissed for what he took to be the 'ferocious individualism' of its argument that society was an artificial construction of humans contrary to their real natures (Durkheim, 1974c).

Robert Alun Jones's (1999: 272–5) study of Durkheim's social realism offers an account of this reinterpretation of Rousseau. Emphasising that Rousseau's 'state of nature' was a *psychological* rather than a *historical* construct, Durkheim saw in this notion an attempt to distinguish the things we owe to society from the things that are part of our psychological nature. He argued that the harmony of Rousseau's natural man with his physical environment was a reflection of the fact that he lived only in a world of sensations but, as the physical world put obstacles in the path of humans, intelligence evolved beyond instinct and sensation, the value of cooperative action became recognised, and individuals formed into groups that then gave rise to social inclinations, rules and ethics. As Jones (1999: 300) notes, what Durkheim found support for in Rousseau's work was the idea that society was not only a real, natural phenomenon, but also 'a *particular, distinctive* part of nature, a reality *sui generis*'. This helped him establish the idea that the sociological study of society should be focused on 'social facts', which he defined as ways of acting characterised by external constraint, generality and independence of their individual manifestations (Durkheim, 1982a: 59). These 'facts' are, in other words, *distinctively social* in that they cannot be reduced purely to individuals, but they are also *natural* in the sense that the social world is not an artificial imposition upon nature, but a specific development within it.

Durkheim's view of society also built on the work of Montesquieu, whose interest in 'what was real and concrete rather than ideal and abstract' challenged Enlightenment rationalism and appealed to Durkheim's sense of the complexity of social life (Jones, 1999: 237). It might also be said that Montesquieu's conception of the 'general spirit' (*esprit général*) of a society appealed to him more than Rousseau's notion of the 'general will' (*volonté générale*). As Watts Miller (1996: 48) has noted, for Durkheim social facts are independent of *will*. The notion of a 'general spirit', on the other hand, is close to Durkheim's idea that each society is characterised by a specific hyper-spirituality. In this respect, Durkheim's work also builds on Comte's interest in the 'spiritual' power of society, however, which Comte identified with the non-rational foundations of social orders, and which he sought to nurture through his 'Religion of Humanity'. For Comte, this would complete the social transformation begun by medieval Catholicism, but would do so in a human, sociological form, stripped of theological beliefs in supernatural forces (Lévy-Bruhl, 1903). In this French sociological tradition, then, society continues to be associated with a kind of 'social miracle', which is why religion and society are inextricably entwined rather than separate as for Weber and Simmel. This 'miracle', its hyper-spirituality, expresses experiences of transcendence, felt obligations and patterns of recognition and interdependence, but emphasises the human rather than the divine sources of these phenomena.

None the less, Durkheim had to confront the problem (central to the German sociological tradition) that, in modern societies, the hyper-spiritual dimensions of social life appeared to be in decline, and he sought to deal with this in two ways. First, in Durkheim's early work there is a sense of the loss of some of the 'spiritual' energies that attract individuals into social wholes, analogous to the secularisation narratives arising from the German tradition. This is evident in his account of the shift from 'mechanical solidarity' to 'organic solidarity', mirroring Tönnies's *Gemeinschaft/Gesellschaft* distinction to some extent (Durkheim, 1984). What is notable, however, is that he continues to emphasise *solidarity*, refusing to accept that social relationships can be reduced to contracts between individuals. Consequently, after *The Division of Labour*, Durkheim adopted a second position, abandoning the mechanical/organic distinction altogether, and seeking to orient his sociological project towards an illumination of a hyper-spirituality constitutive of all societal forms: specifically with regard to the modern West, he came to express the view that post-Christian religious forms would emerge out of this hyper-spirituality (Durkheim, 1974b: 34; 1995: 429). Here, however, it can be argued that Durkheim dismissed the continuing significance of Christianity too readily, failing to appreciate its continued influence upon Western societies. This argument can be supported, ironically, by looking at his account of aspects of Christian history, wherein he draws attention to divisions at the heart of Christianity that can illuminate analogous divisions in contemporary Western societies.

Divided society

In *The Evolution of Educational Thought* (1977) Durkheim draws attention to a cultural contradiction endemic to Christian belief and practice. He notes that Christianity's origins are inextricably entwined within Graeco-Latin influences that carry within them a 'pagan spirit' entirely contradictory of theological doctrines concerning God and His Creation. This contradiction was not simply a logical contradiction, but one that affected action in the temporal world since it involved divergent accounts of natural and super-natural realities, while Christianity also encouraged a culture of learning that, in drawing sustenance from classical literary, philosophical and artistic sources, ensured the persistence within daily life as well as within doctrine of an internal contradiction that could never be overcome (Durkheim, 1977: 21–2). As Archer (1995: 231–3) suggests, in offering this account of Christian development, Durkheim thereby developed an unsurpassed account of how cultural contradictions can constrain choices and actions over huge tracts of time.

The validity of Durkheim's interpretation of this particular contradiction between sacred (Christian) and profane (classical) elements in the history of the Church is no doubt open to question, since many writers would argue that these two elements are actually characterised by much greater continuity than he allows (see Rist, 2002). Nevertheless, it is an important insight that, because societies exist in the *longue durée*, evolving cultural systems can carry within themselves the patterns, assumptions, ideas and beliefs of what has gone before. In view of this insight, it is possible to see contemporary 'secular' society in a fresh light. This is so not only in relation to some of the apparently secular forms of philosophical and sociological theory considered in this chapter that clearly contain religious elements, but also in relation to a host of other examples. Current concerns with 'choice' and 'autonomy', for example, and the generally anti-institutionalist orientation that tends to go along with them, might also be traced back directly to the Protestant Reformation (Rist, 2002: 59). Furthermore, current debates about medical ethics and the 'sanctity of human life' tend to be framed in a broadly Christian way. Indeed, Parsons (1978) has argued that a specifically Christian notion of the 'gift of life' has come to form the basis for the apparently 'secular' ethics of the modern medical profession.

In short, it can be argued that 'secular' culture carries within itself the Christian elements that it seeks to repudiate and, as Durkheim argued regarding Christianity's Graeco-Latin origins, it is hard to see how this repudiation will ever be complete without secular culture destroying itself. This is not to say that we are all 'anonymous Christians' (Rahner, 1979), only to suggest that the Christian influence upon the Western world is such that, even if we consciously reject much of this legacy, its constraining power remains relevant in terms of some of the limits it sets in relation to contemporary agency, and in terms of the resistance it affords when we seek to break free of it. Against this argument, it is possible to anticipate criticisms that this treats human agents as 'cultural dopes' who are not fully aware of the characteristics and consequences of their actions; a criticism that might be made by Giddens (1984), for example, given his emphasis on knowledgeable agents able to reflexively monitor their actions. Giddens's approach, however, tends to overestimate the knowledgeablity of actors and agents, in a manner similar to rational choice theorists (Mellor, 2000: 280). In contrast to such views, it can be noted that it is highly improbable that individuals or groups, however 'reflexive' they are, can ever know everything that impinges upon choices, decisions and orientations. Furthermore, in a society that represents itself as 'secular', religious influences on action and belief are unlikely to be grasped fully, even if, in reality, they remain significant. It is for this reason that a sensitive engagement with historical changes is important, otherwise sociological arguments can express, uncritically, very particular theological points of view.

In this regard, it is notable that, while the German tradition of sociological thought about society might capture many elements of the apparent 'disenchantment' of the modern world, it tends to endorse, as a sociological reality, what is in origin a specifically Protestant view of the religion/society division based on a rejection of the idea that society has any 'spiritual' dimensions. This is not to say that sociological views associated with this tradition are simply 'Protestant', or to deny the significance of those Protestant theologies that *do* recognise the hyper-spiritual basis of society (Torrance, 1985). What is claimed, rather, is that the unacknowledged influence of views of society that have a specifically Protestant history can encourage sociological theorists to underestimate the significance of two things. First, theorists might underestimate the degree to which the idea that religion and society are fundamentally separate is a culturally and historically specific one (see Asad, 2002). Weber's (1978: 432–3) argument that religions have their origins in the 'other-worldly' *charisma* of individuals, which is progressively robbed of its power by rationalisation processes in society, reflects this pattern. Second, theorists might underestimate the degree to which the religion/society division is actually *unsustainable* theoretically. Cameron's (1991) study of the Reformation, for example, identifies this factor as a significant influence on the return to Catholicism by some Protestant peoples. The unsustainable character of the religion/society division is even evident in the history of New England Puritanism, where a rigid opposition to all Catholic notions of sacred space eventually gave way to a return to a form of sacramentalism and the construction of sacred spaces symbolic of its own congregational solidarity (Wilson, 2002). In fact, the emergence of such phenomena can be read as evidence of the causal significance of hyper-spiritual forces even within religious traditions that, theologically, refuse to countenance them.

To return to the subject of nation-states touched on earlier in this chapter, it is also notable that the unsustainability, ultimately, of the religion/society division is also evident in relation to their current evolution. The emergence of the religion/society division was also tied to the post-Reformation reconstruction of national and universalist tendencies within Christianity, thereby encouraging the emergence of modern nation-states: 'nations' existed within medieval 'Christendom', but nation-states start to emerge along with the fragmentation of Christendom into demarcated Christian 'religions'. The tension between national and universal tendencies within medieval Christendom did not, however, cease with the development of modernity. Giddens (1987b: 263) has noted that the development of modern nation-states has, from the beginning, depended on a reflexively monitored set of international relations that have, since the beginning of the twentieth century, taken on an increasingly globalised character (see also Robertson, 1992; 55). In this regard, it is possible to see the increasing importance of institutions such as the European Union as evidence of a resurgence of something akin to medieval Christendom. Hastings (1997: 122), for example, has noted that all the influential figures in the creation of the EU, such as Schuman, Adenauer, Delors and Santer, have been 'socially minded' Catholics committed to moving beyond the nationalisms that supplanted Christian internationalism in the late Middle Ages (see also Siedentop, 2000). Even those 'global networks and flows' discussed by Urry amongst others, however, suggest that a return to something closer to a medieval universalism may be emerging. Falk's (1995: 35) vision of a developing 'global civil society', endorsed by Urry (2000: 211) despite his post-societal orientation, suggests just such a movement.

Alongside such developments, of course, there is also an evident increase in the importance of factors such as *ethnicity* for the construction of societies in certain parts of the globe, especially in Africa and the former Yugoslavia, which suggests a resurgence of a local, rather than a universalist, orientation that is to a large extent hostile to those dominant modern notions of a 'nation' able to embrace different ethnicities (Hastings, 1997). Furthermore, within Western societies other processes of fragmentation have developed alongside those globalising forces that point towards an emergent 'global civil society'. The collapse of many traditional religious, social and political groupings into increasingly expansive 'culture wars' is significant here (Hunter, 1991). Yet ethnic conflicts in places such as the former Yugoslavia and cultural conflicts in Western Europe and the USA can be characterised as a resurgence of religion rather than the ongoing process of societal marginalisation implied by secularisation theorists. With regard to ethnic conflicts, for example, the recent hostility and bloodshed between different ethnic groups in Yugoslavia is rooted in conflicts between Catholic Christians, Orthodox Christians and Muslims that have centuries of violence and distrust underpinning them (Hastings, 1997: 137). With regard to Western Europe, it is also too easy to confuse the lack of churchgoing with the irrelevance of religion (Davie, 2000). It has to be acknowledged, of course, that there have been significant changes in the character and role of Christian beliefs and practices over time, and that some of the more recent of these changes appear to be of a radical sort. None the less, these radical changes need not simply be associated with 'secularisation', where this signals the increasing societal irrelevance of religion. In this regard, de Certeau and Domenach (1974: 11–12) have made the interesting suggestion that Christian influences continue to play a very significant role in Western societies, but that these have become uncoupled from the churches: what we are witnessing, they argue, is the disintegration of the 'ecclesiological constellation' rather than the disappearance of Christianity, as Christian beliefs, symbols, signs and assumptions circulate within contemporary culture in an increasingly unpredictable and ambivalent form (see also Hervieu-Léger, 2000: 159).

In conclusion, rather than imagining that the past has simply been 'swept away' by modernisation or postmodernisation processes (Giddens, 1990: 4), it is worth recalling a comment attributed to William Faulkner: 'The past is not dead. It's not even past' (see Strenski, 2002: 111). This resonates with Durkheim's argument that the present can only be understood in relation to the past because the past is, through the constraints, influences and potentialities with which it confronts us, thoroughly alive within the present (Durkheim, 1977: 15). In this respect, the Christian influence upon Western societies cannot be associated with the 'dead past' but, as I have suggested, can be noted even in a variety of contexts that appear to have a secular character. The purpose of the next chapter is to explore this covert Christian influence upon Western societies further through an engagement with Durkheim's account of how 'collective representations' embed social realities within the consciousnesses of individuals.

Notes

1. In fact, the term 'civil society', which was first used in a sixteenth-century text by Luther, reflects underlying Protestant assumptions about the need to base social orders on the interests of individuals rather than the spiritual dynamics inherent within collectives (Hill, 1966; Ozment, 1992).

2. With regard to the anti-clericalism of modern France, the French Revolution is usually held to represent a key moment in the movement towards a 'secular' society and away from the beliefs and practices of Catholic Christianity. Van Kley (1996), however, has argued convincingly that the French Revolution has *religious* origins, specifically in the development of notions of political liberty amongst Jansenist Catholics. What he emphasises is that it was only as the Revolution progressed that a Catholic endorsement of absolutism against Jansenists and Protestants helped fan the flames of anti-clericalism and thereby divide France into ardent secularists and ultramontanist Catholics, both of whom were eager to interpret the Revolution as an assault on France's Christian past.

3. Given this significant dependence on Catholic concepts, and his very strong antipathy to Protestantism, it is easy to see how Comte's religion has come to be referred to as 'Catholicism minus the Christianity' and 'positivist wine poured into medieval bottles' (Nisbet, 1993: 58). None the less, as Lévy-Bruhl (1903: 16) expresses it, Comte was confident of fulfilling the Catholic programme of the Middle Ages better than Catholicism itself did. Thus, contrary to Bossy's (1985: 171) account of the rupture of 'religion' from 'society' after the Reformation, for Comte they were still a totality: the recognition and reinforcement of this (intellectually and *liturgically*) was to be the mission of sociology.

6

Tacit Society

In previous chapters, it has been argued that sociological theories that place a particular emphasis on the decline of society tend to deal unsatisfactorily with the fact that it is not simply an idea, but a real, complex and temporally grounded phenomenon which, while contingent upon human potentialities, none the less imposes significant obligations upon people, even in contexts that appear to be thoroughly individualistic or utilitarian. In developing this argument, it is possible to reveal further problems with post-societal perspectives by expanding upon one of the central themes of the last chapter, namely the covert persistence of specifically Christian ways of viewing humanity and the world. As Charles Taylor (1989: 104) has observed, even in 'the most secularist quarters of our lay civilisation', Christian imagery, concepts and moral assumptions are present, despite ostensible denials of the Western religious heritage. While the last chapter touched on these with regard to the Christian historical context out of which modern philosophical and sociological conceptions of society have emerged, the concern of this chapter is to make sense of the continuing, covert presence of Christian influences within various strata of contemporary Western societies. The key to making sense of these influences rests on the development of a satisfactory understanding of how society becomes embedded within the consciousness of individuals.

Michael Polanyi's (1967) notion of a 'tacit dimension' in society is relevant in this respect. This notion refers to a substratum of knowledge that can elude our conscious, rational formulations and theories about the nature of the world, but which nevertheless shapes the meanings and understandings of ourselves and the social realities within which we live. It is a notion, however, that goes against the grain of much social and cultural theory. In both Europe and the USA, some influential ways of attempting to deal with questions about the embedding of society within individuals have not focused upon unconscious or tacit phenomena, but upon the importance of *reasonable* or *rational* dialogue for nurturing individual commitment to a social order characterised by consensus (Habermas, 1987, 1989b; Rawls, 1971, 1993). Habermas's notion of 'communicative rationality' and Rawls's vision of an 'overlapping consensus' grounded in public reason are influential examples of such theoretical approaches. In each case, however, assumptions about the inherent or potential rationality of individuals, and the possibilities for some sort of 'pure' rational communication, lean these theories towards abstract and idealist visions of society rather than a critical investigation of how things really are. This is evident with regard to Habermas's discussion of the 'ideal speech' situation (Delanty, 1997), but also with regard to Rawls's account of a 'well-ordered society' (Rawls, 1999:

361): neither of these things actually exist, because humanity's embodied potentialities, out of which societies emerge, are considerably more diverse than these theories allow. This is not to say that humans are not thinking creatures with capacities for a rational critique of their social circumstances, only that a great deal of what goes on in society is neither rational nor fully conscious.

In contrast to such approaches, Durkheim's vision of the hyper-spiritual dynamics inherent to social realities is sensitive to the fact that many of the key aspects of society are shaped by a pre-rational substratum of knowledge. As Gane (1983b: 4) has suggested, Durkheim was an early adherent of the idea that unconscious phenomena have a significant impact upon patterns of social integration. His vision of the nature and social power of 'collective representations' is an important part of his account of such phenomena. This vision is a complex one, however, since it not only touches upon the social significance of ideas, symbols and beliefs, but also raises further questions about human agency and the status of particular forms of knowledge in society (Durkheim, 1982a: 39, 1984: 56; Stedman Jones, 2001: 66). The complexity of Durkheim's arguments is indicated by the fact that he has been interpreted as a social constructionist and epistemological relativist with an entirely inadequate account of agency (Archer, 1995; Jones, 1999), but also as someone entirely opposed to relativism and with a strong interest in human action and freedom (Watts Miller, 1996; Stedman Jones, 2001). He has, furthermore, been portrayed as someone hopelessly contradictory or confused about these issues (Lukes, 1973; Edwards, 2002). The argument offered here, however, is that Durkheim's understanding of collective representations offers a sound basis for understanding how society becomes embedded within the consciousness of individuals in ways that are often tacit rather than reflexively and rationally understood. The first part of this chapter is devoted to exploring his work in these respects, in dialogue with contemporary social theories that appear to call his views into question. Significantly, many of these critiques tend to challenge Durkheim for not being sufficiently constructionist rather than for being too much of an epistemological relativist.

Following this is a critical assessment of Serge Moscovici's 'social representations' theory. Moscovici's distinctive contribution to the contemporary development of social psychology has rested on his elaboration of the concept of 'social representations', and his attempts to demonstrate its theoretical and methodological value (for example, Moscovici, 1976, 1988, 1989, 2001).[1] The differences between Durkheim's and Moscovici's projects are often unjustifiably exaggerated, but what Moscovici adds is a valuable account of the persistence of certain 'core themata' within the fluid, shifting configurations of social forms and processes that characterise modern life, and the role of social representations in the world-views of even those who claim not to believe in them. On the other hand, he leans towards a much more social constructionist view of society than Durkheim, principally due to his tendency to prioritise discursive communication above other patterns of representation, allowing some of his followers to use social representations theory to endorse the de-traditionalisation arguments of writers such as Habermas and Giddens. Contrary to these, the rest of the chapter focuses on three different strata within social reality that are dependent upon tacit forms of knowledge resistant to reflexive deconstruction.

First, various attempts to explore the sociological significance of 'everyday life' are discussed in relation to what Bourdieu has referred to as the 'doxic', or taken-for-granted knowledge enfolded in the social habitus (Fowler, 1997: 2), though, following Taylor (1989), the specifically Christian aspects of this taken-for-granted character are emphasised. Second, the presence of a tacitly Christian way of structuring conceptions of social life within various modern notions of 'public' and 'private' life is discussed as a key example of how a core sociological dichotomy can rest on a religious substratum. Third, through a brief account of Said's (1978) thesis on 'Orientalism', the role of tacit assumptions in inter-societal relations is considered, looking at the different role of Christian and Islamic representations in Said's arguments. In conclusion, I shall suggest that a focus on how the tacit dimensions of societies continue to shape the consciousnesses of individuals calls into question those sociological visions that too readily assume 'a disappearance of the social bond and value breakdown' (Lash and Featherstone, 2001: 17), or dismiss the notion of representations as anachronistic in a 'global information society', where mobility, flows and movement appear to dominate over a more stable symbolic structuring of reality, identity and meaning (Touraine, 1989, 1995; Castells, 2000; Urry, 2000; Gilroy, 2001).

Representing society

Durkheim and Mauss (1963) argue that, to understand any society, it is necessary, first of all, to understand its system of symbolic *classification*. They not only note, as many others have done, that all societies attempt to classify diverse types of phenomena into categories that can make sense of the relations between different dimensions of human experience, but they also argue for the *social* origins of all classification systems. In building this argument, they suggest that when we examine systems of classification, we are not dealing with 'pure ideas' but with societies represented in collectively recognised forms. Collective representations express a unity of knowledge and the hyper-spiritual dynamics of the group represented through collective concepts, symbols and values (Durkheim and Mauss, 1963: 84–5). This concern with representations as expressions of collective life is evident throughout Durkheim's work, however, including *The Rules of Sociological Method* (1982a), and *The Elementary Forms of Religious Life* (1995). In the former work, while distinguishing his social realism from philosophical forms of realism that held individuals and society to have a reality independent of their relations, Durkheim (1982a: 34) argues that social life is 'made up entirely of representations'. In the latter, he argues that society as a *sui generis* reality is expressed through the collective representations emergent from human relations: again challenging philosophical arguments that reduce social life into individuals or individuals into social life, he argues that collective representations express 'an immense cooperation that extends not only through space but also through time' (Durkheim, 1995: 15).

This social realist view of representations has not gone unchallenged in sociology. Urry (2000: 5), for example, observes that it is common for sociologists to acknowledge there is something 'more' in social life than individuals, or the aggregation of individual actions, but suggests that the nature of this 'surplus' is hard to define. He notes that society has been conceived of in various forms, from a functionally integrated social system to institutionalised forms of alienated consciousness, but that none of these definitions has reflected a common consensus or achieved a general acceptance. According to him, however, it is only Durkheim's view of society as a specific and autonomous realm of facts separate from 'nature' that has achieved some sort of general consent, despite the lack of agreement about what these 'facts' are. Yet, for Urry (2000: 26), following Game (1995), this view rests on an erroneous attempt to impose cognitive order on the 'fluidities of sensuousness' that blur the boundaries of 'society' and 'nature'. The globalised 'mobilities' affecting bodies, ideas, images and institutions in contemporary societies make Durkheim's error explicit, and demand 'new rules of sociological method' (Urry, 2000: 210).

According to Urry, Durkheim's error rests on his understanding of society as a *conceptual order* underpinning the apparent fluidity and flux of day-to-day life. Associating Durkheim's notion of collective representations with concepts, which are 'authoritative', he argues that Durkheim's dismissive view of 'sensuous representations', which are 'non-authoritative', condemns sociology to a process of abstraction where the analyst must seek out the conceptual order lurking underneath the apparently random flows of time and space that seem to characterise social life.[2] In short, sociology, as the 'science of society', must, in the Durkheimian view, commit itself to an ahistorical, static and cognitive view of social life, insensitive to the dynamism of fluid, sensually experienced change. If this was ever valid, suggests Urry (2000: 27), and he implies it was not, it is certainly not so now: the increasing adoption of metaphors of movement, liquidity and flux characteristic of much recent social and cultural theory demonstrate how such an approach is now anachronistic (Bachelard, 1983; Deleuze and Guattari, 1986; Braidotti, 1994; Game, 1995).

Nevertheless, this argument misrepresents Durkheim in three ways. First of all, Durkheim (1995: 15) does not associate 'collective representations' simply with *concepts*: the representations through which a society expresses itself are emergent from a dynamic, inter-relational combination of ideas and feelings, and they can take various symbolic forms that include the conceptual, the iconic and the mythological.

Second, even if we concentrate our attention on concepts as forms of collective representation it is clear that they are not the abstract impositions of the social scientist upon a 'sensuous' flux, but are real phenomena emergent from the embodied, ontologically open patterns of interaction between individuals and society. Concepts are indeed reflective of humans as 'social beings', as opposed to the sensations characteristic of 'individual beings' (Durkheim, 1995: 275), but individuals do not become social beings through concepts but through the hyper-spiritual dynamics out of which collective representations emerge (Durkheim, 1995: 220–1). In short, rather than reflecting any cognitivist assumptions on Durkheim's part, his focus on the sociological significance of collective representations rests on his interest in the *sui generis* phenomena that constitute a pre-rational substratum to society.

Third, rather than suggesting that concepts are 'fixed and immutable', Durkheim's argument is merely that they are 'relatively unchangeable', in contrast to sense representations, because they are the means through which communication becomes possible: individual sense experiences can change by the second, but concepts remain less changeable otherwise we would not be able to understand each other (Durkheim, 1995: 434–5). In attempting to make sense of social complexity, Urry (2000, 2003) tends to focus very heavily upon random, chaotic phenomena, so it is easy to see how he comes to reject Durkheim's sense of an emergent order within social reality. None the less, this order is neither as 'ahistorical' nor as 'static' as he imagines it to be, given Durkheim's (1977: 15) emphasis on the dynamic processes through which temporal phenomena impose themselves upon individuals as layers of emergent strata. In fact, for him, it is this attention to temporality that necessitates a recognition of the fact that everything is not arbitrary, random and ephemeral, since certain ways of making sense of ourselves and the world can exist over very long periods of time, even if these ways of making sense are so deeply embedded within us that we are not fully conscious of them (Durkheim, 1977: 11).

For Durkheim, then, collective representations have to be assessed in relation to broad issues concerning human capacities, agency and the hyper-spirituality of society as an emergent reality. If they are not, then a social constructionist argument that all knowledge is entirely limited by the social and cultural circumstances of its immediate context becomes inevitable (Nicholson, 1990). Such arguments may be valuable in terms of emphasising the socially situated nature of knowledge, and in drawing attention to unacknowledged bias in scholarly accounts of social reality, but these factors do not necessarily lead to epistemological relativism if humanity's embodied being-in-the-world is acknowledged as the common basis upon which culturally variable representations emerge. In this regard, Game's *Undoing the Social* (1991) which offers a vision of sociology as a 'fiction' unable to represent the real, identified with the embodied encounter with the everyday, is unsatisfactory: just as Deleuze's (1977) account of embodiment emphasises its constructed character, so too Game's 'body' provides no bulwark against deconstructionist analysis. As becomes clear in her critique of Durkheim's account of representations, the body is reduced to 'fluidities of sensuousness' amenable to social constructions, but with no inherent potentialities for emergent forms of knowledge that transcend the circumstances of the present (Game, 1995; Urry, 2000).

Holistic society

In contrast, Moscovici's social representations theory takes its inspiration from the arguments of Durkheim in challenging the behaviourist and cognitive theories that have dominated social psychology. Like Piaget (1965: 145), who also sought to develop the notion of collective and individual representations, Moscovici (2001: 26) emphasises that it is not enough to stress the social nature of thought: the dynamic, unavoidably interactive 'holism' of collective thought must be demonstrated. He seeks to do this through emphasising that representations 'set out the field of activity and inform the members of the social system of their rights and duties, of a sense of belonging' (Moscovici, 2001: 21). This is quite close to Parsons's (1951, 1969) emphasis on the normative patterning of social action within a social system, which also has Durkheimian sources, though Moscovici, like Durkheim, pays more attention to the *symbolic* character of this patterning: 'Things in themselves mean nothing; people must *represent* them and make them signify, that is, they must give them a meaning using a symbol' (Jovchelovitch, 2001: 176).

It is important to be clear about what Moscovici does and does not add to Durkheim's arguments. It has been suggested, for example, that Moscovici's adoption of the term 'social representations', rather than 'collective representations', fills a gap in Durkheim's analysis, in that Durkheim did not account adequately for the bridge between the individual and the social world (Philogène and Deaux, 2001: 5). This is not so, however, as social representations (in Moscovici's model) and collective representations (in Durkheim's model) have essentially the same role: both types of representations serve to constitute, and express, a collective reality through networks of social interactions. What distinguishes Moscovici's focus on *social* representations is his concern with the 'plurality of representations and their diversity within a group', given the fact that modern societies are highly differentiated, pluralistic and heterogeneous in many respects (Moscovici, 1988: 219). This has some similarities with Gurvitch's (1949: 13) focus on differential patterns of representations in relation to the 'poles' of 'I', 'Other' and 'We', in the sense that he also seeks to develop Durkheim's work in the direction of a more micro-sociological approach. Nevertheless, Moscovici, like Durkheim, is also interested in relatively enduring patterns of representation, which he usefully designates as influential 'themata' within particular societies.

For Moscovici, the symbolic creation and codifications of meanings through representations are manifest in several forms: first, certain underlying themata are simply assumed in any culture, and can take the form of beliefs, maxims or categories; second, some of these themata have a 'core' character that means they pattern other beliefs and 'maintain the stability of the network of communicated knowledge'; third, various types of 'arguments' (classifying, topical and performative) reinforce and replicate systems of social representations through systematically relating concepts, images and emotions to core themata (Moscovici, 2001: 31). Thus, the belief that 'all people are equal', for example, is something many people in Western societies share, and, after being present in the Western system of representations for many centuries, has now become a 'core' element of modern culture. Nevertheless, even though it is now, to a large degree, taken for granted by many, it is still the subject, directly or indirectly, of various types of arguments concerning issues such as gender, race and class, which relate topical concerns back to this core way of representing human reality. A key point to bear in mind, however, is that, much of the time, such representations are not only accepted without the benefit of a reflexive and reasoned engagement with their intellectual, moral or political merits, but can allow for the emergence of philosophical arguments that deny the grounds of their own production.

Moscovici (2001: 27) gives an interesting example of a social representation that denies the grounds of its own emergence when he refers us again to Margaret Thatcher's claim that 'There is no such thing as society. There are only individuals.' As Moscovici suggests, Thatcher ostensibly denies what, in reality, she affirms: her notion of the 'individual' is a collectively constructed representation that is tied to specific notions of humanity, and to specific accounts of the nature of human association. These representations have a long history in certain forms of Protestant theology and liberal political philosophy, as well as being elaborated in the neo-classical economic forms that influenced her arguments directly. Without this collective context for her words, Thatcher's statement would have been meaningless. Thus, it might even be said that when Urry (2000: 12) suggests that 'maybe Thatcher was oddly right when she said there is no such thing as society', he is acknowledging the symbolic force of the system of representations she drew upon, and contributing to the cultural elaboration of these representations through his own, reconstructed vision of sociology, even though he argues that Durkheim's notion of collective representations is now an outmoded tool for social analysis.

Where Moscovici seems to agree with Urry (2000) and Castells (2000), however, is in his rejection of Durkheim's emphasis on the universal sociological significance of religion. For Durkheim (1995: 34–6), the social processes through which collective life is constructed have a religious character symbolically represented in the ubiquitous and absolute distinction between sacred and profane. Moscovici's view of this argument is ambiguous. On the one hand, he endorses Durkheim's arguments as a 'unique and impressive achievement' expressing something fundamental about human society (Moscovici, 1993: 37; 2001: 24). On the other hand, he associates modernity with the abandonment of the sacred/profane polarity (Moscovici, 1993: 337), and cites the decline of religion in support of his arguments concerning the shift from collective to social representations, thereby allowing his interpreters to adopt a fairly robust secularisation thesis (Moscovici, 1988: 219; Jovchelovitch, 2001: 167).[3] For him, the decline of *collective* representations, which embrace a whole society, is coterminous with the decline of the sacred because of the shift from a society where there are widely accepted beliefs and rituals to one where 'conversations and communications between individuals become historically more important' (Moscovici, 1988: 219). This emphasis on conversations signals a departure from Durkheim's focus on the embodied basis of representations, and explains the more social constructionist tenor of Moscovici's writings.

Although Moscovici (2001: 19) suggests that representations can take 'iconic', image-based forms as well as conceptual, linguistic forms, he focuses especially on the latter. He prioritises the fundamental importance of conversation in human life and argues, for example, that 'a social representation is *discursified* thinking, that is a symbolic cultural system involving language'. This departs from Durkheim (1995: 436), who sees language as a system of collective representations but does not identify representations in general only, or even largely, with language. Representations have a communicative function, but this is not necessarily linguistic but often emotional: collective representations work on the emotions and the senses to transform objects by investing them with symbolic power (Durkheim, 1995: 228). Indeed, it can be noted that, by prioritising language, Moscovici moves away from Durkheim's fuller understanding of the embodied basis of representations towards the sort of linguistically oriented cognitivism central to the writings of Habermas. In both cases, it might be said that both Moscovici and Habermas leave us with a somewhat disembodied view of humans as defined by their capacity for talking. Criticising Durkheim's neglect of the sociological importance of linguistic understanding, for example, Habermas (1987: 57) argues that social realities are no longer shaped by rituals, symbols or emotional energies, but through communicative discourse; an argument that clearly has some continuities with Moscovici's focus on discursive communication. From here, however, the two diverge. For Habermas (1987: 77), in line with the rationalism that dominates his thought, the power of the sacred in modernity is translated into 'the authority of an achieved consensus' established on the basis of 'criticisable validity claims'. Moscovici's work, on the other hand, is free of such rationalism and the speculations about consensus, truth and the possibility of 'ideal speech' situations that tend to go along with it. This has not stopped Moscovici and Habermas being used together, however, to endorse a highly questionable picture of the development of modern societies.

Jovchelovitch (2001: 167), for example, stresses the value of social representations theory in accounting for the 'more fluid dynamic of modern societies, where worldviews and practices are contested and negotiated, and the space for a homogenous, unquestioned, and single view of the world is very limited indeed'. For Jovchelovitch (2001: 165), 'social representations are a form of symbolic knowledge intrinsic to public life', but 'traditional' and 'de-traditionalised' societies construct and express symbolic knowledge in different ways. Drawing principally on Habermas (1989b), she suggests that we are now living in an age that has 'gradually freed itself from tradition and unquestioned historical orderings and sought in rational debate and democratic dialogue the response for matters of common concern' (Jovchelovitch, 2001: 168). For Jovchelovitch (2001: 170), where 'traditional' societies were characterised by the central significance of the 'emotional dimension of the social bond', de-traditionalised modernity is characterised by reflexivity, dialogue and negotiation (Beck et al., 1994; Heelas et al., 1996). This means that the 'overtotalising conception of the social' evident in Durkheim's notion of collective representations is no longer of value, since these totalising forms are 'resistant to experience, argumentation, and logical proof'; in other words, collective representations embody all the characteristics that are antithetical to de-traditionalised modernity (Jovchelovitch, 2001: 169–70).

Even so, it is possible to highlight five major problems with the sort of argument offered by Jovchelovitch. First, notions of de-traditionalisation tend to work with a faulty conception of 'traditional' societies. As Levine's (1985: 54) discussion of the Amhara of Ethiopia makes clear, for example, 'traditional' societies are much more diverse, complex, inherently flexible and subject to recurrent change than many in the modern West tend to imagine.[4] Second, the suggestion that collective representations manifest an 'overtotalising conception of the social' is misleading. Durkheim (1974a: 24) argues that 'The representations that form the network of social life arise from the relations between the individuals thus combined or the secondary groups that are between the individuals and the total society.' In other words, collective representations are manifest between individuals and social groups other, and smaller, than the 'total society'. In this respect it is also worth noting that Durkheim's (1995) arguments about collective representations are developed through an analysis of a plurality of clans and tribes. There are three further problems, however, all of which are worth concentrating on in more detail as they reflect a sociological neglect of the tacit dimensions of society.

A third problem with notions of de-traditionalisation concerns the fact that reflexivity, dialogue and rational debate may be prized values in certain sectors of contemporary life, but the degree to which they shape everyday social realities for the majority of people is, to say the least, highly dubious. In fact, all the most influential sociological studies of everyday life (which actually offer a very broad range of theories and arguments) tend to deny the pervasiveness or, in some cases, the significance of such phenomena. A fourth problem concerns the fact that notions of de-traditionalisation tend to underestimate, and often to ignore completely, the degree to which the exercise of rationality and reflexivity in a modern 'secular' society actually takes place through collective representations that have a specific religious history. In this regard, the distinction between 'public' and 'private', which has been hailed as a 'core sociological dichotomy', is particularly worth discussing as it represents one of the 'core themata' of modernity (Jenks, 1998; Slater, 1998). Finally, it has to be noted that Western representations of non-Western cultures not only have characteristics that endure over large stretches of time, and are often resistant to reflexive construction, as Said's (1978) account of 'Orientalism' has demonstrated, but also manifest the continuing significance of Western society's religious substratum. These three problems relate to different social strata, from face to face interactions, through representations of public life within one type of society, to inter-societal relations, but all of them raise issues that demand some sort of reflection upon Western societies' tacit dimensions. The following three sections of this chapter explore them in greater detail.

Everyday society

In an aside that touches upon the sociological neglect of gardening, Turner and Rojek (2001: 228) have sought to remind social and cultural theorists, who tend to get much more excited by technological changes, that, judging by what people do during the weekend, 'Britain seems to be a country in which the garden gnome possesses more cultural relevance than the cyborg'. This suggestion draws attention to the tendency of much postmodern thought to ignore how most people actually live their lives. Featherstone (1992: 159) has observed that postmodernism has been associated with a positive evaluation of local and popular cultures, suggesting 'an increasing sensitivity to the more complex levels of unity, to the syncretism, heterogeneity, and the common taken-for-granted, "seen but unnoticed" aspects of everyday life'. None the less, Baudrillard's (1988b) accounts of the 'hyper-reality' of the contemporary world, for instance, where everything is now 'simulation', suggest little contact with the everyday lives of most people, and little desire to account for the representations through which they make sense of social realities. Bauman (1992a: 155), it can be noted, has to remind Baudrillard that there is life outside television, and that people have to eat, and grapple with some of the harsh realities of life and work, before they sit down and become immersed in televisual spectacles. He suggests, in fact, that 'It becomes a philosopher and an analyst of his time to go out and use his feet now and again'. In some respects, however, this postmodern neglect of everyday life dovetails with a more general sociological tendency to emphasise its decreasing sociological significance.

The notion of 'everyday life' is by no mean an unproblematic one, and sociologists have used the term to represent a broad range of phenomena, of differing degrees of importance, covering the taken-for-granted aspects of daily belief and practice, the pre-institutional reproduction and maintenance of social orders, the embodied, sensual or playful, sense of being together, and the heterogeneity of lived interaction (Featherstone, 1992: 161). One important tradition of analysis, however, represented by writers such as Lefebvre (1971), Habermas (1981, 1987) and Heller (1984), has focused on the 'colonisation' of everyday life by patterns of instrumental rationalisation. Owing a significant debt to Weber's (1991) vision of modern rationalisation processes, this tradition of interpretation, although it invests value in everyday life, nevertheless sees it as increasingly suffering under the impact of broader social, political and economic forces, and, therefore, in a sense, increasingly less significant sociologically. Here, the 'macro' dimensions of society shape, transform and threaten the 'micro' interactions of individuals, implying that rationalisation has a 'self-propelling momentum and universalising force which turns it into a logic of history beyond human intervention' (Featherstone, 1992: 62). Such analyses offer a characteristically fatalist reading of everyday life, where the tacit, taken-for-granted dimensions of society are gradually being obliterated by more powerful social forces.

Focusing on the 'micro' rather than the 'macro' dimensions of social life, however, Schutz's (1962) phenomenological account of everyday life and Goffman's (1969) sociological study of interaction rituals have also offered influential accounts of everyday life, as has Geertz (1983) through his analysis of 'common sense'. In each case, there is an emphasis on the complex, but usually unacknowledged, rules that structure human interaction in context-specific ways. As Scheff (1990: 37), noting the development of Schutz's work in Garfinkel's (1967) 'ethnomethodology', has suggested, the conclusion that can be drawn from such work is that 'the meaning of all human expressions is contextual'. Here, abstract notions of vast social and historical changes, such as Habermas's concept of the 'colonisation of the life-world', and his equally abstract vision of resistance to it in the 'communicative rationality' of an 'ideal speech situation' (Delanty, 1997), are avoided in favour of a detailed examination of specific situations and their representational meanings. In this regard, it is notable that Garfinkel's more recent work (2001) has explicitly detailed his debt to Durkheim, and that Anne Rawls (2001: 65) has used him as an example of how Durkheim's concern with enacted social practices can give rise to fine-grained empirical work.

Ethnomethodological and phenomenological studies can, for all their attention to context, exhibit a fundamentally *cognitive* view of meaning construction. Howes (1991: 6) has noted this bias in Geertz's work, exemplified by his view of cultures as ensembles of 'texts', while Levine (1995: 282) has noted Schutz's emphasis on the subjective meanings of individual actors. This subjectivist concern with the cognitive construction of meaning, typically through *conversation*, is also evident in the sociology of religion developed by Berger (1990), whose debt to Schutz is significant. Contrary to Rawls's suggestion that such studies might fruitfully build on Durkheim's work, the danger of this approach is that it can reinforce sociology's 'fallacy of misplaced abstraction', by prioritising ideas and beliefs in the manner of the 'cultural turn' she rejects, thereby endorsing the idea 'that there is no escape from the relativism of competing sets of beliefs, and competing sets of meanings, each of which defines a competing reality' (Rawls, 2001: 63).

In fact, Bauman (1992a: 40) has suggested that the development of relativistic forms of postmodern sociology was encouraged by Garfinkel and Schutz, through their exposure of the brittleness and endemic fragility of society, which is dissolved 'into a plethora of multiple realities and universes of meaning'.

Although de Certeau (1984) and Maffesoli (1989, 1996) have also been identified with postmodern theory, however, they avoid the extremes of relativism and macro-level abstractionism through their accounts of everyday life in terms of a powerful sociality that resists rationalisation processes. Thus, for de Certeau (1984: xi), in contrast to the emphasis on discourse and conversation characteristic of many social and cultural theories, everyday life has to be understood in terms of tacit 'ways of operating', or *doing things*, rather than patterns of reflexive or rational negotiation. In this regard, he notes the 'clandestine' incorporation of products of the dominant patterns of rationalisation and utilitarianism into forms of life centred on the subterranean sociality that Durkheim identified with the hyper-spiritual substratum of society (de Certeau, 1984: 31). What is particularly notable about de Certeau's work, however, is that he not only addresses the religious dimensions of society in general terms, but also directs our attention to the specifically Christian undercurrents within Western societies, though he does so in a highly ambiguous fashion.

As Torrance (1998: 85) has pointed out, throughout the history of thought, various accounts have been offered of that self-subsistent reality upon which contingent things and events depend, and on the way in which they depend on it. De Certeau's position is a distinctively Christian one, and accords with von Balthasar's (1982: 67) theological vision of a God who is revealed through the apparently accidental and chaotic patterns of social and natural life that none the less point towards a meaningfulness contingent upon the incarnate Christ. For de Certeau, in his more optimistic writings, even in a society that understands itself to be secular as the (post)modern world does, the 'common life' of believing, embodied beings remains alive to emergent theological possibilities, regardless of how many people attend churches, because Christ, for him, did not inaugurate a social institution so much as a *form of practice* which, though it may have become anonymous, is nevertheless working itself out in the ebb and flow of social life (Ahearne, 1996: 500–1; see de Certeau, 1987; Buchanan, 2000). In short, beneath the contingent patterns of day-to-day life a deeper contingency, of humanity upon God, is revealed. On the other hand, de Certeau's picture of everyday life sometimes has a rather tragic dimension that to an extent mirrors the work of Lefebvre (1971) and Heller (1984). Focusing particularly on the immense social influence of phenomena such as the media, in some of his writings he finds less room for the successful exercise of the strategies of everyday life as it is increasingly colonised by the information-driven banalisation of reality (de Certeau, 1984: 186). In contrast, Maffesoli's account of everyday life is consistently affirmative of its inherent potentiality.

Like Urry (2000), Maffesoli discusses the fluid networks, associations and movements of contemporary persons, as well as the aestheticism and ephemerality of many social and cultural phenomena. Characteristic of Maffesoli's account, however, is the recognition that it is Durkheim's conception of society that constitutes the basis for a satisfactory explanation of these phenomena. Although Durkheim's notion of 'collective effervescence' is often associated with the large-scale social upheavals through which social life is reordered or revitalised, he also argued that the emotionally stimulating character of society is manifest in even the most ordinary, everyday interactions, such as in the feelings of neighbourliness aroused by living in proximity to others (Durkheim, 1995: 213). Maffesoli builds on Durkheim's arguments in his account of the pervasiveness of *puissance*, a vital energy which he identifies with ways of 'keeping warm together' in the often inhospitable climate of modern rationalisation processes, permeating everyday life in the form of a 'basic sociality' manifest in neighbourhoods, groups, tribes, sports and workplaces (Maffesoli, 1996: 32, 42).

For Maffesoli (1996: 126), a recognition of the importance of this 'basic sociality' entails an engagement with 'proxemics', with the 'love of the nearby and the present' that marks everyday life. This attention to the embodied proximity of others is often overlooked in some accounts of contemporary social life. Urry's (2000: 40–1) suggestion, for example, that the Internet is now the principal metaphor for best expressing the contingent, fluid character of contemporary social life, implies an abstract, disembodied and inhuman experience of the present. This may, of course, be true for some people (including some academics). Robertson (1992: 177), however, has warned of the dangers of developing theories of global social and cultural changes that ignore the immense significance of the *local* as a dimension of social experience, treating the local–global along 'micro–macro' lines that prioritise the 'macro', though he too tends to interpret the local in terms of global changes. Jenkins's (1999) anthropological work on the immense importance of locality, family and collective memory in English everyday life, on the other hand, notes the continuing significance of what he calls 'local particularity'.

By 'local particularity', Jenkins means ways of acting and thinking that are specific to a particular place, and continue to be passed down through different generations. Contrary to Urry's (2000: 129) focus on the 'time–space desynchronisation' of family life prompted by changes in working patterns, eating habits and the development of video technologies, Jenkins (1999: 129) suggests that 'local society is family-based and women-centred', not only in terms of advice, support and services, but also in terms of recreation and leisure activities. Discussing the Kingswood area of Bristol, for example, he notes that 'It is not unusual for four generations of a family to live within half a mile of each other'; local marriages are the norm, and daughters, in particular, tend to live close to their mothers who become the centres of quite extended family networks rooted, very firmly, in the traditions and collective memories of a specific geographical area (Jenkins, 1999: 129).

This assertion of the importance of locality, family and tradition goes against the grain of much contemporary sociology. For Jenkins (1999: 69), however, it is important to note that 'tradition exists not as a survival, in opposition to the present and to progress, but within the present and as part of it'. In this regard, he emphasises that the association of many of the core values of local society with older people cannot be taken as evidence of the gradual erosion of tradition: not only is the authority of older people recognised by younger members of local society, but, as older members die, others take their places (Jenkins, 1999: 131). This attentiveness to the endurance of traditional patterns of living may challenge some key sociological assumptions about modernity, but it also recalls Goffman's (1969) interest in the highly ritualised patterns that shape our day-to-day interactions with others, and, on a broader scale, Bourdieu's (1977) interest in how particular habits can endure over large stretches of time and between generations. Bourdieu's (1977: 72) definition of the *habitus* as a 'system of durable, transposable dispositions' builds on Durkheim's interest in the power of society to shape individuals' experiences of themselves and the world, and reminds us of the fact that all sorts of traditions, habits and customs continue to influence our daily lives, even if we are not aware of these most of the time (Lemert, 2002: 42).

Bourdieu's emphasis on the taken-for-granted ('doxic') knowledge enfolded in the habitus, drawn from Durkheim and Mauss's discussion of representations in *Primitive Classification* (1963) (Fowler, 1997: 2), suggests that the power of society is present for us in our day-to-day encounters in ways that go beyond cognitive frameworks of meaning, in the sense that society can instil pre-cognitive, embodied dispositions towards particular forms of action and experience. Mauss's (1950) account of the 'techniques of the body' characteristic of different societies, and passed down through generations, emphasises this even more clearly: Mauss notes several examples where decisions to embark upon cross-cultural collaboration and action come up against embodied dispositions resistant to other forms. As with Maffesoli's interest in 'proxemics', and again building on Durkheim's work, there is recognition of the fact that society is not simply an abstract idea, but a reality embedded within human consciousness and our embodied dispositions towards particular types of actions. What is also worth noting, however, is that the 'doxic' knowledge enfolded in the habitus is representative of a set of social dynamics that can extend through very large periods of time (Durkheim, 1995: 15; Jenkins, 1999: 69). In this regard, Taylor (1989) has argued that many of the underlying assumptions, values and dispositions people bring to everyday life, whether this is considered in terms of the meaning-constructing character of its 'micro' dimensions or threats to its vitality from 'macro' level colonisation processes, have specifically Christian origins.

Taylor (1989: 216) notes that the Protestant Reformation led to an enhanced status for what had previously been seen as 'profane', namely the ordinary, everyday life of individuals and communities. The roots of this 'affirmation of ordinary life' go deeper, to the biblical emphasis on God, as Creator, affirming the inherent goodness of life and being, but Protestantism helped nurture this tacit potentiality within Christian tradition to the degree that everyday life became infused with spiritual potentiality (Taylor, 1989: 218, 221). Much of this argument is consistent with that of Weber (1991), for whom Protestantism established clearly defined values that made sense of this-worldly activity in relation to God, and thereby promoted an ethically informed pattern of rational action that possessed a substantial affinity with the 'spirit of modern capitalism'. For Weber, however, this Protestant re-evaluation of everyday life resulted in the stimulation of rationalisation processes that eventually undermined modernity's religious foundations. Taylor's analysis, while not denying the broadly anti-Christian orientation of many aspects of modernity, raises questions about the degree to which these foundations are still important. His argument is that modernity tends to suppress the spiritual roots of the systems of knowledge through which we make sense of social and natural phenomena, but these remain important not only in terms of establishing a satisfactorily historical understanding of contemporary societies, but also in terms of looking beyond present moral, political and social conflicts to the common substratum of tacit assumptions that structure debates about phenomena such as the instrumentalisation of contemporary society (Taylor, 1989: 488).

From this point of view, the apparent opposition between, for example, Maffesoli's celebration of the interpenetration of sacred and profane in everyday life and Habermas's (1981, 1987) critique of its colonisation by modern instrumentalism conceals a common dependence on particular Protestant assumptions. Indeed, while also drawing upon distinctively Catholic ideas such as the 'communion of the saints', Maffesoli (1996: 158) praises Luther's contrast between the institutional church and the 'invisible' *ecclesia* as something that captures the pluralism and *puissance* of the masses, but does not pause to consider whether this unexpected convergence between Protestant theology and postmodern theory is more than coincidental. Further to this, it can be noted that the similarity between Habermas's (1987: 77) 'linguistification' of the sacred and Protestantism's unique interest in the power of language in the construction of new forms of community also suggests the endurance of distinctively Christian 'core themata' in contemporary societies (Moscovici, 2001: 31). This suggestion is also pertinent to aspects of society other than everyday life, including those relating to the 'public' and 'private' dimensions of society. These, in contrast to the more obviously 'doxic' character of everyday existence, have been, and remain, subject to a great deal of reflexive and rational scrutiny, debate and justification. Even so, it is arguable that there is also a tacitly Christian dimension to these representations of social life.

Acephalous society

Modern representations of public/private spheres have a long history that is often interpreted in terms of the gradual secularisation of Western society, even when it is acknowledged that the philosophers who did most to codify them were committed Christians (see Seligman, 1992; Weintraub, 1997). As with the modern 'affirmation of ordinary life', however, there are grounds for suggesting that such representations remain tied to specifically Christian understandings of individuals and society, though some of these understandings cut across modern notions of public and private, and some underpin them directly. Karl Polanyi (2001: 268) touches upon the former type when he argues that Christianity bequeathed to modernity a belief in the uniqueness of the individual and the oneness of mankind. Dumont's (1970) study of the caste system in India, which emphasises the absence of these beliefs in much Indian thought and practice, reinforces Polanyi's argument (see also Siedentop, 2000). Focusing on the development of modern conceptions of political authority, however, O'Donovan (1999: 246) emphasises the significance of specifically Protestant ideas for the emergence of what he calls an 'acephalous society'; that is, the development of a self-consciously secular society driven by unconscious forces from within rather than a conscious commitment to Christian truth. Consequently, while it was only in the nineteenth century, in England, that the idea of *privacy* emerged and it should be recognised that, strictly speaking, its application to other historical periods is anachronistic (Duby, 1988a: ix), it must also be acknowledged that modern notions of public and private have developed over the *longue durée* of Western religious history.

Georges Duby (1988b: 509–10) has discussed how, in the medieval period, people lived in the midst of collectivities, rarely experiencing solitude: even spheres of social life we would now deem 'private', such as the life of hearth and home, were collectively oriented 'households', rather than havens for individuals. This started to change, he suggests, as the Catholic Church sought to intensify individuals' Christian devotion and practice, such as when the Lateran Council of 1215 imposed obligations upon Christians regarding confession and penance before communion at Easter (Duby, 1988b: 533). None the less, in fostering the interior devotion of individual Christians within a Catholic vision of the essentially collective nature of faith and salvation Christian religiosity could never become a purely 'private' matter in the modern sense (Duffy, 1992: 92–3). With the emergence of Protestantism in the sixteenth century, however, a 'privatisation' of religiosity became more evident, particularly with respect to the strong emphasis upon the intensity and purity of individual faith central to Luther's doctrine of justification by grace (Ruel, 2002: 107; see Rupp, 1975). As O'Donovan (1999: 209) suggests, Luther converted Augustine's distinction between the spiritual and the secular 'into an inner–outer distinction, between the realm of the mind and the heart on the one hand, and the realm of social relations on the other'. From this point onwards, the

Christian stands at a distance from society. As noted in previous chapters, this distance took a number of different forms, ranging from the internalism of Lutheranism to the Calvinist commitment to reorder the world in a manner pleasing to God (Taylor, 1989: 227), but eventually resulted in a separation of 'public' and 'private' spheres so clear that even devout, evangelical Christians, in drafting the First Amendment to the US Constitution, fervently assented to the separation of church from state in order that the state could not 'interfere' in what was principally a matter of private conscience (O'Donovan, 1999: 245). A key point to note here, however, is that such phenomena do not amount to 'secularisation' in any simple sense, since the underlying representational structure of what is understood as 'public' and 'private' is still defined in essentially Protestant terms.

This representational structure is still evident today. Seligman's (1992) account of contemporary understandings of society in the USA, for example, illuminates fundamental continuities between America's religious origins and its present day characteristics. He emphasises that the specific relationship between private and public spheres in American society means it is both 'the paradigm of modern societies' and thoroughly 'Protestant' in its essential nature: the public arena is actually 'neutral' and 'devoid of autonomous value', only becoming meaningful as a social arena when morally validated individuals bring their private concerns to bear upon it (Seligman, 1992: 134–5). He is *not* suggesting that the public arena is unimportant or lacks value, then, only 'that it lacks autonomous value in and of itself. The value accruing to the public space is a function of the universal value attributed to the social actors (those morally autonomous individuals) acting and interacting in the public realm' (Seligman, 1992: 135). One consequence of this is that the public sphere can become characterised by a cacophony of voices seeking to assert their individual 'rights', with the legislature unable to mediate between irreconcilable visions of these (Seligman, 1992: 136), but this Protestant vision of the public sphere has also given rise to constructive attempts to find ways of mediating this pluralism of individual rights-based claims upon society.

These more constructive conceptions of the relationship between public and private spheres also have a recognisably Protestant character, even if this is generally concealed by a representational system that is, ostensibly, religiously neutral. In this regard, it is notable that John Rawls (1999: 619–21), one of the most influential and respected theorists of American political liberalism, argues very strongly for the neutrality of the public arena in relation to religion, even asserting that religious individuals must 'translate' their religious convictions into the language of 'public reason', so that the constitutional protection of the rights, liberties and dignity of the individual is not compromised by the imposition of any one 'comprehensive doctrine' that might seek to shape social life to particular religious goals (see also Rawls, 1993). On the face of it, this does not look like a religious argument, and, indeed, it has been suggested that Rawls's political vision, even if it does not actively endorse secularism, basically views religion as being irrelevant to a flourishing liberal democracy (Song, 1997: 220). It is possible to criticise Rawls's views on the basis that they simply ignore the manifest importance of religious commitments in contemporary public life, particularly in the USA (Casanova, 1994). As Jeremy Waldron (2002: 237–9) has argued, however, a more fundamental problem with Rawls's vision is that it avoids confronting difficult questions about the religious grounds of egalitarian commitments, failing to see that his political conception of the human individual as a morally responsible, reasonable and free agent arises out of, and arguably still depends upon, the sort of theology of natural law that was central to the Protestant social and political theory of Locke. In this regard, the peculiar absence/presence of religion in such views has, perhaps, a specifically American character.

As O'Donovan (1999: 245) suggests, the Christians who helped frame the First Amendment, which articulates the sort of separation of church and state that Rawls is defending, actually *presupposed* the current existence and future vitality of a Protestant society and culture, and it is possible, at least, to raise the question of whether something similar is presupposed in Rawls's work, even if he refuses to acknowledge it. In this regard, it is worth noting Parsons's (1960, 1963) studies of contemporary American values, not only because of his stress upon the enduring significance of specifically Protestant views for the American social system, but also because of his awareness of the fact that these views are so deeply established in the substratum of American society that, to many Americans, they do not look 'religious' at all.

As Robertson (1991: 154) has noted, Parsons recognised that modern societies in general, and the USA in particular, were increasingly dependent upon the voluntaristic 'inputs' of individuals, but that these, nonetheless, operated within a distinctive religious and moral ecology that allowed the individual conscience to be shaped in particular ways (see Parsons, 1966; Bourricaud, 1981; Bellah et al., 1992). Rejecting arguments about the death of the Protestant ethic, Parsons saw Christian values as informing the cultural value system of modern America, in the sense that its Protestant heritage continues to provide a 'pre-contractual' foundation for the development of modern life so that its 'secular' orders still approximate to the normative models provided by religion (Parsons 1978: 168, 240). In Durkheim's terms, what Parsons is talking about is the individual internalisation of the 'conscience collective', the normative patterning of individual decisions and choices through the incorporation of collective values into the personal identities of individuals. Without this incorporation, which in Weber's terms can also be referred to as a 'calling', Parsons (1978: 320) holds that the 'instrumental apparatus of modern society' could not function (Shilling and Mellor, 2001: 94).

Viewed in the light of Parsons's arguments, Rawls's (1999: 620) assertion that, in the public sphere, for the sake of creating consensus individuals must translate their religious convictions into 'neutral' forms of public reason, could be interpreted as a *concealment* of religion rather than a denial of its fundamental social significance, since the view of religion, society and consensus offered by Rawls has particular, unacknowledged theological roots. Similar comments can be made about European social theory. Grace Davie (2000, 2001), for example, has noted the widespread 'tacit understanding' amongst large sectors of the European population that the churches continue to have an important public role (see also Beckford, 2003: 54–5). Much European social theory, however, has an ostensibly secular character that tends to ignore such understandings. It is also arguable that such theory can depend upon a specifically religious form of symbolic classification, though this is even more covert due to a tendency to express a more manifest antipathy to religion. Habermas, for example, has an emphasis on the necessity of translating religious commitments into a communicative rationality appropriate to the public realm that is apparently very similar to that of Rawls. For Habermas (1987: 77), however, the creation of the public sphere is dependent upon a post-Enlightenment commitment to a secular polity (see Rochlitz, 2002). As Calhoun (1997: 83) notes, for Habermas, the public sphere is an arena for 'rational–critical discourse'. The private sphere is, in contrast, associated with individual interests, which is where he locates religion. Thus, this self-consciously secular tradition of thought depends upon a notion of rational individuals, but defines rationality in relation to a critical faculty that allows people to participate in a public sphere where 'the public good' is distinct from private interest, and defined on a collective, consensual basis that has no religious dimension. Public life is an arena for rational–critical debate, not a place where religious goals can be worked out.

This view has continuities with Protestant traditions of religiosity, in the sense that religion is located in a representation of the private sphere that arguably depends upon a Christian demarcation of 'secular' and 'religious' spheres of action. The difference with Rawls is that, for Habermas, the public sphere is defined in relation to what Rawls would call a secular form of 'comprehensive doctrine'. Here, the public sphere is not envisaged as a 'neutral' space for the mediation of individual rights, but conceptualised in relation to a vision of secular liberation, ideally characterised by a dialogue between free and equal individuals dominated only by the merits of argument. There are two further things worth noting about Habermas's argument, however. First, it is utopian: he recognises that the contemporary organisation of politics, bureaucracy and labour not only fails to embody this ideal in practice, but also often serves to actively oppose it (Habermas, 1987). Second, this utopianism does not simply rest upon a failure to take religion seriously (Lemert, 1999), but can be identified with the Kantian tradition of Western philosophy, where Christian commitments to practical benevolence, the recognition of 'higher goods' and the need for an ethic of just and responsible social action become translated into an abstract and rationalised form of secular philosophy (Taylor, 1989: 84–6). Given this influence of Kant, which is also evident in the work of Rawls, insisting upon the 'translation' of religious commitments into forms of 'public reason' or 'communicative rationality' conceals the fact that a prior translation has already taken place: what look like 'secular' philosophical concerns have already been framed in Protestant terms.

Following from this, it is clear that using Habermas's arguments to support claims about de-traditionalisation, secularisation and the decline of collective representations, as Jovchelovitch (2001) does, is highly problematic: not only does Habermas's position apparently endorse a certain way of representing the 'secular' world of modernity, rather than simply reflecting an attempt to make sense of certain social changes, but his own 'secular' form of theory is itself emergent from a particular Christian tradition and retains some of its assumptions. While these contradictions in Habermas's work raise questions about its merit, however, similar contradictions are manifest in a much more extreme form in the work of others. Edward Said's (1978) highly influential account of the Western tradition of 'Orientalist' scholarship, which has done a great deal to encourage the development of 'post-colonial' studies, exhibits a set of contradictions that mean his arguments are both suggestive and deeply flawed. It is precisely because Said defines himself as a 'secular critic' of society that he is keen to identify the centrality of tacitly (and, for him, perniciously) Christian assumptions in Western representations of non-Western cultures (Said, 1994: 89; Hollis, 2001: 306; Said and Ashcroft, 2001: 279). Even so, partly because Islamic societies do not recognise this distinction between the religious and the secular (Asad, 2002), and partly because, as a secularist, he is reluctant to acknowledge the social significance of religion in general terms, he fails to accord Islam an equally powerful role in society.

Deconstructing society

Said's (1978: 2) argument is that 'Orientalism' is based upon a distinction between Orient and Occident that is both ontological and epistemological. For him, representations have a far greater power than for Durkheim, since he follows Foucault in expressing the idea that epistemology determines ontology; that is, he supports the view that reality is defined *exclusively* through representations (Said, 1978: 3). He argues that Western 'knowledge' about the Orient *creates* the Orient, classifying Orientals as irrational, depraved, childlike and 'different' in contrast to Occidentals who are rational, virtuous, mature and 'normal' (Said, 1978: 40). For Said (1978: 12), this 'knowledge', which is distributed throughout aesthetic, scholarly, economic, sociological, historical and philological domains, is actually a coherent pattern of representations that he identifies with colonial dominance over non-Western societies. While he outlines several features of these representations, however, he places great importance on their religious origins.

For him, Christianity is not only understood to have been a key influence upon the construction of Orientalist discourse and hegemony, permeating all sorts of areas of cultural and political life, but is also credited with establishing an enduring pattern whereby the Orient was 'accommodated to the moral exigencies of Western Christianity' (Said, 1978: 67). Indeed, it is claimed that Orientalism, as a 'form of paranoia', arose initially from Christian visions of Muhammad as an impostor seeking to usurp the place of Jesus (Said, 1978: 72), but its influence continued through the development of modernity and into the present. Even where Western ideas and practices appear to be 'secular', in fact, Said identifies them with Christianity. Thus, figures as diverse as Schlegel, Wordsworth, Chateaubriand, Bouvard and Comte are presented as proponents 'of a secular post-Enlightenment myth whose outlines are unmistakably Christian' (Said, 1978: 115). Even contemporary books and articles on Islam are deemed to perpetuate medieval Christian antagonism towards it as a heretical form of Christianity (Said 1978: 209, 287). As far as Said (1978: 121) is concerned, the religious influences upon the West did not disappear in modernity but were 'reconstituted, redeployed, redistributed in the secular frameworks'; a suggestion he also repeated with regard to more recent concerns about Islamic terrorism against the 'Christian West' (Said, 1997: xxix). In short, for Said, Christianity is not simply complicit in the development of Orientalism, but a key feature of its origin, development and persistence. This attributes to Christianity an immense significance in terms of its social and cultural power and, in that sense, is consistent with some of the arguments offered in this chapter. None the less, Said's engagement with the social significance of religion is a highly partial one.

Islam, it can be noted, has a highly problematic, often contradictory presence in Said's work. At many points Said criticises Western scholars for emphasising differences between Christianity and Islam, or for suggesting that the two religions should be approached in significantly different ways (for example, Said, 1978: 276, 282, 297, 299, 306). Despite this, Said's treatment of Christianity and Islam are markedly, and significantly, different. When he discusses the fact that Islam 'dominated or effectively threatened European Christianity' up until the end of the sixteenth century, for example, he does so in relation to the development of *European* Christian imperialism, rather than the military expansion of the Islamic empire (Said, 1978: 74). Even with regard to the Middle East, and in contrast to the apparently great influence of Christianity in the West, Said seems keen to play down the impact of Islam upon the lives of people. Said (1978: 278, 299) criticises Gibb, for example, for stressing the importance of Islam in relation to all areas of life in the Middle East, and also criticises Halpern's (1962) observation that Western assumptions about the autonomy of politics and economics from religion do not apply in Middle Eastern society: for Said, this is an 'invidiously ideological' portrait of Islamic societies. In fact, he more recently emphasised that 'Islam' 'defines a relatively small proportion of what actually takes place in the Islamic world', and argues that the 'vociferously polemical Orientalists' who endorse the view that Islam has a broader social and cultural significance are using their scholarly obfuscations to attack the Middle East and to stir up anti-Islamic feeling (Said, 1997: xvi). Contrary to Said's views, however, Jalal al-'Azm (1981: 11) has suggested that many of the Orientalists' claims about the ubiquity of religion in Middle Eastern societies are correct, no matter how difficult the appreciation of this fact might be for modern Westerners.

Said's reluctance to credit Islam with the kind of social and cultural significance he attributes to Christianity in the West stems from his self-consciously 'secular' standpoint, which not only reflects his basic antipathy to religion, but also serves to obscure the religious assumptions evident in his own arguments. With regard to the former issue, he argues, for example, that beneath the 'veneer of religious cant' in Jewish, Christian and Muslim traditions 'a seething cauldron of outrageous fables is revealed, seething with several bestiaries, streams of blood, and innumerable corpses' (Said, 1993: 78; Kennedy, 2000: 78).[5] This accords with his image of himself as a 'secular critic' (Said and Ashcroft, 2001: 279), and his belief that 'the true intellectual is a secular being' (Said, 1994: 89; Hollis, 2001: 306). As Hart (2000: 10) has suggested, where, for Durkheim, religion is the moral force inherent within social life, for Said it is something 'immoral and demoniac' because it limits the free enquiry that is the essence of secular criticism.

Nonetheless, while this strong hostility to religion is clearly an important element of Said's 'secular criticism', his basic assumptions about the desirability of the autonomy of politics and economics from religion, like those of Rawls and Habermas, suggest a covert set of religious assumptions lurking beneath his ostensible secularity. Said, though born in Jerusalem, had a Christian background and was educated in British and American schools (Kennedy, 2000: 5), which might explain why his distinction between the religious and the secular is such a key element of his thought. Asad's (2002) argument that academic studies of religion tend to take this specifically Christian dualism into the study of religions such as Islam, is of note here, and perhaps helps explain Said's tendency to replicate problems he identifies in the scholarship of others. Consequently, he can unmask the religious assumptions lurking in the apparent secularity of writers such as Comte (Said, 1978: 115), but he does not address the idea that this duality is itself religious. For Said, indeed, this dualism is not simply a more or less useful way of studying religion, but is a basic principle of his entire theoretical approach to the study of society, culture and literature, and a key dimension of his self-identification as an intellectual. Consequently, despite his critique of what he regards as the pernicious Christian influence upon representations of Islamic societies, it can be said that Said's own work is framed at the most basic level by systems of symbolic classification rooted in Christian history.

However, a further reason for Said's inability to deal with the general social significance of religion in a satisfactory manner relates to his inadequate theory of representations. It has been suggested that 'Foucault is perhaps the most important single theoretical source for Said' (Kennedy, 2000: 25). In this respect, Foucault's (1972) argument that that there is no such thing as a 'true' representation of anything, since everything is constructed by discourse, is a key idea for Said, who argues that he is interested in 'the internal consistency of Orientalism and its ideas about the Orient', and not 'any correspondence, or lack thereof, with a "real" Orient' (Said, 1978: 5). The inverted commas around 'real' signal the purity of the Foucauldian intent here, as does his account of how representations fabricate a sense of the real that does not actually exist (Said, 1978: 23). His suggestion that *Orientalism* is 'basically an anti-essentialist book and I don't really have any-thing to say about an "Orient"', reflects this debt to Foucault (Said and Ashcroft, 2001: 277). Nevertheless, at times his post-structuralist decon-structionism gives way to a form of secular humanism that offers an entirely different understanding of representations. He argues, for example, that the nexus of power that creates 'the Oriental' involves 'obliterating him as a human being' (Said, 1978: 27, 231), and, at the end of the book, he talks explicitly of a 'human reality' beyond ideological representations of the Orient (Said, 1978: 326). Furthermore, he argues that, without the cor-rupting influence of Western representations of the Orient, 'there would be scholars, critics, intellectuals, human beings, for whom racial, ethnic and national distinctions were less important than the common enterprise of promoting human community': in this sense, he considers Orientalism's fail-ure to illuminate real human experience as a *human* failure as much as an intellectual one (Said, 1978: 328).

This contradiction regarding the representations theory Said is using, together with the problems that arise from his adoption of a 'secular' standpoint, mean that his account of the tacitly religious dimensions of society is, ultimately, unsatisfactory. Indeed, despite his appeal to a fuller understanding of humanity than Orientalist representations allow, his own vision of the human constitution of social reality is limited by fail-ure to engage with the hyper-spiritual dynamics, and their religious expressions, that give rise to particular systems of representation. In con-trast, Durkheim's vision of representations as emergent from the embod-ied patterns of relations between individuals and society not only looks far more intellectually compelling, but also offers a more satisfactory basis upon which to relate the particular characteristics of different soci-eties to general human potentialities and characteristics. For Durkheim, humanity was a product of the diverse cultures, histories and geographies within which people live, but he was also interested in common elements of human behaviour (Janssen and Verheggen, 1997: 296). For Moscovici (2001: 14–15) too, one of the principal benefits of the social representa-tions approach is that it focuses on the common patterns of meaning and identity construction that find expression in the diversity of human cul-tures. None the less, a further manifestation of the 'post-human' orienta-tion of some contemporary social theories is evident in the focus on 'post-representational' forms of society. These would not only appear to render redundant many of these questions about human particularity and generality, but would also displace debates about the conscious and unconscious dimensions of social reality in favour of questions about technological possibilities and dangers. Consequently, these deserve serious attention.

Post-representational society

This chapter began by raising questions about the embedding of society within the consciousness of individuals, noting that social theories centred on notions of reasonable or rational dialogue fail to account for the unconscious processes through which social realities, as phenomena emergent from the embodied potentialities of human beings, are constituted. Drawing on Michael Polanyi's notion of the 'tacit dimension' of human knowledge, it was suggested that Durkheim's notion of collective representations and, to some extent, Moscovici's development of this concept, could help explain how the hyper-spiritual or religious substrata of societies could come to shape their particular self-understandings. From there, the rest of the chapter dealt with the various degrees to which these tacit dimensions were explicitly or implicitly present in accounts of sociological theories of everyday life, Western conceptions of public and private life, and Orientalist representations of Islamic societies. The notion of a 'post-representational' society, however, suggests that social realities must be conceptualised in a manner radically different to any of the approaches considered so far.

Lash and Featherstone (2001) have offered a brief but illuminating summary of the key issues to be confronted in this respect, developing their arguments in dialogue with Taylor's (1994) exploration of the politics of 'recognition' in a multicultural society. Following Taylor, they emphasise that the recognition of human dignity and authenticity is a key thematic of modernity. However, while he stresses the role of recognition in relation to self-identity (see Taylor, 1989), they add that recognition, 'grounded in reciprocity and unity of purpose … is also the source of modernity's social bond' (Lash and Featherstone, 2001: 14). In this respect, they draw on the arguments of Durkheim, Mauss and Lévi-Strauss to show that in modernity, even where there has been the danger that the social bond will break down, modern nations provided resources for reconstituted and individualised versions of the social bond. In the 'global information society', however, claims for recognition come from a multiplicity of cultures rather than a 'national *Kultur*', while the inclusive social bonds of modernity have broken down, leaving only a 'de-traditionalised, transformed and fragmented' world determined only by the information flows of 'the communications order' (Lash and Featherstone, 2001: 15-16). Here, in so far as such a thing continues to exist, 'the social bond comes more and more to resemble the *communication*' (emphasis in original), standing apart from everyday social relations in the compressed, machine-mediated flow of information that 'avoids completely the question of representation', taking place 'outside of symbolic structures – in the real' (Lash and Featherstone, 2001: 16; Hardt and Negri, 2000). In fact, in this post-representational world, recognition 'becomes making sense of the information and communitational flows', values 'are disengaged from structures and are set free into the general flows', and intersubjectivity becomes mediated through technology (Lash and Featherstone, 2001: 17). In Hayles's (1991) terms, representation, grounded in human relationships, no longer works in a 'post-human' world.

Lash and Featherstone's arguments, which complement many of the views of writers such as Urry (2000, 2003) and Castells (2000), exhibit some of the characteristics discussed in previous chapters, notably the tendencies towards technological determinism and grand claims about epochal transformations in Western societies, allied to a false restriction of Durkheim's notion of society to the modern nation-state. What is of particular note, however, is their evacuation of the human from 'the real': here, the human is identified with the realm of the symbolic, while the real is identified with information flows. None the less, the theoretical sources they draw upon in developing their account of this post-representational world are often expressly hostile to such an interpretation. One of their sources, Zizek (1989), for example, does *not* interpret the 'excess' of the real in a way that lends itself to talk of informational flows and machine-mediated communication. On the contrary, Zizek (2002) has recently argued in very clear terms that using the notion of the 'real' in this sort of way actually obfuscates the reality of the human condition in the contemporary world. It is also notable that Lash and Featherstone's arguments rest on a misinterpretation of Bataille's notion of the 'general economy', which they define as 'the space in which the social bond had broken down'. Contrary to the suggestion that Bataille was 'Durkheim and Mauss's most important opponent' (Lash and Featherstone, 2001: 16), he actually followed Durkheim in his argument that the general economy is not the space where the social bond is absent, but where it comes into being, expressing the exuberance and effervescence of life (Bataille, 1991: 10).[6]

Rather than offering visions of a post-representational world of 'excess', what Bataille and Zizek share is a commitment to a fuller sense of what it is to be human than that acknowledged in modernity, and in much modern social theory. Indeed, while Lash and Featherstone (2001: 16) reference Zizek and Deleuze together as advocates of a notion of the real 'in excess of Durkheim's symbolic', Zizek (2002: 30) attacks Deleuze's 'monotonous' discourse on 'the decentred proliferation of multitudes and non-totalizable differences' which occludes the real forces within society. What Lash and Featherstone also miss is the fact that, for Zizek, this emphasis on real forces raises religious questions, and brings him close to an implicit endorsement of the kind of natural law basis for sociological theory offered by philosophers such as MacIntyre (1984, 1988). For MacIntyre, the theology of natural law provides an essential foundation for the study of society since it grounds emergent social realities in the inherent (God-given) capacities and potentialities of human nature relative to notions of individual and common good. While developing his arguments in an ostensibly different tradition of social and cultural analysis, Zizek clearly recognises, and endorses, such notions of the good. Thus, it is Zizek's (2002: 29; emphasis in original) '*love for humanity*' that leads him, following 'Christ's famous words about how he has come to bring the sword and division, not unity and peace', to oppose the fascism, racism and economic and technological imperialism that tends to be hidden by 'the hegemonic liberal multiculturalist ideology'. In contrast to this ideology, which talks of such 'evils' but can never engage with their underlying causes because of its inability to look beyond a language of 'differences', Zizek (2002: 65) offers an unashamedly universalist commitment to the human grounded in theology.

In the light of this, and despite the differences in philosophical language characteristic of their work, Bataille and Zizek are actually closer to the attempts of Taylor (1994) and his colleagues to 're-think human values in the context of particular cultures', rather than to Lash and Featherstone's (2001: 1–2) starting point of 'difference' and not 'universalism'. Indeed, although they unfavourably contrast the universalism of the 'hallowed halls of Princeton' with the poverty and ethnic diversity of the London borough of Lewisham, it is the lack of a universalist concern for general, real features of human society that limits their analysis (Lash and Featherstone, 2001: 2). It is for this reason that the notion of a post-representational society tends to lack a moral dimension, since, as Taylor (1989: 5) expresses it, morality depends upon an ontology of the human. Such an ontology is, none the less, evident in the renewed interest in rights, responsibilities and obligations that has tended to develop alongside the processes discussed by Lash and Featherstone. As May (2002: 159) suggests, 'there is a growing notion of a global civil society alongside, or perhaps within, the global information society', challenging some of the economic and technological processes that would render the world 'post-human'. This reassertion of society should not be seen as a radical counter-movement to the epochal changes brought about by information technology, however, but simply the continuance of some of the elementary patterns characteristic of humans as social beings. Indeed, as May (2002: 160) has commented, 'The emergence of the information society may change some of the forms in which our interactions take place, but the substance of our lives will remain the same: the need for sustenance, the need for companionship, the need to work to live'.

Beyond these 'needs' listed by May there are many other aspects of social life that endure within the 'information society', even if these are often identifiable only in the 'tacit' dimensions of society. Taylor's (1989: 520) attempt to uncover the Christian moral sources of modern notions of selfhood buried under the language of secularism, utilitarianism, naturalism or various kinds of rationalism is particularly significant in this regard, but the broader influence of Christian orientations discussed in this chapter also suggests the need for a further engagement with the religious underpinnings of contemporary societies, and with questions about how these continue to shape contemporary orientations, aspirations and needs. If, however, these Christian underpinnings are not simply unacknowledged but firmly denied, then this raises questions about the long-term consequences of this denial. Castells (1998: 1) offers a clear manifestation of this denial when, despite acknowledging that the date of the millennium is defined by the Gregorian calendar of Christianity, he dismisses Christianity as 'a minority religion that is bound to lose its pre-eminence' as representation becomes shaped by 'real virtuality' rather than religion. As another 'secular critic' dreaming of fulfilling Enlightenment hopes for a more just social order, however, his embrace of the emancipatory potentialities of technology, allied to a rejection of religion, means that he is unable to grasp what Virilio (1984) envisages to be the dangerous and inhuman consequences that flow from the attempted elimination of modernity's Christian origins. These dangers, which are not only related to technology but to the increasing pervasiveness of a reductive utilitarianism, become even more pressing in the context of a 'clash of civilisations' (Huntington, 1996), where other societies begin to reassess their own moral and religious sources and increasingly define themselves in opposition to the West. These are the concerns of the following chapter.

Notes

1. This concept has formed the basis for a significant assault on the dominance of behaviourist and cognitive forms of social psychology (see Farr and Moscovici, 1984; Jodelet, 1989; Guimelli, 1994; Chaib and Orfali, 2000; Deaux and Philogène, 2001). Just as Durkheim originally envisaged sociology to be a sort of 'collective psychology', so too Moscovici has attempted to revitalise the *social* dimension of 'social psychology' through a fresh engagement with Durkheim's sociological vision (see Durkheim, 1974b: 34; Moscovici, 2001: 24).

2. His argument is as follows: 'For science it is necessary to abstract from these flows of time and space in order to arrive at concepts ... Durkheim views concepts as beneath this perpetual, sensuous, surface flux. Concepts are outside of time and change ... They are fixed and immutable and it is the task of science to reveal them' (Urry, 2000: 26; see also Urry, 2003: 59).

3. In general, Moscovici's reading of Durkheim is too subtle to associate the decline of the sacred simply with the decline of institutionalised forms of religion. Like Bataille (1992), he recognises that symbols of the sacred are representations of the passionate energies that flow through collective life, and cannot be confined to those social forms that, in common usage, denote 'religion' (Moscovici, 1993: 50).

4. Indeed, Levine (1985: 11) emphasises that the attempt to portray such societies as monolithic and inflexible reflects distinctively Western, post-Enlightenment myths rather than sociological reality (see also Shils, 1981).

5. Consequently, however wronged or misrepresented he believes Muslims and Islam to be, he is not about to endorse Islam as a valuable way of thinking and living. With regard to his native Palestine, for example, Said was clear that he wanted a secular, rather than an Islamic, future for it (Walhout, 2001: 250).

6. Even more than Zizek, Bataille's thought appears to be entirely antithetical to any notion of a machine-mediated reality: in fact, his notion of the general economy is developed in opposition to the commodification of the human that he saw as the consequence of modern industrialism and the marginalisation of religion (Bataille, 1991: 129).

7

Resurgent Society

One of Urry's key arguments about contemporary social and cultural changes is that what looks like 'emergent global order' is, in reality, better characterised as 'constant disorder and disequilibrium'. Referring to phenomena such as the rise of religious 'fundamentalism' and the spread of Western consumerism, he argues that national governments may seek to 'dampen down' some of the chaotic forces spreading across different social contexts but their local powers can have little impact upon tendencies towards disequilibrium that are global in character (Urry, 2000: 208–9; see also Beck, 2000: 11). The implication here is that societies, which are local, are relatively powerless and insignificant in relation to global flows and forces, thus necessitating a post-societal form of analysis. Similar implications are evident in a range of other types of social, economic and political studies, particularly amongst those that interpret global changes through market models concerned with the free flow of capital (Stiglitz, 2001). It is also notable, however, that this stress on the relative insignificance of society in relation to global forces tends to co-exist with the view that religion has become separated from particular societal contexts. In market-oriented theoretical models, this takes the form of reducing religion to one more global commodity to be bought and sold in an increasingly free market (Iannaccone, 1997). Within more culturally oriented models, religious belief and activity become symbolic of those global forces that render societies insignificant. Thus, for Urry (2000: 209), *jihad* can be associated with the 'identity politics' of the new 'global disorder' rather than with particular societal or traditional religious forms.

The aims of this chapter are to suggest that such views are misconceived, and to propose a more productive way of assessing some contemporary social and cultural conflicts. Within a sociological perspective that acknowledges the contingency of social and cultural forms upon human characteristics and potentialities, that takes sufficient account of the *sui generis* dimensions of societies as emergent forms, and that seeks to engage with the hyper-spiritual orientation towards transcendence built into social relationships, the idea that social and religious forces can become entirely chaotic or commodified phenomena, cut adrift from particular societal forms, looks highly implausible because it ignores the specifically human basis of social and cultural realities. Indeed, from a social realist point of view, the true character of some of the contemporary global transformations that mark the present can only be understood if they are analysed in relation to the human, societal and religious contexts that facilitate their emergence. In this regard, what looks like a post-human, post-societal or post-religious set of global flows and markets to writers such as Urry and Castells can be, in reality, understood as the *resurgence* of those phenomena such global transformations appear to render obsolete. Further to this, there are three key arguments developed throughout this chapter, all of which can help illuminate the resurgent significance of societies and their intimate connections with religions.

First, it is argued that Huntington's (1993, 1996) 'clash of civilisations' thesis is of value in that it directs sociological attention to the fact that between 'national societies' and 'global disorder' there are emergent civilisational forms that need to be taken seriously; second, it is argued that the global resurgence of Islam can be understood as a resurgence of *society*, rather than some sort of 'fundamentalist' rejection of modernity; and third, it is argued that this Islamic resurgence provides a further stimulus to the reassessment of the Christian legacy for Western societies. In relation to the first of these arguments, the intention here is to establish the idea that some of the most important global conflicts and problems facing the world today may indeed be transcendent of particular societies but that this does not render society redundant any more than participation in society renders individuals insignificant: societies not only remain important because 'civilisations' are emergent from them, but also because civilisations necessarily find their expression through particular societal forms. Further to this, and building upon the arguments about the hyper-spiritual dimensions of society discussed in earlier chapters, it is argued here that civilisations develop specific characters through the influence of their religious substrata.

With regard to the second of these key arguments, it has already been noted that a significant feature of Durkheim's account of society is the recognition of an ambiguity at its heart, in the sense that the social energies that can be a stimulus for heightened moral sensibilities can also provoke barbarism, violence, oppression and fanaticism (Durkheim, 1995: 213, 417). Further to this, Karl Polanyi (2001: 265) has argued that, historically, the resurgence of society against the dehumanising utilitarianism of the market economy has taken a number of extreme forms, including those of fascism and communism. Specifically, his argument is that in a world apparently dominated by market forces two extreme options can impose themselves upon people regarding the reality of society: the first, adopted by liberal philosophy, is 'to remain faithful to an illusionary idea of freedom and deny the reality of society'; the second, expressed through fascism and communism, is 'to accept that reality and reject the idea of freedom' (Polanyi, 2001: 266). Originally written in the 1940s, Polanyi's argument here helps throw new light on the post-September 11th world: the first of these options reflects a dominant view within certain sections of the Western world; the second option is, arguably, close to that taken up by many contemporary followers of Islam.

While Polanyi ostensibly focuses on these two options, however, he implicitly offers a third: his concern for the uniqueness and autonomy of individuals, balanced by an acceptance of the reality of society as a necessary context for a life of freedom and justice, has, as he acknowledges, Christian sources (Polanyi, 2001: 268). Polanyi's critique of economic reductionism was grounded in a firm sense of the Western world's religious heritage, and he was a committed Christian socialist (Roth, 2003). More recent critiques of contemporary social and cultural patterns in the West by writers such as Zizek (2000, 2002) and Virilio (2002) also look to Christian sources for a vision of the Western world that transcends economic and technological forms of reductionism. These theoretical writings are significant because they raise questions about whether particular forms of social life necessarily depend upon particular types of religion; indeed, post-September 11th, these questions seem all the more important given the fact that increased suspicion about the motives and actions of Muslims within Western societies has been matched by a noticeable firming up of patterns of Christian identification (Fetzer and Soper, 2003). In this respect, following the example of writers such as Said (1978, 1997), it is all too easy to interpret any such firming up of Western identities against those of other societies and cultures in 'racist' terms. This is, nevertheless, a simplistic and reductionist approach that does not allow for the possibility that religious factors can be much more important than racial ones, aside from the fact that it ignores the racial diversity within Islamic and Western contexts. It should also be noted that Zizek and Virilio are explicitly hostile to all forms of xenophobia and racism. It is Huntington (1996), however, in an account of the contemporary 'clash of civilisations' that has been both highly influential and highly contentious in its reassessment of international political, social and cultural conflicts, who offers a particularly strong emphasis upon religious factors above others. This account, and related arguments by other authors, is a good place to begin a discussion of the contemporary resurgence of religion and society.

Hyper-national society

The term 'clash of civilisations' was first used by Bernard Lewis (1990) to refer to the resurgence of conflicts between Islam and the West, but Samuel Huntington's development of this idea in an article (1993), and then a book of the same title (1996) has proved a particularly influential, if much disputed, contribution to political debates about emerging global conflicts. While Urry's (2000: 19) consideration of an emergent global level of social and cultural relations focuses on its post-societal characteristics, in the sense that various mobilities, flows and chaotic forces are presumed to circulate independently of societies, Huntington's arguments centre on a notion of 'civilisations' which sees them as phenomena transcendent of, but emergent from, societies. His notion of 'civilisation' draws from a number of sources, and includes a number of different features, though it relies heavily upon Durkheim and Mauss's (1971) focus on civilisation as an emergent 'moral milieu' encompassing particular groups of nations or societies, and Braudel's (1980, 1994) idea that civilisations endure, and develop, over the *longue durée* of human history (Huntington, 1996: 41–4). Although Huntington considers a number of sources for different forms of civilisation, he emphasises the importance of religion in particular. Indeed, in view of his arguments, a civilisation can be considered as a phenomenon that encompasses a number of societies united by a common religious substratum: this applies not only to those societies defined by their identification with Islam, but also structures what we mean by 'the West', since this is constituted by societies that have evolved along specifically Christian lines even if this evolution is obscured by the difference in nomenclature.

In this regard, Huntington's arguments are consistent with some of the themes developed in this book: he argues, in fact, that 'Western Christianity, first Catholicism and then Catholicism and Protestantism, is historically the single most important characteristic of Western civilisation. During most of its first millennium, indeed, what is now known as Western civilisation was called Western Christendom' (Huntington, 1996: 70). Furthermore, he also emphasises that Christianity's significance is not merely historical. Discussing the Christianisation of parts of Africa and Asia, for example, he notes that 'the most successful protagonists of Western culture are not neoclassical economists or crusading democrats or multinational corporation executives. They are and most likely will continue to be Christian missionaries' (Huntington, 1996: 65). Also, in his account of the current evolution of the European Community, he suggests that its borders are essentially those of Western Christendom from five hundred years ago, and that this Christian pattern of identification still 'provides a clear criterion for the admission of new members to Western organisations' (Huntington, 1996: 158, 160). In this regard, even though the USA, as an overwhelmingly Christian society, is often contrasted with the more secular environs of Europe, the substratum of European societies also remains religious: 'Christian concepts, values and practices nonetheless pervade European civilisation' (Huntington, 1996: 305). Indeed, Huntington argues that, while the undermining of Christianity would seriously threaten Western civilisation, there is no likelihood of this in the short or medium term. For him, however, a real threat to Western civilisation is present in the spread of Islam, across the globe and within Western societies through patterns of economic migration. This idea that Islam manifests a 'threat' to Western civilisation is, of course, a contentious one, particularly for those Muslim minorities peacefully living and participating in European and American societies. None the less, Huntington's arguments about Islam can be broken down into three main parts, all of which raise important points about the relationship between religion and society.

First, he follows Maxime Rodinson in recognising that Islam and modernisation do not clash, since the successful economic and scientific modernisation of society is in no sense forbidden by Islamic law (*shar'ia*), and, consequently, he asserts that the explicit or implicit assumptions by many Westerners that modernisation and Westernisation go hand in hand are false: 'In fundamental ways, the world is becoming more modern and less Western' (Huntington, 1996: 78; see Pipes, 1983). Following this, he emphasises that even when Western consumer goods circulate extensively within

Muslim societies they tend to have a negligible impact upon religious orientations: indeed, he argues that it is only modern Western arrogance with regard to other societies, and Westerners' ignorance about the basis of their own civilisation, that leads to such assumptions about the power of consumer-related economic and cultural processes (Huntington, 1996: 58). In fact, the resurgence of Islam has been characteristically associated with young, modern-oriented, well-educated urban populations, not conservative, backwards looking, older generations (Huntington, 1996: 101; see Lannes, 1991; Esposito, 1992). Here, Huntington is acknowledging that religion can be very deeply embedded within societies, and that the Western assumption that modernisation and secularisation necessarily go hand in hand reflects a failure to grasp the real sources of the most powerful social representations through which people make sense of society and the world. In short, much of what is 'modern', including technological, scientific and market-related processes, can have a significant impact upon certain strata within societies, but does not necessarily reach down into the hyper-spiritual and religious levels of social reality that shape societies as *sui generis* phenomena.

A second factor Huntington emphasises, which builds upon his recognition of the deeply embedded power of religion, is that the contemporary resurgence of Islam cannot be associated with an 'extreme' minority, but with a *general* reassertion of Islamic beliefs and practices evident in personal commitments and actions, as well as in the social, political and philosophical orientations through which Islamic societies structure their activities, and in the increasing attempts by Muslim states to build international Islamic coalitions (Huntington, 1996: 110; Hillal Dessouki, 1982: 9–13; Esposito, 1992: 12). What is significant here is that Huntington resists the modern sociological assumption that strong religious commitments are characteristic of only a small, 'deviant minority' or those types of society deemed to be somehow less sophisticated and knowledgeable than those of the West (Berger, 1990). On the contrary, he not only challenges Western arrogance in this respect, but also points towards the fundamental significance of religion for contemporary social, political and cultural theory: what he recognises is that strong Islamic commitments are not the preserve of individuals or particular groups of individuals, but of societies and, beyond them, of civilisations.

A third factor Huntington (1996: 217) emphasises, however, which is particularly significant in terms of his claims about an Islamic 'threat' to Western civilisation, and which follows from the two factors noted above, is that the 'underlying problem for the West is not Islamic fundamentalism', but Islam in general. Here, he is interested primarily in the subject of religion and violence. As Huntington (1996: 217) stresses, Western political leaders have tended to state that violent acts in the name of Islam are perpetuated by an 'extreme' minority, that Islam is in essence a religion of peace, and that 'moderate' Muslims condemn such violence when it occurs. He not only suggests that these claims lack evidence, however, but also argues that 'Fourteen hundred years of history suggest otherwise' (Huntington, 1996: 209), and claims that 'Muslims make up about one-fifth of the world's population but in the 1990s they have been far more involved in intergroup violence than the people of any other civilisation' (Huntington, 1996: 256). Indeed, following James Payne's (1989: 124) study of differential patterns of militarisation in Christian and Islamic societies, he argues that the fact of the 'Muslim propensity towards violent conflict' is undeniable (Huntington, 1996: 258). Again following Payne, he notes that the embodiment of Islam as a 'religion of the sword' is manifest in the example of Muhammad, who was a military commander as well as a religious leader (Huntington, 1996: 263; Payne, 1989: 127). In this regard, although both Christianity and Islam are monotheistic, universalistic faiths with a tendency to see the world in 'us-and-them' terms, Christ and Muhammad offer radically different religious models with regard to the type of actions that can be considered religiously legitimate. Indeed, Huntington (1996: 264) argues that Islam, alone among all the major religions of the world, tends to promote a violent struggle against those populations that refuse to accept its superiority.

Huntington's claim about an Islamic propensity towards violence is, clearly, one of the most contentious aspects of his arguments. This concentration on one particular aspect of Islam, which arises from his focus on international political conflicts, does not offer a comprehensive and detailed vision of Islam in general terms, and runs the risk of ignoring internal debates about the legitimate uses of violence, as well as the wealth of diverse theological views and social practices that have constituted various forms of Islam. None the less, it is also clear that Qur'anic texts, the analysis of history, and even the arguments of many Muslim apologists provide some support for his arguments. Not only are there many Qur'anic texts that urge violent battle against all those who refuse to accept Muhammad and Islam,[1] but the most comprehensive and historically detailed of the many recent discussions of *jihad* emphasises the centrality of war to Islam as it has been practiced historically (Bat Ye'or, 1996). As Bat Ye'or (1996: 40) expresses it, 'The aim of *jihad* is to subjugate the peoples of the world to Allah, decreed by his Prophet Muhammad'. Indeed, she argues that, far from being exceptional, *jihad* has been the norm in Islamic history (Bat Ye'or, 1996: 251).[2] In a more apologetic vein, Nasr (1988: 73) acknowledges that Islam offers a 'positive symbolism of war', in which the 'holy war' against *internal* impulses leading away from religious righteousness and the *external* 'holy war' against enemies of Islam are part of one inseparable process, since nothing other than 'some kind of precarious peace' can be possible until the defeat of all those forces that oppose submission to God's will. Consequently, while Huntington clearly offers a limited account of Islam, it is, arguably, not an inaccurate one.

The sociological significance of this argument rests on its recognition of the differential social consequences of particular religious traditions. In this regard, while the 'clash of civilisation' thesis might justifiably be criticised for offering a view of inter-societal relationships that offers little hope for any common sense of purpose or solidarity across religious divides, it nevertheless builds on a tradition of social theory that dates back to Weber, for whom such differences were also of great significance. Viewed within a social realist perspective, it is possible to mitigate the bleakness of Huntington's analysis by noting that differences in religion and society emerge from common human conditions and characteristics, and that, therefore, potentialities for mutual 'recognition' and emergent forms of solidarity are always present (Taylor, 1994). This should not detract from the fact that such differences are real, however, since, as emergent phenomena, they continue to be of irreducible contemporary significance, and help us to understand why it is that in those parts of the world where Buddhist, Hindu, Sikh or other religions dominate, some of the same economic, political and cultural resentments that mark Islamic societies have *not* resulted in a 'holy war' against the West.

The arguments offered by Huntington have, of course, been subject to a great deal of criticism. Skidmore's (1998) comments are symptomatic of many of these in that he suggests Huntington offers a too homogeneous picture of Islamic societies, and that, more broadly, he underestimates the significance of economic forces and overestimates the significance of religious ones. What is notable here, aside from the merits or demerits of Huntington's arguments about the specific character of Islam, is the reluctance to accord religion any sort of fundamental social and political significance. A similar reluctance is evident in Eisenstadt's (2000) attempt to add subtlety to Huntington's analysis by agreeing that religions provide broad civilisational frameworks for contemporary social and political developments, but none the less arguing, in the manner of Giddens (1990, 1991a), that these religions have been reflexively reconstructed through modern cultural, economic and political processes. In short, religion remains of secondary importance when viewed in relation to modernity, even if the resurgence of religion necessitates the development of a notion of 'multiple modernities'. Notably, these sorts of arguments have tended to prevail amongst sociologists even after the Islamic terrorist attacks on the World Trade Center in New York on September 11th 2001, as well as amongst international relations theorists, who have been even more reluctant to acknowledge the public vitality of religion (Philpott, 2002).

Violent society

Written before the events of September 11th, Huntington's account of Islam within his 'clash of civilisations' thesis raises important questions about the degree to which different religious traditions can impact upon individuals and societies in diverse ways. In contrast, a number of assessments of these events by prominent social and cultural theorists have tended to push these questions aside, a tendency characteristic of many recent studies of Islam (see Ellul, 1996: 18). Indeed, rather than

Huntington, a number of European sociologists have followed Said (1978, 1997) in their attempts to make sense of these events, focusing on Western tendencies to misrepresent Islam, rather than dealing directly with questions about the degree to which Islam might offer religious legitimations for violence that cannot be confined to a 'deviant minority' of 'extremists' or 'fundamentalists'. Said, while acknowledging that 'there *has* been a resurgence of emotion throughout the Islamic world', and that economic problems and anti-democratic practices have contributed to this, blames the West for provoking problems through its 'indiscriminate' attacks upon Islam in the media, scholarship and 'pro-Israeli books and journals' (Said, 1997: xv–xvi, xxi). Here, Islamic 'fundamentalism' is portrayed as a response to the historic and continuing injustices of the West, not as anything that reflects continuities with earlier patterns of Islamic thought and practice (see Voll, 1987).

Using Said as a theoretical source to help make sense of the post-September 11th world looks highly problematic, however, since he tends to burden the West with all the responsibility for all conflicts with Islam. This ignores the fact that, as Jalal al-'Azm (1981: 19) points out, powerful representations of other cultures are not confined to the West, but occur in all societies, and Islamic cultures often operate with an 'Orientalism in reverse'. Further to this, as Benthall (2002: 2) has noted, Huntington's vision of a 'clash' between Islam and the West is actually an inversion of the classical Islamic division of the world into two camps, the *dar al-Islam* (the 'realm of Islam') and the *dar al-harb* (the 'realm of war', that is, of the 'unbelievers') (see also Bat Ye'or, 1996: 40). None the less, following Said's line of thought, Turner (2002: 115) interprets the 'negative images' of Islam in the post-September 11th West as 'a revival of Orientalism'. Here, the new 'Orientalist' critique is directed towards Huntington (1993, 1996), Fukuyama (1992, 2002) and Schmitt (1996a, 1996b, Schmitt et al., 1996). Similarly, while Kellner (2002: 148) does not accuse Huntington of reinforcing an essentially Western hegemonic pattern of discourse, he argues that his 'binary model of inexorable conflict between the West and Islam' 'lends itself to pernicious misuse', and that Huntington misrepresents Islam through homogenising it, thereby ignoring internal arguments within Islam about modernity and the legitimate use of violence.

As Turner (2002: 109) notes, however, Huntington *is* attentive to conflicts within Islam, particularly regarding ethnic differences but also between different Muslim countries. Furthermore, it can be noted that Huntington devotes attention to religious, political, economic and demographic factors affecting Muslim societies, though he interprets all of these as tending towards the intensification of hostilities towards the West. Turner (2002: 103-4), however, views the notion of a contemporary 'clash of civilisations' as a distinctively Western phenomenon, rooted in religious and political misrepresentations of Islam, and suggests that it cannot be understood fully without recognising the influence of the political theology of Carl Schmitt (1996a, 1996b; Schmitt et al., 1996), which has had a significant impact on recent American political science and foreign policy (see McCormick, 1998; i ek, 2002: 109). Turner (2002: 107–8) emphasises Schmitt's Roman Catholic theological commitments in his account of how Schmitt saw in Catholicism a defence against cultural relativism, and how Schmitt developed a political theology that divides the world into 'friend' and 'foe'. It is in these (Catholic) terms that Islam can be represented as an enemy expressing religious values contradictory of those that underpin the Western world. For Turner, rather than Islam representing a real threat to the real underpinnings of Western civilisation, what Schmitt and Huntington express are fears expressive of a long history of Christian misrepresentations of Islam; these fears, furthermore, arise from a marginal (Catholic) religious viewpoint rather than from the 'liberal denominational Protestantism' that has an 'elective affinity' with capitalism in its relativism and consumerism (Turner, 2002: 117).

Turner, like Habermas (1989a), is clearly unsympathetic towards Schmitt's arguments, seeing him as an essentially conservative figure, despite acknowledging his influence upon both left and right in American political science. Nevertheless, Schmitt, like Huntington, takes religious factors seriously rather than reducing them into economic grievances, legitimations of consumerism or culturally relative misrepresentations of other 'more important' factors. In accusing Huntington, Fukuyama and Barber of 'the recreation of Orientalism', Turner (2002: 112), in contrast, offers a highly selective, and ultimately unconvincing, account of religion.

There are many aspects of Huntington's arguments that Turner does not engage with, including the point that young Muslims can combine a liking for Coke, jeans and pop music with a devotion to Islam that can extend to martyrdom (Huntington, 1996: 58), but the key problem with Turner's critique is that he does not take religion seriously as an elementary feature of society. Although Turner's work in the sociology of religion has focused on the relationship between religion and power, social control, economics and historical development (see Turner, 1991), his location of the *origins* of religion in 'unmediated inner experiences' presupposes that religion and society are fundamentally distinct phenomena (see Turner and Rojek, 2001: 131). There are two things to note about this. First, it reflects Turner's debt to Weber, who expressed a similar view, and it informs his argument that *jihad* 'refers primarily to an internal spiritual struggle', and that its social/military dimensions are 'secondary' (Turner, 2002: 112). Second, however, Turner's view of religion leads him to underestimate the sociological significance of Islam as a historical reality.

In the past, Turner (1991: 32–3) has suggested that the pessimism of Said's analysis of Orientalism can be overcome by focusing on the essential *sameness* of different cultures or religions, a focus exemplified by his simplistic equation of *jihad* with the Crusades.[3] Post-September 11th, seeking to counter contemporary 'misrepresentations' of Islam, Turner (2002: 112) also argues that Islamic and Christian forms of 'fundamentalism' are essentially interchangeable, though he does not seem to take either very seriously:

indeed, he questions whether such forms of fundamentalism, along with 'individualistic Protestantism', can survive the eroding influence of Western consumer culture: 'What remains to be seen is whether, in the long run, the world of pure entertainment is triumphant over that of the sacred' (Turner, 2002: 117).

Benjamin Barber's (1995) *Jihad vs. McWorld* has similarities in this respect. For Barber, the conflict between Islam and the West is merely one aspect of a broader conflict between the tribal politics of *jihad* and the consumerism and secularism represented by McDonald's. Turner's (2002: 111) suggestion that the terrorist attack on the World Trade Center towers, embodiments of Western capitalism, can be read as an illustration of Barber's symbolic dichotomisation is an example of the influence of his arguments. Yet they express a highly selective engagement with the significance of religion for society. Barber's (1995: 9) use of the term *jihad*, for example, separates it from its Islamic origins and applies it to a range of other phenomena that he believes embody 'militant' rejections of modernity. Some of these usages are manifestly absurd: with regard to France, for example, the renewal of interest in bagpipes amongst Bretons is presented as one form of 'European Jihad' (Barber, 1995: 172). Other usages exemplify broader tendencies to equate Islamic beliefs and practices with other types of religious phenomena. With regard to 'American Jihad', for example, Barber (1995: 212) equates Islamic 'Holy War' with the Protestant 'fundamentalist' critique of liberalism. As Barber notes, such equations are common (see Marty and Appleby, 1991), but they often depend upon a neglect of historical facts. The term 'fundamentalism' has a specifically Protestant and American history, where it originally signalled the rejection of *liberal* Protestant views of the culturally conditioned character of biblical texts: the unchangeable 'fundamentals' emphasised, particularly those relating to the inerrancy of scripture, had deep roots in Protestant history, but also arose in relation to long-standing difficulties within this tradition regarding the interpretation of biblical texts that were 'inspired' by the Word of God (Ammerman, 1987; Shepard, 1987; Munson, 2003). In view of this, the application of the term 'fundamentalism' to an Islamic context, though now widespread, looks inherently problematic, since *all* Muslims would reject the idea that Qur'anic teaching is in any sense culturally conditioned following their belief that the Qur'an was dictated by God to Muhammad (Rippin and Knappert, 1986).

One thing that follows from applying the notion of 'fundamentalism' in this general way, however, is that, just as those Protestant Christians who have a literalist view of biblical teaching can be seen as an 'extreme' or 'fundamentalist' minority, so too a distinction between 'moderate' and 'fundamentalist' Islam becomes possible. It is this distinction that facilitates statements as general and as historically and sociologically naïve as the following: 'Fundamentalists can be found among every religious sect and represent a tiny, aggravated minority whose ideology contradicts the very religions in whose name they act' (Barber, 2001: xv). Contrary to this view,

Huntington's (1996: 258) emphasis on a *general* 'Muslim propensity toward violent conflict' is, of course, highly contentious if not inflammatory, but raises legitimate questions about the degree to which Islam provides resources for a theological legitimation of violence absent in other religious traditions. In this respect, it is right that Turner (2002: 114) and Kellner (2002: 148) note the existence of contemporary Muslim voices challenging 'militant' interpretations of Islam. None the less, sensitivity to the dangers of offering a too homogeneous account of particular religious traditions is not the same thing as the rejection of any notion of inherent religious characteristics. As Lindholm (1997: 748) has suggested, for some people in the West the whole notion of a 'distinct cultural heritage' has come, under the influence of writers such as Said, to be regarded as an oppressive act of Western dominance that seeks to obliterate the multiplicity and creative flux through which people construct meaningful lives. Lindholm quite rightly draws attention to the liberal utopianism underpinning such arguments, and their lack of an engagement with social reality. In contrast, a social realist view of contemporary religious changes not only takes distinct heritages seriously, but also recognises that these must be considered in relation to distinctively societal dynamics and characteristics.

Virulent society

Polanyi's (2001) account of the emergence of communism and fascism in response to the social fragmentation wrought by free market economics offers a potentially fruitful way of making sense of why Islam has become resurgent in the *present*, for he interprets such phenomena in terms of the resurgence of society. Echoing Durkheim's analysis of religion, Polanyi (2001: 245–7) emphasises the dynamic, emotional underpinnings of communism and fascism, and their capacities for responding to some of the chaotic, destabilising aspects of modern economic processes by nurturing an ideology of the group against notions of universal brotherhood. This is not to say that the emergence of phenomena such as communism and fascism can be reduced into economic factors, only to suggest that they represent a certain kind of 'moral' and 'religious' response to the tendency of economics to deny the reality of society. For Polanyi, in fact, free market economics are dangerous in two senses: first, they are dangerous because, in ignoring social obligations, bonds and forms of solidarity, they can produce inhuman ways of living and working; secondly, however, they are dangerous because those hyper-spiritual aspects of social realities they ignore or actively oppose can reassert themselves in virulent forms manifest as an authoritarian denial of individual freedom and an aggressive militarism towards outsider groups (Polanyi, 2001: 266–7).

In some respects, the resurgence of Islam can be interpreted in similar terms, though not in those proposed by Fukuyama (2002).[4] As Huntington (1996: 98) suggests, the broader resurgence of religion of which the Islamic revival is a part is a reaction against 'secularism, moral relativism and self-indulgence, and a reaffirmation of the values of order, discipline, work, mutual help and human solidarity'. Much of Barber's (1995, 2001) analysis is also consistent with this argument. Echoing Polanyi, Barber (2001: xvii) suggests that the global spread of *laissez-faire* economics, which denies the reality of society, has stimulated a backlash evident in the resurgence of Islam in many parts of the world. This backlash, however, is to do with moral and religious conflicts, not simply with economic grievances or political pressures attendant upon globalisation (Davetian, 2001). Contrary to Urry's (2000: 209) association of *jihad* with the 'identity politics' of a new, post-societal 'global disorder', in fact, the resurgence of Islam does not signal the demise of society but its revitalisation. In Polanyi's terms, what Kepel (1994) has called '*la revanche de Dieu*' is the resurgence of *society* in the face of its global denial. The antagonism expressed by even 'moderate' Muslims towards what is perceived to be the West's consumerism and absence of values, as well as their belief that the West is determined to destroy the Islamic community, suggest this kind of resurgence (Huntington, 1996: 214; Vertigans and Sutton, 2001; Lewis, 2002).

As I have already noted, however, this resurgence does not, contrary to Barber's view, tend to involve a rejection of the economic and scientific benefits of modernisation, even in its apparently most 'extreme' forms. Indeed, Zizek (2002: 133) suggests that the link between resurgent Islam and European fascism in the earlier parts of the twentieth century is valid in the sense that both are attempts to have 'capitalism without capitalism'; that is, they are attempts to benefit from all that modern economies can offer without suffering societal fragmentation. It is also important to note, however, that the particular character of the Islamic resurgence reflects resources specific to this religious tradition: the 'authoritarian' characteristics of this resurgence, to Western eyes, reflect Islam's rejection of the distinction between temporal and spiritual power central to Christian history (Bat Ye'or, 1996: 256; Lewis, 2002: 96), and the fact that it does not have the emphasis on the uniqueness of individuals that Christianity has bequeathed to Western societies (Siedentop, 2000: 209; Polanyi, 2001: 268). In this regard, resurgent Islam also follows Polanyi's model in its antipathy to democracy, a point that can be developed by returning to Barber's discussion of Islam.

Although Fukuyama's (1992) *The End of History* has been interpreted as an assertion of post-Cold War Western superiority, it has also been suggested that the events of September 11th and their aftermath have called its conclusions into question (Kellner, 2002: 147). In a recent comment on these issues, however, Fukuyama (2002: 58) has reasserted his view of the eventual triumph of democracy and liberal politics over what he calls 'Islamo-fascism'. For him, Islam is an inherently anti-modern religion whose power and influence has been boosted by economic and cultural problems relating to modernisation processes: arguing that hostility to the West is characteristic not only of a Muslim minority, he none the less believes that Muslims will eventually prefer the benefits of Western consumption over Islamic authoritarianism (Turner, 2002: 110). Such secularist triumphalism has been rejected by Barber, who not only views the relationship between democracy and consumption as being far more problematic than this, but who also offers a more considered account of the possible interactions between various forms of religion and democratic politics, and a keener sense of the difficulties of achieving forms of social and religious consensus. Like Fukuyama, however, he fails to appreciate the continuing significance of Christian orientations for the development of democratic societies, and thereby underestimates the degree to which they underpin even his own arguments.

Although he notes de Tocqueville's argument that democracy depends upon religion (see also Bergson, 1979; Maritain, 1986), Barber (1995: 210) not only distinguishes democracy from any particular religious form, but also distinguishes it from modernity (which he defines in 'secular' terms). Consequently, although he notes that Islam is 'relatively inhospitable to democracy', and that Muslim societies are happier to import Western technology than Western social and political institutions, he none the less argues that democracy should not be associated with the corrosive secularism Muslims fear: on the contrary, democracy can accommodate Islamic beliefs and practices in the same way that it accommodates the 'fundamentalist' Protestantism of America's 'Christian Right' (Barber, 1995: 205–11). There are, however, two major problems with these arguments. First, they do not take sufficient account of the fact that the American experience of democracy does not simply 'accommodate' Protestant Christianity: it was *created* through it, and retains foundational assumptions about temporal and spiritual domains inherent to this religious tradition (Taylor, 1989: 399; O'Donovan, 1999: 245). Second, following from this, Barber's arguments leave him in a poor position from which to see how the religious assumptions in his own vision of how 'global democracy' might be secured. In this respect, it is notable that, in arguing for the necessity of a global 'civil society' to counteract the corrosive McDonaldization of the world, he returns to de Tocqueville's vision of nineteenth-century America as an embodiment of his democratic vision (Barber, 1995: 282).[5] He is in good company in this respect, since, as I discussed in Chapter 6, figures such as Rawls, in the USA, and Habermas, in Europe, have similar blind spots when it comes to religious presuppositions in their writings. Even so, while these problems with Barber's arguments raise questions about the nature and value of his analysis, they also direct our attention to broader questions about the role of Christianity in relation to contemporary Western societies.

Suicidal society

If the contemporary resurgence of religion can be seen as an attempt to recover 'a sacred foundation for the ordering of society' (Huntington, 1996: 96; Kepel, 1994: 2), then, for the West, this recovery necessitates an engagement with its Christian legacy. In this regard, it is worth noting that Payne's

(2003) use of Huntington's clash of civilisations thesis to elucidate the complex role of Orthodox Christianity in Greek society, and the tensions between Orthodox theology and European notions of Human Rights that arise out of Catholic and Protestant traditions, suggests the continuing vitality of this 'sacred foundation', in certain societies at least. Similarly, numerous studies such as that of Wanner (2003) testify to the growing importance of revitalised forms of Christianity in Eastern Europe. Nevertheless, thinking principally of the USA and Western Europe, Huntington's book concludes with a vision of a 'suicidal' Western civilisation, despite the more optimistic tone of some of his statements elsewhere. Here, it should be noted that the continuing strength of American forms of Christianity in private and public life suggests limits to such claims with regard to the USA (see Warner, 1993; Casanova, 1994), though the greater strength of self-consciously 'secular' perspectives within Western Europe, which often align themselves with 'multicultural' repudiations of the West's religious heritage, underlines the suggestiveness of Huntington's analysis. Here, echoing Durkheim's (1995: 315) account of how societies die when the beliefs, traditions and aspirations of the collectivity are no longer felt by individuals, he discusses the decline of civilisations in similar terms, and raises questions about the West's will to renew itself (Huntington, 1996: 303).

Virilio's (2002) post-September 11th critique of Western societies, while arising out of a very different tradition of thought to that of Huntington, offers a complementary, though even harsher, assessment of the 'suicidal' state of Western civilisation. For Virilio (2002: 10), the history of the modern West can be read as a striving to be 'rid of God', though this is not an argument about 'secularisation'. Indeed, within his Catholic perspective, this striving has been a key aspect of certain forms of Protestantism, such as Calvinism, where the doctrine of predestination and an iconoclastic suspicion of human embodiment encouraged a broader, nihilistic 'hatred of matter' (Virilio, 2002: 11–12). It is in the modern 'techno-scientific imagination', however, that this striving reaches its most extreme, 'Satanic', form since humanity becomes enslaved to the pursuit of an immortality, beyond good and evil, that ultimately results in the elimination of the human (Virilio, 2002: 16, 19, 28). Consequently, for him, the suicidal nihilism of the Islamic terrorists on September 11th has to be placed alongside the suicidal 'techno-scientific mysticism' of the West (Virilio, 2002: 37). Indeed, he interprets the September 11th attacks as *Satanic*, precisely because the 'rich Muslim students, military men and technicians' involved in these terrorist acts had fallen 'inadvertently into the biblical company of Lucifer' through their acceptance of the promise of modern techno-scientific progress emanating from the West (2002: 66). While these arguments have a characteristically apocalyptic tone, Zizek's (2002) more measured assessment of the same events has some similar features.

Along with Virilio, Zizek (2002: 40) identifies a nihilistic tendency within the West as well as among the Islamic terrorists, which he associates with Nietzsche's account of 'passive' and 'active' forms of nihilism respectively. Also agreeing with Virilio, he rejects the notion that Islam has any innate propensity to violence and, instead, interprets the 'clash of civilisations' as a clash *within* the one dominant civilisation of global capitalism (Zizek, 2002: 41). Indeed, he suggests that 'the Muslim fundamentalists are not true fundamentalists, they are already "modernists", a product and a phenomenon of global capitalism – they stand for the way the Arab world strives to accommodate itself to global capitalism' (Zizek, 2002: 52). There is an element of economic reductionism in Zizek's argument here: he explicitly says so, in fact (Zizek, 2002: 42), but his argument is also notable in that, like Virilio, the events of September 11th are somehow deemed to be the West's own fault. Rather than locating this fault in the 'Satanic' temptations of techno-science, however, Zizek's arguments are closer to those of Barber in focusing on the destructive implications of global capitalism, though he goes further than Barber in the sense that *jihad* is not an act of *resistance* to capitalism, but a further manifestation of the nihilism it actively endorses. Leaving aside the fact that Zizek's economic reductionism effectively robs the Muslim terrorists of any moral responsibility for the killing of thousands of people, such arguments at least have the merit of directing our attention to questions about the sort of societies Western democracies have become. Indeed, just as Virilio (2002: 79) talks of 'our enfeebled, senile democracies', Zizek (2002: 64–5) discusses how European and American societies are increasingly losing their grip on social reality through the relativism, multiculturalism and solipsism encouraged by the globalised spread of market forces. In this regard, Zizek is worth discussing further since, while he resists the apocalyptic Christian Messianism of Virilio, he none the less argues for the necessity of building on the West's Christian legacy, even in a society that understands itself as 'multicultural'.

Although Huntington finds it difficult to imagine the Christian foundation of Western civilisation disappearing completely, he criticises the dominant ethos of 'multiculturalism' for actively denying the European religious, philosophical and political heritage, and thereby promoting a cultural amnesia that will make the West vulnerable to internal decay and external threats (Huntington, 1996: 305). While it is all too easy to dismiss such arguments as 'conservative ideology' (Kellner, 2002: 148), it is notable that they are also echoed in those more radical political writings cognisant of the fact that multiculturalism emerged as the more progressive forms of politics associated with socialism fell into decline (Zaretsky, 1995: 245). Here, the real coexistence of different religious and cultural orientations is not the issue: what is subjected to criticism is multiculturalism as an *ideology*.

The ideological aspects of multiculturalism have been discussed by a number of writers (Vertovec, 1996; Hjerm, 2000; Alexander, 2001). These aspects can take quite different forms, ranging from a commitment to a 'relativising universalism' that anticipates the development of an intercultural global society, through to a valorisation of difference that appears to reject any form of universalism (Alexander, 2001: 237). In each of these forms, however, there is an ideological critique of existing or historical patterns of

Western societies, and an expressed desire to move towards some sort of 'post-national, multicultural polity' (Werbner, 2003; see Commission, 2000). A key feature of 'multiculturalism' in this sense is the philosophical and political *disaggregation* of social totalities into a multiplicity of differences: thus, the identification 'American', for example, has to be prefaced by some disaggregating signifier relating to race, gender, sexuality and so forth (Zaretsky, 1995: 244).

Yet, as Zizek (2002: 64–6) argues, this concern for differences operates, paradoxically, as a *hegemonic ideology*, where 'Hollywood meets the most radical postcolonial critique of ideological universality' in their common advocacy of 'an infinite task of translation, a constant reworking of one's own position' that reduces the attempt to grasp universality into an ultimately solipsistic 'respect for Otherness'. Here, the advocacy of multiculturalism effectively denies the reality of society and the reality of a common humanity, thereby frustrating the possibility of real religious, moral and political critique. In this respect, it is worth recalling that Braidotti's (1994 12–13) 'nomadism', discussed in Chapter 2, places a very strong emphasis upon the importance of multiculturalism within particular societies, and even within the self, rather than simply across different types of society (see also Minh-ha, 1989), but does so within a philosophical system that 'despises mainstream communication' and 'common sense', and endorses a highly subjectivist account of what constitutes culture and society (Braidotti, 1994: 16). For Zizek (2002: 78), such postmodern relativisations of any notion of truth grounded in the reality of humanity and society not only constitute an essentially *reactionary* retreat from real engagement with the world into a comfortable subjectivism, but also exhibit a *deception* : the multiculturalist 'respect for Otherness' conceals an inability to engage with others as they really are. For Zizek (2002: 90), it is this deception that explains the liberal endorsement of 'moderate' Islam against its 'fundamentalist' forms: it is 'the tolerant liberal version of the "war on terrorism" which ultimately wants to save Muslims themselves from the fundamentalist threat'.

Zizek's reassertion of the reality of humanity and society in order to develop a satisfactory critique of contemporary social and cultural forms has been echoed in other writings emanating from the Marxist tradition of social theory. Michael Burawoy's (2003: 193) combination of Gramsci's theory of 'civil society' and Polanyi's Christian socialist critique of economic reductionism, for example, argues that a satisfactory form of social theory must 'give pride of place to society alongside but distinct from state and economy'. What is notable about Burawoy's arguments is that, although they are framed in the terms of a 'Sociological Marxism', they draw upon those aspects of Gramsci's and Polanyi's work that are most suggestive of a Durkheimian influence. It has been noted before that Gramsci's 'hegemony' resonates with Durkheim's 'collective conscience', and Weber's concern with the social ethics of religions, in making sense of both the 'spontaneous', 'religious' consent of the masses to the prevailing social order, and the generation of social and moral solidarity (Lockwood, 1992: 325). Burawoy (2003: 219) builds on this, and Polanyi's concern with the reaction of society to market forces, to argue that classical Marxism was too focused on the functioning of states to appreciate the crucial role of society in providing a substratum of beliefs, values, ideas and orientations that can endorse or challenge particular state forms. What Burawoy neglects, however, is the religious dimensions of Polanyi's arguments. In contrast, Zizek's reassertion of the reality of humanity and society against postmodern relativism follows Polanyi in taking an explicitly Christian form.

Charitable society

Zizek's (2000) *The Fragile Absolute* is a Marxist defence of the West's 'Christian legacy'. For him, the 'return of the religious dimension' in much contemporary social and cultural life is, in many respects, deplorable because it is manifest, in the West, as an obscurantist postmodern 'spiritualism' that dissolves social reality into a multiplicity of meaningless flows (see Heelas, 1996). In contrast, what he finds in Christianity, uniquely among all religious forms, is a belief that 'the *temporal* Event of Incarnation is the only path to eternal truth and salvation. In this precise sense, Christianity is a "religion of Love": in love, one singles out, focuses on, a temporal object which "means more than anything else"' (Zizek, 2000: 96). Here, for Zizek, the struggle to grasp objective meaning in a world of particularity and difference becomes the most pressing religious demand placed upon individuals and societies: contrary to postmodern theory, people cannot be reduced into symbolic codifications of 'Otherness' which offer opportunities for self-realisation, but are real, unavoidable *neighbours* whose very particularity confronts the individual with universal demands and obligations that cannot be ignored (Zizek, 2000: 109). This is why, for him, a proper engagement with the nature of society in the contemporary Western world necessarily involves an engagement with its Christian legacy. In this regard, it is notable that, in reference to Saint Paul, Zizek (2000: 145–6) recalls the fundamental principle of *charity* that, as I discussed in Chapter 5, provided the religious basis for medieval conceptions of social life that have cast their shadow over Western views of society ever since.[6]

It has already been noted that, historically, the highest Christian calling has been the nurturing of the 'social miracle', where salvation and social solidarity were inseparably linked (Bossy, 1985: 57), and that contemporary theology's greatest challenge can still be found in the illumination of ultimate truth through the emergent convictions and experiences arising from 'the social sub-structure of knowledge' (Torrance, 1985: 112). Zizek's invocation of charity as the social and religious medium through which particularity and universality are reconciled not only points to the continuing vitality of this religious tradition of thought, even in the unlikely setting of cultural studies, but also touches upon a number of important considerations regarding some of the conflicts, divisions and problems surrounding

Western societies that are of broader social and sociological significance. Above all, it suggests that there are three identifiable routes through contemporary social and cultural complexity, and that only one of them builds on the humane values inherent to the West's religious and moral legacy. In terms of the 'clash of civilisations', the first of these routes involves identifying Islam as the 'enemy' of Western civilisation, and preparing for the state of 'total war' envisaged by Virilio (2002: 82); the second, indicative of the 'passive nihilism' discussed by Zizek (2002: 40), involves the relativisation of real religious, moral and political problems within a vacuous multiculturalist ideology; the third route, however, engages directly with the West's religious legacy and endorses neither nihilism nor a false utopianism. On this route, moral obligations towards others are recognised as the foundations of all human social relationships, and these are understood to be as unavoidable as they are beyond deconstruction. Such a route does not, of course, have anything to do with naïve assumptions about the goodwill of others: the letter of Saint Paul to which Zizek refers was written when Christians faced persecution and death. In this respect, the manifest jubilation amongst many Muslims after September 11th cannot be taken lightly (Barber, 2001: xv). Nevertheless, within this tradition, the obligation to behave with charity towards others remains inviolable even if others do not recognise it.

Zizek's invocation of charity is also significant, however, with regard to those forces within Western societies that seek to deny the reality of society, whether this is done on the basis of an economistic individualism or the foundationless constructionism of postmodern philosophy. As I have suggested at a number of points throughout this study, social and cultural theories offering post-societal or post-social visions of the contemporary world tend, despite their philosophical differences in other respects, to reinforce the nominalist view of society promoted by neo-classical economic theory and those sociological forms of sociology influenced by them. In Polanyi's terms, they endorse a 'liberal' philosophical view of social reality that denies its *sui generis* aspects, which helps explain why both post-societal sociology (Urry, 2000) and rational choice theory (Stark and Bainbridge, 1985, 1987) tend to define themselves against the sociological realism of Durkheimian theory. Such theories and philosophies do not exist in a social vacuum, however. On the contrary, they have arisen within a broader 'pattern of derision and contempt for dependence' that directly confronts the religious underpinnings of Western civilisation (Bauman, 2001: 72). Here, the biblical injunction to be 'my brother's keeper', which confronts humanity with the ontological fact of mutual dependence, and forms the basis of the Western moral tradition, is not only ignored but actively dismissed as states cut back welfare provision and put more and more areas of social life at the mercy of 'markets' of one sort or another (Bauman, 2001: 72).

While Bauman (2001: 80) argues that this biblical injunction manifests the human quality of a society and the measure of its ethical standard, many contemporary social and cultural theories elect to follow one of the two routes through contemporary complexity that seek to abandon the West's religious legacy. Thus, mirroring the nihilistic vision of a 'total war' between civilisations, some forms of social theory (such as rational choice based approaches) offer a Hobbesian vision of social life as a mass of competing self-interests forever on the brink of a war of all against all. On the other hand, mirroring the 'passive nihilism' of multiculturalism, social theories influenced by postmodern philosophy abandon the engagement with social reality for what is often a highly subjectivised exploration of notions such as 'hybridity', 'nomadism', or *différance*. As Zizek (2002: 86) has suggested, however, social reality does not disappear just because postmodern sociologists no longer know what it is: on the contrary, it just continues on its course, often throwing up challenges and dangers that necessitate careful, considered thought. It might be said, indeed, that the whole 'clash of civilisations' problem appeared while many sociologists were just not paying attention to social reality. Even after September 11th, however, Touraine (2003), for example, persists in his attempts to redefine sociology as the study of the *absence* of society, the disappearance of social actors, and the destruction of social bonds. While this sort of disciplinary development is not unique – the emergence of forms of 'negative theology' focused on the 'death of God' prefigure it – it is not only bizarre but, as Bauman's focus on moral obligation implies, irresponsible.

Discussing the ethical theories of Levinas (1974) and Løgstrup (1997), Bauman (2001: 171, emphasis in original) emphasises that both of them 'posit responsibility as the *never ending, eternal human condition*', and the fact that this ethical demand is a pre-rational presence in our social relations, forever demanding that 'the word is made flesh'. In Bauman's case, it is the presence of this ethical demand that ensures his sociological work has a persistent moral dimension, that underpins his case for a 'sociology of postmodernism' rather than a 'postmodern sociology', and that means his account of 'society under siege' is a critique rather than a celebration (Bauman, 1992a, 2002).

In this regard, Zizek's (2000) suggestion that charity acts as the social and religious medium through which particularity and universality can be reconciled and Michael Walzer's (1994: 1–11) argument that human society 'is universal because it is human, particular because it is society' have much in common with Bauman's moral vision of sociology. What both Zizek and Walzer are keen to emphasise is that there are certain universal aspects of the human condition, and that there are certain universal moral obligations inseparable from these, though they cannot be apprehended apart from their particular societal contexts. Huntington (1996: 318) uses Walzer's argument to support his case for an approach to international politics that seeks to recognise commonalities, accept diversity and renounce universalism. Zizek's approach has much in common with this but, like that of Bauman (2001), demands more: in this approach the universal religious and moral obligations that emerge from, and have to be exercised within, the particularity of human social relationships mean that a sensitivity to social and cultural diversity cannot slip into a relativism that endorses moral indifference or inaction. This is why, for both of them, tendencies towards the deconstruction of society in forms of utilitarian or postmodern thought have to be resisted: in the end, such approaches are thoroughly de-humanising, even if they appear in the garb of a celebration of cultural diversity.

Taken together, the arguments of Zizek, Walzer and Bauman also suggest a productive way out of the 'clash of civilisations' considered in this chapter. The analysis of the resurgence of religion and society offered here has pointed towards the inadequacy of those sociological visions of contemporary conflicts as 'chaotic' phenomena within post-societal 'global flows', and found much to endorse in Huntington's sensitivity to the importance of particular religious forms in understanding contemporary global conflicts. In this respect, Huntington's arguments that Islam can embrace modernity without embracing Western institutions and values, that the Islamic resurgence cannot be identified with an 'extreme' minority, and that Islam offers legitimations for violence not found in other traditions, should be taken seriously by sociologists, even if some of these arguments demand qualifications and raise further sets of questions. While the evidence of a number of assessments of the events of September 11th suggest the continuing lack of a serious engagement with the fundamental sociological significance of religion for society, however, the arguments of Zizek and Bauman, in particular, suggest that a proper reassessment of the Christian foundations of Western societies might provide contemporary social theory with some valuable resources for engaging with contemporary global challenges and conflicts: rather than accepting those visions of a dichotomous structuring of social reality offered by either Huntington or by Islamic accounts of the 'lands of Muslims' and the 'lands of war', what the Christian notion of charity demands is a real attentiveness to irreducible difference and particularity that cannot be separated from a sense of solidarity and moral responsibility that is universal and inviolable.[7] The necessity of further sociological reflection upon this notion can be illuminated by recalling Durkheim's arguments concerning the moral dimensions of sociology which, despite other differences, have much in common with the arguments offered by Zizek and Bauman.

As Jenkins (1998: 91) has noted, for Durkheim, the sociologist expresses and participates in the circulation of those social forces that are described and analysed in sociological studies. In other words, since sociology 'participates in these forces, it may contribute to them: the sociological vocation is inescapably political and ethical, because it is a human practice'. This understanding of sociology departs from the naïve objectivism of positivist visions of a 'value-free' social science, and from the extreme relativism of postmodern philosophies (see Sayer, 2000: 174–5). It demands that sociologists take responsibility for the arguments, implications and consequences of their academic work, since these surely have some sort of an effect upon the collaborative endeavour that is human life, however modest, contingent and limited they might be. In this regard, shying away from difficult questions about the real challenges and conflicts emergent from different religious and societal contexts is both sociologically unsustainable and morally irresponsible, as is that collective amnesia, widespread amongst sociologists, concerning the specifically Christian foundations of Western societies. On the other hand, however, allowing the recognition of difference to evolve into visions of dichotomous civilisations that discount the common human characteristics, potentialities and obligations that underpin divergent forms of society is not only likely to provoke further conflicts, but is also sociologically questionable in that it ignores the complex human dynamics through which social realities are consituted.

Further to this, Zizek's (2000) invocation of the Christian understanding of charity in order to grasp universal demands and obligations in a world of real, unavoidable neighbours cannot be dismissed as simply a reflection of his theological commitments. It is also thoroughly sociological, in Durkheim's sense of the term, in that it takes seriously the irreducible reality of society and the moral responsibility of the analyst in seeking objective meaning in a world of particularity and difference, thereby seeking to make a positive contribution to the development of the social dynamics in which all human beings participate. It is also sociological, however, in its recognition of the fact that a proper engagement with the emergent particularity and difference that is contingent upon universal human characteristics and potentialities necessitates a fresh engagement with the Christian legacy for the Western world since, as Durkheim (1982b: 211) proposed, sociology cannot ignore the historical contexts out of which particular forms of social and cultural life emerge. To neglect such considerations, in favour of the sort of 'negative sociology' offered by writers such as Touraine, would surely prove fatal to any attempt to develop a satisfactory understanding of contemporary Western societies and the challenges they face in a context of increasing global complexity, and might also stimulate further movement towards the sort of 'clash of civilisations' discussed by Huntington. As Polanyi's analysis of an earlier period of history makes clear, an inability to grasp the complex reality that constitutes a society, including its essential religious dimensions, is liable to result in dangerous forms of counter-movements. In view of this, contemporary sociology should avoid replicating the errors of an earlier generation of liberal philosophers, and should, therefore, resist the temptations of those 'active' and 'passive' forms of nihilism that deny the reality of society and those religious forces that give a society its particular characteristics (Zizek, 2002: 40).

Notes

1. The fact that the Qur'an legitimates violence against those who are deemed to be enemies of Islam is surely incontrovertible: it urges Muslims to 'fight in the way of God with those who fight with you ... And slay them wherever you come upon them' (Sura 2: 186; see also Sura 22: 40); it emphasises that, 'Prescribed for you is fighting, though it be hateful to you' (Sura 2: 214); it stresses that Muslims must 'slay the idolaters wherever you find them, and take them, and confine them, and lie in wait for them at every place of ambush' (Sura 9: 5; see also Sura 4: 90); it says 'When you meet the unbelievers, smite their necks' and make 'wide slaugh-

ter among them' (Sura 47: 4); and it urges Muslims to embrace martyrdom, saying that 'whoso-ever fights in the way of God and is slain, or conquers, We shall bring him a mighty wage' (Sura 4: 76; see also Sura 9: 125). The fact that the Qur'an is understood to be the unmediated Word of God, rather than the Word of God mediated through humans (as in the case of the Christian and Hebrew Bibles), and the fact that Muhammad himself spread Islam through military con-quest, reinforce the seriousness with which these texts concerning *jihad* must be taken since they limit the degree to which Qur'anic texts can be reinterpreted in the light of changed social and cultural circumstances (see Rippin and Knappert, 1986; Lewis, 2002).

2. Bat Ye'or (1996: 40) argues that, in Islamic tradition, 'Mankind is divided into two groups, Muslims and non-Muslims. The former compose the Islamic community, the *umma*, who own the territories of the *dar al-Islam* governed by Islamic law. Non-Muslims are *harbis*, inhabitants of the *dar al-harb*, the lands of war, so called because they are destined to come under Islamic jurisdiction, either by war (*harb*), or by the conversion of their inhabitants … every act of war in the *dar al-harb* is legal and immune from censure'. For Ellul (1996: 21), in the light of this historical study, Islamic 'terrorism' is not an 'extreme' perversion of this reli-gion, but a return to its traditional policy (see also Pipes, 2003).

3. This equation ignores the fact that *jihad* was a feature of Islam from the start, manifest in the examples of Muhammad and his early followers and legitimated by the Qur'an (Lewis, 2002). In contrast, all the New Testament Gospels agree that Christ admonished those of his disciples who resorted to the sword when the authorities came to arrest him (Matthew 26: 47; Mark, 14: 48; Luke, 22: 47; John, 18: 11), while, more generally, non-violence is repeatedly held up as a Christian ideal (e.g. Matthew, 5: 9, 38). Furthermore, Christianity existed for over a thousand years before the first Crusade, which itself cannot be considered apart from questions about European reactions to Islamic military activity (Bat Ye'or, 1996: 89, 140, 49–50; Lewis, 2002: 4).

4. Fukuyama's (2002) notion of 'Islamo-fascism' is a highly problematic one since, contrary to Huntington, he not only believes that Islam and modernity are essentially incompatible, but also equates modernity with essentially Western values to do with democracy and individual freedom: in this view, the link between Islam and fascism is made in the sense that Islam is deemed, like fascism, to be a dangerous but temporary reaction to the gradual universalisation of these values.

5. It is also notable that Barber (1995: 293) presents Pat Buchanan's critique of the myth of 'Economic Man' as an embodiment of the new 'American Jihad' launched by conservative Christians, but his own critique of the economic reductionism and imperialism of 'McWorld' has exactly the same intention, namely the constraint of economic forces by a robust 'civil soci-ety'.

6. The biblical text reads as follows: 'If I speak in the tongues of mortals and of angels, but do not have love, I am a noisy gong or a clanging cymbal. And if I have prophetic powers, and understand all mysteries and all knowledge, and if I have all faith, so as to remove mountains, but do not have love, I am nothing. If I give away all my possessions, and if I hand over my body so that I may boast, but do not have love, I gain nothing … Love never ends. But as for prophe-cies, they will come to an end; as for tongues they will cease; as for knowledge, it will come to an end. For we know only in part, and we prophesy only in part; but when the complete comes, the partial will come to an end … For now we see in a mirror, dimly, but then we will see face to face. Now I know only in part; then I will know fully, even as I have been fully known. And now faith, hope and love abide, these three; and the greatest of these is love' (1 Corinthians 13; Zizek, 2000: 146).

7. Anthropological research on Muslim charitable practices has noted significant common-alities with Judaeo-Christian traditions, but also that Muslims are often reluctant to extend charity beyond the confines of their own communities (Benthall, 2002: 2). This might reflect the fact that the Qur'an endorses the importance of charity very strongly (Sura 107), but also says 'Let not the believers take the unbelievers for their friends, rather than the believers' (Sura 3: 25, see also Sura 3: 113).

8

Conclusion

In the course of this book, it has been argued that many theoretical critiques of the notion of society have offered views of social life insufficiently sensitive to the fact that human beings, even when they are postmodern social and cultural theorists, cannot avoid what Archer (1995) has aptly called 'the vexatious fact of society'. For Archer, society is a 'vexatious' phenomenon because it is of human constitution, yet resistant to individual and collective efforts to transform it in accordance with particular ideals and projects, and because it often changes in ways that no one wants. Furthermore, it constrains our actions even when we are reflexively aware of our roles in it through our own activity (Archer, 1995: 1–2). While this understanding of society's 'vexatious' characteristics focuses on the stubborn resistance of societal forms to particular human projects, however, Durkheim (1982a: 57) offers a more positive vision of society as *a collective way of being* emergent from, and expressive of, what it is to be human. Common to both, however, is the recognition that society is a real, unavoidable phenomenon for human beings and, by implication, for social theory.

It is this recognition that has shaped the social realist arguments developed over the preceding chapters. In building these arguments, each chapter has been structured around various representations of society within a broad range of social and cultural theories. The principal focus of each chapter, however, has been on the elucidation of one of six dimensions of society that can help revitalise its sociological study, and reveal the over-hastiness of those who seek to abandon it for post-societal forms of sociology. The dimensions discussed here have not, of course, offered an exhaustive account of all that society is. None the less, each dimension was chosen in order to illuminate a distinctive and important aspect of society, and to demonstrate the value of returning religious concerns to the centre of sociological theory. The conclusions that can be drawn from each of these chapters reinforce the sense that society is a 'vexatious' reality in several senses.

As I argued in Chapter 2, a characteristic of many forms of contemporary social theory, and not only those that adopt notions of a 'post-societal' or 'post-social' age, is the resort to various forms of linguistic, technological or economic reductionism. Because society is a multidimensional reality, however, constituted as an inter-relational, *sui generis* totality, it is resistant to such reductionism. This is not to say that such forms of social theory have nothing to contribute to the analysis of contemporary social and cultural life, only that they fail to deal with the *complexity* of society in a satisfactory way. It is clearly the case that sociologies centred on technological or economic changes, for example, capture something true about the way the world is today, and that they can help illuminate some of the difficulties inherent to the development of a satisfactory understanding of society.

Many of these approaches, however, seem to presuppose that humanity and society are infinitely malleable forms subject to endless reconstruction. Consequently, they tend to exaggerate the world reconstructing power of particular types of phenomena, allowing the notion of society to disappear into informational flows or global markets, depending upon which authors we read.

What the complexity theories developed in the natural sciences have emphasised, however, is that reality has to be apprehended as 'interconnected wholeness' characterised by specific ontological features (Adam, 1990: 59). By analogy, the evident partiality characteristic of some contemporary social theories can only be overcome by appreciating that society is also a complex totality, possessing specific ontological characteristics emergent from the embodied human beings who constitute it. This is important, because without sufficient attentiveness to the ontological dimensions of society as a complex reality, social theorists can find themselves being lured into making all sorts of extreme, and often highly implausible, claims about the contemporary world. Within some social theories, for example, a wholly unconstrained excitement nurtured by some technological developments leads to visions of the 'disappearance' of society, humanity and religion that look more like science fiction than sociological analysis. A prime example of this type of thing is provided by Baudrillard (1988a: 51), who claims that 'for mutants there can no longer be any Last Judgement ... for what body will one resurrect?' (see Gane, 2003: 161). Within contemporary social and cultural theory, however, Baudrillard's claim is by no means an eccentric one.

Urry's (2000: 77–8) rejection of a 'species-specific' model of sociology in favour of focus on various human/technological 'hybrids', and Haraway's (1991) interest in 'cyborg cultures', for example, complement Baudrillard's vision of our 'mutant' present. In this regard, it is worth noting that Urry's model allows him to see religious organisations such as Al-Qaida as 'mutant' forms constituted through technological flows and networks (Urry, 2003: 132). The problem with such views, aside from the fact that moral questions about killing people for religious reasons are obscured by the language of science fiction, is that they not only ignore the degree to which many contemporary social forms can depend upon beliefs, practices and traditions that have deep roots in the *longue durée* of human history, even if they currently express themselves, in part, through electronic communications media, but also that they fail to account satisfactorily for those sensual, emotional, cognitive and moral capacities that ensure our social reality is indeed a 'species-specific' phenomenon, characteristically constituted in the awareness of our own mortality (Bauman, 1992b). Consequently, it is hardly surprising that writers such as Castells (1998), who appears to believe that humans can be reconfigured like computers, can regard Christianity as a bizarre relic of an entirely different world, while others can view Al-Qaida as a 'virtual community', putting it on a par with New Age newsgroups and other manifestations of postmodern lifestyle choices mediated through the Internet (Urry, 2000: 43, 209; Barber, 1995; Rose, 1996).

In view of such arguments, it is hardly a surprise that some have claimed 'social theory has failed intellectually', or that they have accused it of promoting a 'culture of the ephemeral' in sociology, since a 'portentous vocabulary' cannot, in the long run, conceal the lack of a proper engagement with reality (Abell and Reyniers, 2000). To counter such charges against social theory, and to build a more satisfactory account of the ontological dimensions of society as a complex reality, a crucial starting point must be a proper engagement with the real human beings who constitute society. Further to this, as I discussed in Chapter 3, it is important to recognise that society is a *contingent* reality, dependent for its emergence upon the embodied potentialities and powers of human beings. In this regard, one of the most difficult tasks confronting social theory is the problem of how to make sense of some of the most elementary capacities and forces that enable societies to develop and be maintained. Abell and Reyniers (2000: 749), in an attempt to eliminate the 'banalities and truisms' that they believe mark contemporary social theory, argue for the importance of 'technical expertise' in the development of sociological theories, criticising those who have sought 'to construct social theory largely in an "arts" framework as a non-technical endeavour'. None the less, when we are dealing with human beings (and society is a *human* reality) the limitations of such views are all too apparent: the frailties endemic to human life, the reflexive and practical engagement with lived experience, the emotional and moral responses stimulated by inter-relationships, and the contagious circulation of religious forces all testify to a dynamic aspect to social life that cannot be contained within a narrowly 'technical' discourse.

Following Durkheim, I have suggested that reflection upon the contingent character of society illuminates its 'hyper-spiritual' aspects, and the fact that it is possessed of an open-ended, transcendent dimension that necessarily gives rise to emergent religious forms. To some, of course, the notion of 'hyper-spirituality' might, just as much as Castells's (2000) talk of 'timeless time' and the 'space of flows', suggest a 'portentous vocabulary' divorced from the 'technical issues' that should be central to sociological theory. As I have argued, however, sociology has a long history of recognising, and trying to make sense of, some sort of holistic substratum of social energies or forces that underpins a society's more institutionalised dimensions. Here, it is important to stress that not everything in society is immediately available for empirical scrutiny, particularly with regard to the 'enhancement of being' that emerges from our social relationships (Freitag, 2002). The notion of hyper-spirituality, however, goes some way towards accounting for the power of societies to shape human thought and experience, especially in relation to their capacities for directing human consciousness beyond empirical factors towards a fuller grasp of the ontological strata within which individuals and communities make sense of themselves and the world. Rowan Williams's (2000: 59) exploration of the theological possibilities inherent within such a pre-contractual, collective way of being helps illuminate the suggestiveness of this notion for understanding how life in society qualitatively transforms human individuals.

The notion of hyper-spirituality therefore points towards the elementary social, and sociological, significance of religion as a collective engagement with the possibilities of transcendence emergent from the potentialities and limitations of embodied human life, though I have stressed that it is important to see religion as an emergent but *irreducible* phenomenon if we are to appreciate its immense power over the development of individuals and societies. Archer (2000: 185–6) captures the essence of this particular relationship between emergence and irreducibility when she stresses the embodied basis for the development of particular forms of knowledge and experience, before going on to discuss Christianity as a total way of life that radically transforms belief and action. In the writings of Mauss (1969, 1973) and Gurvitch (1964, 1971) the interest in society as a 'total' phenomenon illuminates further the complex intertwining of religious elements within a broad range of social and cultural phenomena. Further to this, the notion of hyper-spirituality helps reveal the limitations of those theoretical approaches that, even if they do not ignore religion completely, treat it as an epiphenomenon of economic, political or technological forces: it might be said, in fact, that such approaches fail to appreciate the full implications of the fact that society is of human constitution.

Consequently, reflection upon the contingency of society, rather than reinforcing some contemporary social constructionist views of the arbitrariness and relativity of particular societal forms, strongly endorses the view that societies have some irreducible characteristics of fundamental sociological significance. In this regard, the discussion of the *necessary* dimensions of society, offered in Chapter 4, further refuted the constructionist view of social reality and dealt with the 'vexatious' character of society directly. Here, it was emphasised that taboos and other rituals of inclusion and exclusion direct the sociological imagination towards obligatory aspects of society and their intimate relationship with forms of social solidarity. More broadly, however, the arguments of Mauss, Bataille and Polanyi were considered as key resources for illuminating how even the most radical economic transformations of the modern world have to be assessed in relation to the hyper-spiritual and religious aspects of society. Further to this, some of the ambiguous characteristics of society were emphasised, including the possibility of authoritarian reassertions of social reality against market forces. In the light of these arguments, the idea that contemporary individuals are free of obligations, rules and traditions can be exposed as a fantasy; on the contrary, since social realities have what Mauss called a 'total' character, they offer all sorts of possibilities for human potentialities to flourish but also impose constraints and obligations upon people that we ignore at our peril. In this chapter it was argued, for example, that the development of fascism and communism in the early twentieth century, and the appearance of violent anti-globalisation movements at that century's end, could all be interpreted as reassertions of society against utilitarian and individualistic currents that sought to undermine its reality.

Sociological accounts of the endless choices and possibilities open to contemporary individuals, however, which focus on 'disembedding mechanisms', and underplay, if not ignore, the degree to which individuals remain embedded in society in other ways, tend to operate with a 'discontinuist' view of history (Giddens, 1990). In their extreme forms, statements concerning the development of 'high modernity', or even the appearance of a 'postmodern' era, can look relatively modest and understated alongside more radical sociological accounts of the contemporary post-societal, post-human and post-representational condition, where the announcement of the 'end of history' is trumped by altogether more ambitious claims about the 'end of time'. The appeal of such views is not hard to grasp. While Giddens's (1990, 1991a) own view of history is open to question, he is surely correct to identify a modern tendency to imagine that all links with the past have been deconstructed and that we live in an era of radical, all-pervasive change. It is this tendency that informs the desire to construct post-societal and post-social models of sociology, and that ensures classical theorists such as Durkheim must be thrown overboard as we set sail across global information flows towards our post-human future: the basic assumption is that he was writing a *century* ago, so how could he possibly have anything to say of relevance to the contemporary world, since everything has changed so radically?

Contrary to such views, a central argument of this book has been that societies must be understood as phenomena that develop across the *longue durée* of human history. In Chapter 5, focused on the *temporal* dimensions of society, the value of a social realist view of time was emphasised: here, it was argued that the irreversible temporal pattern of emergent social forms constitutes the reality within which humans exercise their agency. Consequently, and against the grain of social theories focused on notions of 'instantaneous' or 'timeless' time, I sought to establish the continuing importance of the fact that, across the *longue durée* of Western history, Christian theological perspectives have had an immense influence on the constitution of societies, even if their modern influence has often been obscured by the apparently 'secular' characteristics of Western societies. This claim was supported with regard to medieval visions of temporal and spiritual realities, the hardening up of these in the post-Reformation separation of religion and society, the emergence of social contract theories that elaborated upon this separation or sought to overcome it, and the subsequent incorporation of these concerns into classical and contemporary forms of sociology. A key idea emphasised here was that while Western societies became 'post-Christendom' societies, in the sense that the collective constitution of social life was divested of its *explicitly* theological character, they never became fully 'post-Christian': indeed, it is possible to see Western 'modernity' as the creation of Christianity rather than its secular aftermath (Bossy, 1985; Taylor, 1989; Ozment, 1992; Kumar, 1995; Siedentop, 2000). From this point of view, divergent patterns of sociological interpretation in

German, French and American traditions of thought can all be read as attempts to grapple with problems inherited from Christianity, ranging from a 'Protestant' focus on self-directing subjects constituting social orders through contracts to 'Catholic' accounts of the 'general will', 'general spirit' and the positive polity.

Building upon these arguments, the focus on the *tacit* dimensions of society in Chapter 6 offered an opportunity to illuminate the continuing significance of covert Christian influences upon Western societies. Through Michael Polanyi's (1967) notion of a 'tacit dimension' in society, and the theory of collective representations developed by Durkheim and others, this chapter examined the powerful role of Christianity in the constitution of forms of collective consciousness that are sometimes so fundamental they are simply taken for granted rather than being objects of reflexive scrutiny and critique. In this regard, some of the structures of, and values we place upon, everyday life, together with the division of social life into 'public' and 'private' realms, and the location of Islamic societies within Western patterns of representation, can all be read as examples of how a tacitly religious structuring of collective consciousness is evident within various strata of social reality. With regard to Rawls and Habermas, for example, it was argued that the stress on the need for religious commitments to be 'translated' into forms of 'public reason' or 'communicative rationality' conceals the fact that a prior translation has already taken place: the constitution of 'secular' forms of reason or rationality reflects the influence of specifically Protestant conceptions of the possibility of a religiously 'neutral' social space; conceptions central to those Christians who helped frame the First Amendment to the American Constitution (O'Donovan, 1999: 245).

Waldron's (2002: 238–9) comparison of Rawls and Locke is important, however, for drawing out some of the implications of the contemporary tendency to obscure, or deny, the specifically Christian foundations of many Western ways of thinking about the world and ourselves. As Waldron suggests, Rawls, like Locke, offers a political vision that rests on certain assumptions about equality and the fact that human persons are free agents possessing specific moral powers. For Locke, however, these assumptions are grounded in a firm belief in God and, consequently, political order has, ultimately, to reflect an underlying sense of religious order. For Rawls, on the other hand, the equality and moral powers of human beings are simply self-evident components of a general consensus regardless of particular religious viewpoints (which should be kept out of public life anyway). The weakness of this position is evident in the fact that many Nietzscheans, for example, would have told Rawls that 'all this moralistic talk of agency and moral personality was redundant and reducible nonsense' (Waldron, 2002: 239). In short, many people would not share his assumptions about human nature. To go further, however, it could be said that Rawls's assumptions are not self-evident at all, but depend upon a Christian theology he rejects. Because of this rejection, furthermore, a satisfactory defence of notions of equality and freedom could be compromised. Karl Polanyi's (2001: 268) account of how fascism negated Christian anthropology, and thereby obliterated freedom and democracy, is instructive in this regard.

For those theorists who adopt a more relativistic position than Rawls, however, there are also some potentially troubling aspects. In this regard, it is worth noting Nigel Biggar's (1997: 137) comments on the moral irresponsibility of those intellectuals who have used the individual freedoms nurtured by Christianity to espouse a value relativism that could ultimately deny these freedoms to others. Wildly overstated claims about the 'multicultural' nature of contemporary Western societies exacerbate these dangers, since these too suggest a highly selective engagement with the religious influences upon society. Similar things, though, can be said about those bold contemporary assertions concerning the 'breakdown of the social bond' and the appearance of a 'post-representational' world where social life is reduced to the computational problem of 'making sense of the information' (Lash and Featherstone, 2001). Not only do writers such as Bataille and Zizek, who have been called upon to endorse these views, strongly oppose such forms of reductionism, but they are, again, manifestly selective in their assessment of current trends. This is not to deny that some of the de-humanising processes discussed by such writers are taking place, only to emphasise that they have to be seen in a broader context. In fact, as de Certeau (1984), Maffesoli (1996) and Augé (1992), amongst others, have suggested, people are remarkably resistant to such trends in terms of their capacities for the domestication and subversion of economically or technologically driven projects for social purposes. Even Touraine (2003: 127–9), while asserting that the 'logic of the market' is now the 'non-existent social order', nevertheless notes the existence of a 'heterogeneous set of unfinished, local, barely institutionalised reconstructions of what is usually referred to as the social bond'.

These phenomena are not only evident at local levels, either: as Rumford (2003) has outlined, there is increasing interest amongst many sectors of the European population in the emergence of a new European society, for example, distinct from the political and economic institutions of the European Union. In this regard, it is again important to note that this resilience of society is matched by the persistence of those religious factors largely ignored by post-societal theorists. Although, in drawing up a draft Constitution for the EU in 2003, after much debate, all references to 'God' and 'Christianity' were excluded, with only a more general reference to Europe's 'religious history' included in the text, it is clear that the EU's Christian dimensions remain significant. In a manner not dissimilar to the construction of the US Constitution, the apparent secularity of the EU Constitution not only ignores the fact that the whole idea of 'Europe' is of Christian origin (Rémond, 1999: 109), but also that most of the major figures involved in the construction of the EU have been devoted Catholics (Hastings, 1997: 122). Here, then, although the Christian sources of an emerging trans-national form of society have been partially obscured, is further evidence that sociological denials of the reality of society and the contemporary significance of religion can be overstated (Siedentop, 2000).

Religion, like society, has 'vexatious' characteristics: although of human constitution, it has *sui generis* characteristics that ensure its resistance to those attempts by modern individuals to reflexively reconstruct it in the manner outlined by Giddens (1990), and that severely constrain the attempts of multi-national corporations to harness religious dynamics for commercial gain (Ritzer, 1999). Taken together, in fact, religion and society remain 'vexatious' for contemporary sociology precisely because they will not vanish into those global flows, aggregate outcomes or reflexively constructed lifestyle options that so beguile contemporary theorists. On the contrary, because they are emergent from embodied human potentialities and characteristics, they are unavoidable features of human life, and, by implication, should remain central features of sociological study. None the less, while my arguments in this respect have been developed on the basis of a critical discussion of Durkheim's understanding of society, and through a development of his view of the significance of the general, *sui generis* dimensions of social reality, my concern with *divergent* patterns of religious development has signalled a departure from his view that all religions 'fulfil the same needs, play the same role, and proceed from the same causes' (Durkheim, 1995: 3). This departure allowed for an appreciation of the historical and contemporary significance of specifically Christian influences upon Western societies, but it also facilitated a fresh assessment of the notion of the 'clash of civilisations' thesis offered by Huntington (1996).

In Chapter 7, the discussion was centred upon how this notion of a 'clash of civilisations' can help illuminate the fact that, rather than disappearing, society is actually a *resurgent* phenomenon. This chapter offered three main arguments. First, it was argued that, rather than accepting current impressions of a state of 'global disorder', an engagement with this notion reveals how it is sociologically important to recognise the contemporary existence of distinct 'civilisations' in the world, but that these must be understood as phenomena that emerge from societies and are embedded in them. Further to this, and building upon the arguments about the hyper-spiritual dimensions of society discussed in earlier chapters, it was argued that civilisations develop specific characters through the influence of their religious substrata. Second, it was argued that the global resurgence of Islam could be understood as a resurgence of *society*, rather than some sort of 'fundamentalist' rejection of modernity. Here, it was suggested that Durkheim's (1995) view of the ambiguous aspects of the sacred and society, and Karl Polanyi's (2001) arguments concerning the fact that society can forcibly reassert itself as a reality in the face of market forces, could help throw fresh light upon the Islamic resurgence. Third, it was argued that this resurgence, since it raises questions about the religious foundations of different types of society, provides a further stimulus to the reassessment of the Christian legacy for Western societies. In this respect, it was suggested that the arguments of Virilio (2002) and Zizek (2000, 2002) are particularly significant.

In the course of this discussion, some of the problems relating to

Huntington's (1996: 258) emphasis on a *general* 'Muslim propensity toward violent conflict' were noted, but it was also suggested that he raises legitimate questions about the degree to which different religious forms endorse different types of social action, particularly with regard to the huge differences between the Qur'an and the New Testament in this respect. What was also noted, however, was that sociological reflections upon the terrorist attacks on the Twin Towers on September 11th, 2001 studiously avoided such questions, preferring to endorse Barber's (2001: xv) bland generalisations about the essentially peaceful nature of all religions but for a few 'fundamentalists', or to offer economically reductionist arguments that failed to even raise the question of why Buddhist, Sikh or Hindu responses to the social fragmentation wrought by 'McWorld' have been so different from those in parts of the Islamic world. Here, the failure to take religion seriously as an elementary feature of societies as emergent human realities offers little hope for a satisfactory analysis of some of the conflicts shaping the world today, and certainly can offer little in the way of a constructive response to these. Indeed, Barber's (1995: 172) dislocation of the concept of *jihad* from its Islamic context, and its application to phenomena such as the revival of folk music in Brittany, not only trivialises religion sociologically, it is also morally questionable: given that sociologists participate in the social realities they analyse, they have a responsibility, as Durkheim understood, not to shy away from difficult questions and problems but to confront them directly and seek to make a positive contribution to their resolution. An inability to recognise that there is a fundamental difference between a fondness for traditional bagpipes and a religious injunction to 'slay the idolaters wherever you find them' (Sura 9: 5; see also Sura 4: 90) would not live up to Durkheim's vision of the sociological vocation.

In contrast, I have argued that Zizek's (2000) invocation of the Christian understanding of charity in order to grasp universal demands and obligations in a world of real, unavoidable neighbours is of immense sociological value, as well as being reflective of his theological commitments. Drawing upon Nietzsche's account of 'passive' and 'active' forms of nihilism, Zizek (2002: 40, 64–5) identifies a dangerous inability to deal with social reality evident in the relativism and solipsism that mark much of the contemporary world. His reassessment of the Christian legacy for Western societies, however, recognises that a proper engagement with real particularity and difference must build on the resources and traditions characteristic of the specific historical contexts out of which they emerge. Here, rather than identifying Islam as the 'enemy' of Western civilisation, and preparing for the state of 'total war' envisaged by Virilio (2002: 82), or endorsing the relativisation of real religious, moral and political problems through a vacuous form of multiculturalist ideology, it is accepted that moral obligations towards others are the foundations of all social relationships, and that these are as unavoidable as they are beyond deconstruction. This understanding of what living in society is all about explicitly invokes the 'social miracle' of Christendom (Bossy, 1985), but it also returns us to Durkheim's (1973) vision of society as a moral and a religious phenomenon, wherein the demands of solidarity force us to transcend the temptations of egoism and utilitarianism. As such, it is consistent with Durkheim's social realism, and with his account of the moral obligations incumbent upon the social analyst.

This account is, of course, markedly in contrast to the acquiescent 'post-societal' endorsement of economic and technological forces geared towards the 'hollowing out' of the religious, moral and human dimensions of societies. Touraine (2003: 125), for example, makes the case that 'Over the past few decades, the key to understanding the evolution of sociology has been the desire, whether explicit or not, to destroy the idea of society', but he offers little in the way of questions about the plausibility or desirability of this pattern of sociological evolution; on the contrary, he goes on to argue that, in consequence, we must develop a form of sociology focused on the 'disappearance of social actors' and the 'non-existence' of society. This serves as a *de facto* endorsement of some of the forces that undoubtedly impoverish humanity's contemporary social experience, and that seek to minimise the significance of societies in terms of the sustenance of common obligations, values and meanings. As Bauman's (2001, 2002) recent studies of 'society under siege' emphasise, these forces are significant and need to be taken seriously in the sociological analysis of society. They do not represent all that societies are, however, let alone all that they could be, and certainly cannot constitute benchmarks for satisfactory models of sociological analysis. Zizek's emphasis on the importance of charity, however, can usefully be held up as a reminder to sociologists that the analysis of society involves the engagement with human potentialities and characteristics, and with those emergent forms that simultaneously constrain human beings and allow them to flourish.

In this book, it has been emphasised that society is an emergent reality, contingent upon the embodied dispositions and potentialities of human beings, and characterised by a substratum of hyper-spiritual forces that facilitate the emergence of religious forms manifesting divergent conceptions of the 'transcendental conditions of human togetherness' (Hertz, 1983: 87; Bauman, 2002: 53–4). None of these different elements can be explained away with reference to market forces, technological developments, or the language games of cultural theory; on the contrary, they are real phenomena and making sense of them is located at the heart of what Durkheim termed 'the serious life'. If sociology is to remain, as Durkheim intended, a serious attempt to make sense of the social and cultural processes through which human reality is constituted, then it cannot push aside such considerations, as other 'classical' sociologists also understood. Consequently, before we set about writing 'new rules of sociological method' to mark the arrival of yet another new epoch, we should recognise that we can gain a great deal from a creative re-engagement with the old ones. Until that has been done, or until postmodern fantasies of a post-human world become a reality, which does not, as yet, look very likely, then sociology should remain 'the study of society' and religious issues should constitute one of its key areas of concern.

Bibliography

Abell, P. (1991) 'Introduction', in P. Abell (ed.) *Rational Choice Theory*. Aldershot: Edward Elgar.

Abell, P. (1996) 'Sociological theory and rational choice theory', in B.S. Turner (ed.), *The Blackwell Companion to Social Theory*. Oxford: Blackwell.

Abell, P. and Reyniers, D. (2000) 'On the failure of social theory', *British Journal of Sociology*, 51 (4): 739–50.

Abercrombie, N., Hill, N. and Turner, B. S. (1980) *The Dominant Ideology Thesis*. London: Allen and Unwin.

Abric, J-C. (2001) 'A structural approach to social representations', in K. Deaux and G. Philogène (eds), *Representations of the Social*. Oxford: Blackwell.

Adam, B. (1990) *Time and Social Theory*. Cambridge: Polity.

Adam, B. (1995) *Timewatch*. Cambridge: Polity.

Ahearne, J. (1996) 'The shattering of Christianity and the articulation of belief', *New Blackfriars*, 77 (909): 493–504.

Albrow, M. (1996) *The Global Age: State and Society Beyond Modernity*. Cambridge: Polity.

Alexander, J.C. (2001) 'Theorising the "Modes of Incorporation": Assimilation, Hyphenation, and Multiculturalism as Varieties of Civil Participation', *Sociological Theory*, 19 (3): 237–49.

Allen, N.J. (1998) 'Effervescence and the Origins of Human Society', in N.J. Allen, W.S.F. Pickering and W. Watts Miller (eds), *On Durkheim's Elementary Forms of Religious Life*. London: Routledge.

Ammerman, N. (1987) *Bible Believers: Fundamentalists in the Modern World*. New Brunswick, NJ: Rutgers University Press.

Anderson, B. (1991) *Imagined Communities*. London: Verso.

Archer, M.S. (1988) *Culture and Agency*. Cambridge: Cambridge University Press.

Archer, M.S. (1995) *Realist Social Theory*. Cambridge: Cambridge University Press.

Archer, M.S. (1998) 'Introduction: Realism in the social sciences', in M.S. Archer, R. Bhaskar, A. Collier, T. Lawson and A. Norrie (eds), *Critical Realism: Essential Readings*. London: Routledge.

Archer, M.S. (2000) *Being Human*. Cambridge: Cambridge University Press.

Arendt, H. (1995) *Men in Dark Times*. New York: Harcourt Brace.

Ariès, P. (1977) *The Hour of Our Death*. New York: Knopf.

Armitage, J. (2000) 'From modernism to hypermodernism and beyond: An interview with Paul Virilio', in J. Armitage (ed.), *Paul Virilio*. London: Sage.

Aron, R. (1990) [1967] *Main Currents in Sociological Thought*, Vol. II. London: Penguin.

Aron, R. (1991) [1965] *Main Currents in Sociological Thought*, Vol I. London: Penguin.

Asad, T. (2002) 'The construction of religion as an anthropological category', in M. Lambek (ed.) *A Reader in the Anthropology of Religion*. Oxford: Blackwell.

Augé, M. (1992) *Non-Lieux. Introduction à une anthropologie de la surmodernité*. Paris: Editions du Seuil.

Bachelard, G. (1983) *Water and Dreams*. Farrell, TX: Pegasus.

Balthasar, H.U. von (1982) *The von Balthasar Reader*. (M. Kehl and W. Löser, eds). Edinburgh: T&T Clark.

Balthasar, H.U. von (1989) *The Glory of the Lord: A Theological Aesthetics*, Vol. VII: *Theology: The New Covenant*. Edinburgh: T&T Clark.

Banton, M. (1998) *Racial Theories*. Cambridge: Cambridge University Press.

Barber, B.R. (1995) *Jihad vs. McWorld*. New York: Ballantine Books.

Barber, B.R. (2001) '2001 Introduction' to *Jihad vs. McWorld*. New York: Ballantine Books.

Bataille, G. (1986) 'Writings on laughter, sacrifice, Nietzsche, un-knowing', October, 36.

Bataille, G. (1987) [1962] *Eroticism*. London: Marion Boyars.

Bataille, G. (1988a) [1938] 'The Sorcerer's Apprentice', in D. Hollier (ed.), *The College of Sociology 1937–39*. Minneapolis: University of Minnesota Press.

Bataille, G. (1988b) [1938] 'Attraction and repulsion I', in D. Hollier (ed.), *The College of Sociology 1937–39*. Minneapolis: University of Minnesota Press.

Bataille, G. (1988c) [1938] 'Attraction and repulsion II', in D. Hollier (ed.), *The College of Sociology 1937-39*. Minneapolis: University of Minnesota Press.

Bataille, G. (1988d) *Inner Experience* (trans. L.A. Boldt). Albany: State University of New York Press.

Bataille, G. (1991) [1967] *The Accursed Share*, Vol. I. New York: Zone Books.

Bataille, G. (1992) [1973] *Theory of Religion*. New York: Zone Books.

Bataille, G. and Caillois, R. (1988) [1937] 'Sacred sociology and the relationships between "society", "organism" and "being"', in D. Hollier (ed.), *The College of Sociology 1937–39*. Minneapolis: University of Minnesota Press.

Bat Ye'or. (1996) *The Decline of Eastern Christianity under Islam: From Jihad to Dhimmitude*. London: Associated University Presses.

Baudrillard, J. (1983) *In the Shadow of the Silent Majorities*. New York: Semiotext(e).

Baudrillard, J. (1988a) *The Ecstasy of Communication*. New York: Semiotext(e).

Baudrillard, J. (1988b) *Selected Writings*. Cambridge: Polity.

Baudrillard, J. (1990a) *Cool Memories*. London: Verso.

Baudrillard, J. (1990b) *Fatal Strategies*. New York: Semiotext(e).

Baudrillard, J. (1993) *Symbolic Exchange and Death*. London: Sage.

Baudrillard, J. (2002) *The Spirit of Terrorism*. London: Verso.

Bauman, Z. (1988) 'Is there a postmodern sociology?', *Theory, Culture and Society*, 5(2–3): 217–36.

Bauman, Z. (1989) *Legislators and Interpreters*. Cambridge: Polity.

Bauman, Z. (1992a) *Intimations of Postmodernity*. London: Routledge.

Bauman, Z. (1992b) *Mortality, Immortality and Other Life Strategies*. Cambridge: Polity.

Bauman, Z. (1993) *Postmodern Ethics*. Oxford: Blackwell.

Bauman, Z. (2001) *The Individualized Society*. Cambridge: Polity.

Bauman, Z. (2002) *Society Under Siege*. Cambridge: Polity.

Bauman, Z. and Tester, K. (2001) *Conversations with Zygmunt Bauman*. Cambridge: Polity.

Beaman, L. (2003) 'The myth of pluralism, diversity and vigour: The constitutional privilege of protestantism in the United States and Canada', *Journal for the Social Scientific Study of Religion*, 42 (3): 311–25.

Beck, U. (1992) *Risk Society*. London: Sage.

Beck, U. (2000) *What is Globalisation?* London: Sage.

Beck, U., Giddens, A. and Lash, S. (1994) *Reflexive Modernisation*. Cambridge: Polity.

Becker, G. (1986) 'The economic approach to human behaviour', in J. Elster (ed.), *Rational Choice*. Oxford: Blackwell.

Beckford, J.A. (2003) *Social Theory and Religion*. Cambridge: Cambridge University Press.

Beckwith, S. (1993) *Christ's Body: Identity, Culture and Society in Late Medieval Writings*. London: Routledge.

Beidelman, T.O. (1973) 'Kaguru symbolic classification', in Rodney Needham (ed.) *Right and Left: Essays on Dual Symbolic Classification*. Chicago: University of Chicago Press.

Bell, D. (1974) *The Coming of Postindustrial Society*. Harmondsworth: Penguin.

Bell, D. (1980) 'The social framework of the information society', in T. Forester (ed.), *The Microelectronics Revolution*. Oxford: Blackwell.

Bellah, R. (1973) 'Introduction' to *E. Durkheim on Morality and Society*. Chicago: University of Chicago Press.

Bellah, R., Madsen, R., Sullivan, W.M., Swidler, A. and Tipton, S.M. (1992) *The Good Society*. New York: Vintage.

Benthall, J. (2002) 'Imagined Civilisations?', *Anthropology Today*, 18 (6): 1–2.

Berger, P.L. (1990) [1967] *The Sacred Canopy*. New York: Doubleday/Anchor.

Berger, P.L. and Luckmann, T. (1966) *The Social Construction of Reality.* Harmondsworth: Penguin.

Bergmann, W. (1981) *Die Zeitstruckturen Sozialer Systeme: Eine systemtheoretische Analyse.* Berlin: Duncker & Humblot.

Bergson, H. (1979) *The Two Sources of Morality and Religion.* Notre Dame, IN: University of Notre Dame.

Berking, H. (1999) *Sociology of Giving.* London: Sage.

Bertens, H. (1995) *The Idea of the Postmodern: A History.* London: Routledge.

Besnier, J-M. (1995) 'Bataille, the emotive intellectual', in C. Bailey Gill, *Bataille: Writing the Sacred.* London: Routledge.

Bettelheim, B. (1955) *Symbolic Wounds.* Glencoe, IL: Free Press.

Beyer, P. (2003) 'Constitutional privilege and constituting pluralism: Legal freedom in national, global and legal context', *Journal for the Social Scientific Study of Religion,* 42 (3): 333–9.

Bhaskar, R. (1979) *The Possibility of Naturalism.* Hemel Hempstead: Harvester.

Bhaskar, R. (1989) *Reclaiming Reality.* London: Verso.

Bhaskar, R. (1998) 'Philosophy and Scientific Realism', in M.S. Archer, R. Bhaskar, A. Collier, T. Lawson and A. Norrie (eds), *Critical Realism: Essential Readings.* London: Routledge.

Biggar, N. (1997) *The Good Life: Reflections on What We Value Today.* London: Society for Promoting Christian Knowledge.

Billig, M. (1995) *Banal Nationalism.* London: Sage.

Block, F. (2001) 'Introduction' to K. Polanyi, *The Great Transformation.* Boston, MA: Beacon Press.

Bloom, A. (1987) *The Closing of the American Mind.* New York: Simon and Schuster.

Bobbio, N. (1989) 'The great dichotomy: public/private', in *Democracy and Dictatorship.* Minneapolis: University of Minnesota Press.

Bogard, W. (2000) 'Sociology in the absence of the social: The significance of Baudrillard for contemporary thought', in M. Gane (ed.), *Jean Baudrillard,* Vol. II. London: Sage.

Bohman, J. (1991) *New Philosophy of Social Science.* Cambridge: Polity.

Bossy, J. (1985) *Christianity in the West 1400–1700.* Oxford: Oxford University Press.

Botting, F. and Wilson, S. (1998) 'Introduction', *Bataille: A Critical Reader.* Oxford: Blackwell.

Boulton, D. (1997) *A Reasonable Faith: Introducing the Sea of Faith Network.* Loughborough: Sea of Faith.

Bourdieu, P. (1977) *Outline of a Theory of Practice.* Cambridge: Cambridge University Press.

Bourricaud, F. (1981) *The Sociology of Talcott Parsons.* Chicago: University of Chicago Press.

Braidotti, R. (1994) *Nomadic Subjects.* New York: Columbia University Press.

Braudel, F. (1972) *The Mediterranean and the Mediterranean World.* London: Fontana.

Braudel, F. (1980) *On History.* London: Weidenfeld and Nicolson.

Braudel, F. (1994) *History of Civilisations.* New York: Allen Lane.

Brown, C. (2001) *The Death of Christian Britain.* London: Routledge.

Bruce, S. (2002) *God is Dead.* Oxford: Blackwell.

Buchanan, I. (2000) *Michel de Certeau, Cultural Theorist.* London: Sage/TCS.

Bukert, W. (1983) [1972] *Homo Necans: The Anthropology of Ancient Greek Sacrificial Ritual and Myth.* Berkeley, CA: University of California Press.

Bukert, W. (1987) 'The problem of ritual killing' in *Violent Origins: Walter Bukert, René Girard and Jonathan Z. Smith on Ritual Killing and Cultural Formation.* Stanford, CA: Stanford University Press.

Burawoy, M. (2003) 'For a sociological Marxism: The complementary convergence of Antonio Gramsci and Karl Polanyi', *Politics and Society,* 31 (2): 193–261.

Byrne, D. (1998) *Complexity Theory and the Social Sciences.* London: Routledge.

Caillé, A. (1986) 'Promesses d'une sociologie sacrée', *Bulletin du M.A.U.S.S.,* 19: 4.

Caillois, R. (1950) *L'homme et le sacré.* Paris: Gallimard.

Caillois, R. (1988a) [1938] 'Introduction', in D. Hollier (ed.), *The College of Sociology 1937–39.* Minneapolis: University of Minnesota Press.

Caillois, R. (1988b) [1937] 'The winter wind', in D. Hollier (ed.), *The College of Sociology*

1937–39. Minneapolis: University of Minnesota Press.

Calhoun, C. (ed.) (1992) *Habermas and the Public Sphere*. Cambridge, MA: MIT Press.

Calhoun, C. (1997) 'Nationalism and the public sphere', in J. Weintraub and K. Kumar (eds), *Public and Private in Thought and Practice: Perspectives on a Grand Dichotomy*. Chicago: University of Chicago Press.

Calhoun, C. (1998) 'Community without propinquity revisited: Communication technology and the transformation of the urban public sphere', *Sociological Inquiry*, 68 (3): 373–97.

Calhoun, C. (2000) 'Resisting globalisation or shaping it?', *Prometheus*, 3: 28–47.

Cameron, E. (1991) *The European Reformation*. Oxford: Oxford University Press.

Campbell, C. (1987) *The Romantic Ethic and the Spirit of Modern Consumerism*. Oxford: Blackwell.

Capra, F. (1982) *The Turning Point*. London: Wildwood House.

Casanova, J. (1994) *Public Religions in the Modern World*. Chicago: University of Chicago Press.

Castells, M. (1996) *The Rise of the Network Society*. Oxford: Blackwell.

Castells, M. (1997) *The Power of Identity*. Oxford: Blackwell.

Castells, M. (1998) *End of Millennium*. Oxford: Blackwell.

Castells, M. (2000) 'Materials for an exploratory theory of the network society', *British Journal of Sociology*, 51 (2): 5–24.

de Certeau, M. (1984) *The Practice of Everyday Life*. Berkeley, CA: University of California Press.

de Certeau, M. (1987) *La faiblesse de croire*. Paris: Seuil.

de Certeau, M. and Domenach, J-M. (1974) *Le Christianisme éclaté*. Paris: Ed. du Seuil.

Chaib, M. and Orfali, B. (eds) (2000) *Social Representations and Communicative Processes*. Jonkoping: Jonkoping University Press.

Chatellier, L. (1989) *The Europe of the Devout*. Cambridge: Cambridge University Press.

Cladis, M. (2000) 'Redeeming love: Rousseau and eighteenth-century moral philosophy', *Journal of Religious Ethics*, 28 (2): 221–51.

Cohen, Y. (1978) 'The Disappearance of the Incest Taboo', *Human Nature*, 1: 72–8.

Colas, D. (1991) 'Le moment Luthérien de la société civile', *Philosophie Politique*, 1: 41–54.

Coleman, J. (1990) *Foundations of Social Theory*. Cambridge, MA: Belknap/Harvard University Press.

Collins, R. (1988) 'The Durkheimian tradition in conflict sociology', in J.C. Alexander (ed.), *Durkheimian Sociology: Cultural Studies*. Cambridge: Cambridge University Press.

Collins, R. (1993) 'Emotional energy as the common denominator of rational action', *Rationality and Society*, 5 (2): 203–30.

Commission (2000) *Commission on the Future of Multi-Ethnic Britain*. London: Profile Books.

Comte, A. (1853) *The Positive Philosophy of Auguste Comte*, Vols I, II. London: John Chapman.

de Connick, F. (1995) *Travail intégré, société éclatée*. Paris: Presses Universitaires de France.

Craib, I. (1992) *Anthony Giddens*. London: Routledge.

Cupitt, D. (1995) *The Last Philosophy*. London: SCM Press.

Davetian, B. (2001) 'Moral tensions between Western and Islamic cultures: The need for additional sociological studies of dissonance in the wake of September 11', *Sociological Research Online*, 6 (3): U45–U53.

Davie, G. (2000) *Religion in Modern Europe*. Oxford: Oxford University Press.

Davie, G. (2001) 'The persistence of institutional religion in modern Europe', in L. Woodhead and P. Heelas (eds), *Peter Berger and the Study of Religion*. London: Routledge.

Davies, C. (1982) 'Sexual taboos and social boundaries', *American Journal of Sociology*, 87 (5): 1032–63.

Davies, C. and Neal, M. (2000) 'Durkheim's altruistic and fatalistic suicide', in W.S.F. Pickering and G. Walford (eds), *Durkheim's Suicide*. London: Routledge.

Dayan, D. and Katz, E. (1988) 'Articulating consensus: the ritual and rhetoric of media events', in J.C. Alexander (ed.), *Durkheimian Sociology: Cultural Studies*. Cambridge: Cambridge University Press.

Deaux, K. and Philogène, G. (eds) (2001) *Representations of the Social*. Oxford: Blackwell.

Delanty, G. (1997) 'Habermas and occidental rationalism: The politics of identity, social learn-
     ing and the cultural limits of moral universalism', *Sociological Theory*, 15 (1): 30–59.
Deleuze, G. (1968) *Différence et repetition*. Paris: Presses Universitaires de France.
Deleuze, G. (1969) *Logique du sens*. Paris: Minuit.
Deleuze, G. (1977) *Nietzsche et la Philosophie*. Paris: Presses Universitaires de France.
Deleuze, G. (1979) 'Introduction', in J. Donzelot, *The Policing of Families*. London: Hutchinson.
Deleuze, G. and Guattari, F. (1986) *Nomadology*. New York: Semiotext(e).
Deleuze, G. and Guattari, F. (1988) *A Thousand Plateaus: Capitalism and Schizophrenia*.
     London: Athlone Press.
Derrida, J. (1987) *Positions*. London: Athlone Press.
Derrida, J. (1991) *A Derrida Reader*. Hemel Hempstead: Harvester.
Derrida, J. (1998) [1967] 'From restricted to general economy: A Hegelianism without reserve',
     in F. Botting and S. Wilson, *Bataille: A Critical Reader*. Oxford: Blackwell.
Descartes, R. (1994) *Selected Philosophical Writings*. Cambridge: Cambridge University Press.
Dobash, R.E. and Dobash, R. (1979) *Violence Against Wives*. New York: Free Press.
Dobbelaere, K. (1999) 'Towards an integrated perspective of the processes related to the
     descriptive concept of secularisation', *Sociology of Religion*, 60 (3): 229–47.
Douglas, M. (1966) *Purity and Danger*. London: Routledge and Kegan Paul.
Duby, G. (1988a) 'Preface' to G. Duby (ed.), *Revelations of the Medieval World, A History of
     Private Life*, Vol. II. London: Harvard/Belknap Press.
Duby, G. (1988b) 'Solitude: eleventh to thirteenth century', in G. Duby (ed.), *Revelations of the
     Medieval World, A History of Private Life*, Vol. II. London: Harvard/Belknap Press.
Duffy, E. (1992) *The Stripping of the Altars*. New Haven, CT: Yale University Press.
Dumont, L. (1970) *Homo Hierarchicus*. Chicago: University of Chicago Press.
Dumont, L. (1971) 'Religion, politics and society in the individualistic universe', *Proceedings of
     the Royal Anthropological Institute for 1970*. Oxford: Royal Anthropological Institute.
Durkheim, E. (1907) 'Lettres au Directeur de la Revue néo-scholastique', *Revue néo-scholas-
     tique*, 14: 606–7, 612–14.
Durkheim, E. (1913) 'Deploige, Simon, Le Conflit de la morale et de la sociologie', *Année soci-
     ologique*, 12: 326–8.
Durkheim, E. (1952) *Suicide*. London: Routledge.
Durkheim, E. (1953) [1906] *Sociology and Philosophy*. London: Cohen and West.
Durkheim, E. (1961) *Moral Education*. New York: Free Press.
Durkheim, E. (1963) [1898] 'Incest: The nature and origin of the taboo', in E. Durkheim and
     A. Ellis, *Incest*. New York: Lyle Stuart.
Durkheim, E. (1970) [1888] 'Cours de science sociale', in *La Science sociale et l'action*. Paris:
     Presses Universitaires de France.
Durkheim, E. (1972) 'La science positive de la morale en Allemagne', in A. Giddens (ed.), *Emile
     Durkheim: Selected Writings*. Cambridge: Cambridge University Press.
Durkheim, E. (1973) [1915] 'The dualism of human nature and its social conditions', in R.
     Bellah (ed.), *Emile Durkheim on Morality and Society*. Chicago: University of Chicago Press.
Durkheim, E. (1974a) [1906] 'The determination of moral facts', in *Sociology and Philosophy*.
     New York: Free Press.
Durkheim, E. (1974b) [1898] 'Individual and collective representations', in *Sociology and
     Philosophy*. New York: Free Press.
Durkheim, E. (1974c) [1888] 'Course in social science: inaugural lecture', translated by N.
     Layne in 'Emile Durkheim's Inaugural Lecture at Bordeaux', *Sociological Inquiry*, 44: 197.
Durkheim, E. (1977) *The Evolution of Educational Thought*. London: Routledge and Kegan Paul.
Durkheim, E. (1982a) [1895] *The Rules of Sociological Method, and selected texts on sociology and
     its method*. London: Macmillan.
Durkheim, E. (1982b) [1917] 'Society', in *The Rules of Sociological Method, and selected texts on
     sociology and its method*. London: Macmillan.
Durkheim, E. (1982c) [1908] 'Debate on explanation in history and sociology', in *The Rules of
     Sociological Method, and selected texts on sociology and its method*. London: Macmillan.

Durkheim, E. (1984) [1893] *The Division of Labour in Society*. London: Macmillan.

Durkheim, E. (1995) [1912] *The Elementary Forms of Religious Life* (trans. Karen E. Fields). New York: Free Press.

Durkheim, E. and Mauss, M. (1963) [1903] *Primitive Classification*. London: Cohen and West.

Durkheim, E. and Mauss, M. (1971) 'Note on the notion of civilisation', *Social Research*, 38: 808–13.

Edwards, T. (2002) 'Durkheim, Kant and the social construction of the categories', in T.A. Idinopulos and B.C Wilson (eds), *Reappraising Durkheim for the Study and Teaching of Religion Today*. Leiden: Brill.

Eisenstadt, S.N. (2000) 'The resurgence of religious movements in processes of globalisation: Beyond end of history or clash of civilisations', *Journal on Multicultural Societies*, 2 (1).

Eliade, M. (1959) *Cosmos and History*. New York: Harper.

Elias, N. (1978) *The History of Manners*. Oxford: Blackwell.

Ellul, J. (1996), 'Foreword' to Bat Ye'or, *The Decline of Eastern Christianity under Islam: From Jihad to Dhimmitude*. London: Associated University Presses.

Elster, J. (1989) *The Cement of Society: A Study of Social Order*. Cambridge: Cambridge University Press.

Erikson, E.H. (1965) *Childhood and Society*. Harmondsworth: Penguin.

Esping-Anderson, G. (2000) 'Two societies, one sociology, and no theory', *British Journal of Sociology*, 51 (2): 59–77.

Esposito, J.L. (1992) *The Islamic Threat: Myth or Reality*. New York: Oxford University Press.

Evans-Pritchard, E. (1956) *Nuer Religion*. Oxford: Oxford University Press.

Evans-Pritchard, E. (1965) *Theories of Primitive Religion*. Oxford: Clarendon Press.

Falk, P. (1994) *The Consuming Body*. London: Sage.

Falk, R. (1995) *On Human Governance*. Cambridge: Polity.

Farr, F.M. and Moscovici, S. (eds) (1984) *Social Representations*. Cambridge: Cambridge University Press.

Featherstone, M. (1991) *Consumer Culture and Postmodernism*. London: Sage.

Featherstone, M. (1992) 'The Heroic Life and Everyday Life', in M. Featherstone (ed.), *Cultural Theory and Cultural Change*. London: Sage.

Ferguson, H. (1992) *The Religious Transformation of Western Society*. London: Routledge.

Fetzer, J.S. and Soper, J.C. (2003) 'The roots of public attitudes toward state accommodation of European Muslims' religious practices before and after September 11', *Journal for the Scientific Study of Religion*, 42 (2): 247–58.

Fields, K.E. (1995) 'Translator's introduction: Religion as an eminently social thing', in E. Durkheim, *Elementary Forms of Religious Life*. New York: Free Press.

Foucault, M. (1970) *The Order of Things*. New York: Random House.

Foucault, M. (1972) *The Archaeology of Knowledge*. London: Tavistock.

Foucault, M. (1998) [1963] 'A preface to transgression', in F. Botting and S. Wilson, *Bataille: A Critical Reader*. Oxford: Blackwell.

Fowler, B. (1997) *Pierre Bourdieu and Cultural Theory*. London: Sage.

Frazer, J. G. (1903) 'Taboo: totemism', *Encyclopaedia Britannica*, 9th edition.

Freitag, M. (2002) 'The dissolution of society within the "Social"', *European Journal of Social Theory*, 5 (2): 175–98.

Freud, S. (1930) *Civilisation and its Discontents*. London: Hogarth Press.

Freud, S. (1950) *Totem and Taboo. Some Points of Agreement between the Mental Lives of Savages and Neurotics*. London: Routledge and Kegan Paul.

Freud, S. (1962) *The Future of an Illusion*. London: Hogarth.

Frisby, D. (1992) *Simmel and Since*. London: Routledge.

Frisby, D. and Sayer, D. (1986) *Society*. London: Tavistock.

Fukuyama, F. (1992) *The End of History and the Last Man*. New York: Free Press.

Fukuyama, F. (2002) 'The real enemy', *Newsweek*, Feb: 54-9.

Fulcher, J. (2000) 'Globalisation, the nation-state and global society', *Sociological Review*, 48 (4): 522–43.

Fustel de Coulanges, N.D. (1956) *The Ancient City*. New York: Doubleday.

Game, A. (1991) *Undoing the Social*. Buckingham: Open University Press.

Game, A. (1995) 'Time, space, memory, with reference to Bachelard', in M. Featherstone, S. Lash and R. Robertson (eds), *Global Modernities*. London: Sage.

Gane, M. (1983a) 'Durkheim: woman as outsider', *Economy and Society*, 12 (2): 227–70.

Gane, M. (1983b) 'Durkheim: the sacred language', *Economy and Society*, 12 (1): 1–47.

Gane, M. (1988) *On Durkheim's Rules of Sociological Method*. London: Routledge.

Gane, M. (2003) *French Social Theory*. London: Sage/TCS.

Garfinkel, H. (1967) *Studies in Ethnomethodology*. Englewood Cliffs, NJ: Prentice Hall.

Garfinkel, H. (2001) *Ethnomethodology's Program: Working Out Durkheim's Aphorism*. Boulder, CO: Rowman and Littlefield.

Geertz, C. (1973) *The Interpretation of Cultures*. New York: Basic Books.

Geertz, C. (1983) *Local Knowledge*. New York: Basic Books.

Gehlen, A. (1988) *Man: His Nature and Place in the World*. New York: Columbia University Press.

Gellner, E. (2001) 'The mightier pen: The double standards of inside-out colonialism', in P. Williams (ed.), *Edward Said*, Vol.II. London: Sage, pp. 396–403.

Giddens, A. (1976) *New Rules of Sociological Method*. London: Hutchinson.

Giddens, A. (1984) *The Constitution of Society*. Cambridge: Polity.

Giddens, A. (1987a) *Social Theory and Modern Sociology*. Cambridge: Polity.

Giddens, A. (1987b) *The Nation-State and Violence*. Berkeley, CA: University of California Press.

Giddens, A. (1990) *The Consequences of Modernity*. Cambridge: Polity.

Giddens, A. (1991a) *Modernity and Self-Identity*. Cambridge: Polity.

Giddens, A. (1991b) 'Structuration theory: past, present and future', in C.G.A. Bryant and D. Jary (eds), *Giddens's Theory of Structuration*. London: Routledge.

Giddens, A. (1992) *The Transformation of Intimacy*. Cambridge: Polity.

Giddens, A. (1994) *Beyond Left and Right*. Cambridge: Polity.

Giddens, A. (1998) *The Third Way*. Cambridge: Polity.

Gillette, P.R. (2002) 'A religion for an age of science', *Zygon*, 37 (2): 461–71.

Gilroy, P. (2001) 'Joined up Politics and Post-Colonial Melancholia', *Theory, Culture and Society*, 18 (2–3): 151–68.

Ginsberg, M. (1956) *On the Diversity of Morals*. London: Allen and Unwin.

Girard, R. (1987) 'Generative Scapegoating', in *Violent Origins: Walter Bukert, René Girard and Jonathan Z. Smith on Ritual Killing and Cultural Formation*. Stanford, CA: Stanford University Press.

Girard, R. (1995) [1972] *Violence and the Sacred*. Baltimore, MD: Johns Hopkins University Press.

Godelier, M. (1999) *The Enigma of the Gift*. Cambridge: Polity.

Goffman, I. (1969) *The Presentation of Self in Everyday Life*. Harmondsworth: Penguin.

Gofman, A. (1998) 'A vague but suggestive concept: the "total social fact"', in W. James and N.J. Allen (eds), *Marcel Mauss: A Centenary Tribute*. Oxford: Berghahn Books.

Goldthorpe, J.H. (1998) 'Rational action theory for sociology', *British Journal of Sociology*, 49(2): 167–92.

Gombrich, R. (1980) *Theravada Buddhism*. London: Routledge.

Gould, S. J. (1991) *Wonderful Life*. Harmondsworth: Penguin.

Gouldner, A. (1980) *The Two Marxisms: Contradictions and Anomalies in the Development of Theory*. New York: Seabury Press.

Goux, J-J. (1998) [1990] 'General economics and postmodern capitalism', in F. Botting and S. Wilson (eds), *Bataille: A Critical Reader*. Oxford: Blackwell.

Gramsci, A. (1971) *Selections from the Prison Notebooks*. London: Lawrence and Wishart.

Guimelli, C. (1994) *Structure et Transformation des Représentations Sociales*. Paris: Delachaux and Niestlé.

Gurvitch, G. (1949) 'Microsociology and sociometry', *Sociometry*, XII: 1–31.

Gurvitch, G. (1963) 'Social structure and the multiplicity of times', in E.A. Tiryakian (ed.), *Sociological Theory, Values and Sociocultural Change*. Glencoe, IL: Free Press.

Gurvitch, G. (1964) *The Spectrum of Social Time*. Dordrecht: D. Reidel Publishing Company.

Gurvitch, G. (1971) *The Social Frameworks of Knowledge*. Oxford: Blackwell.

Gvosdev, N.K. (2001) 'Constitutional doublethink, managed pluralism and freedom of religion', *Religion, State and Society*, 29 (2): 81–90.

Habermas, J. (1981) *The Theory of Communicative Action*, Vol. 1. London: Heinemann.

Habermas, J. (1987) *The Theory of Communicative Action*, Vol. 2. Cambridge: Polity.

Habermas, J. (1989a) *The New Conservatism*. Cambridge: Polity.

Habermas, J. (1989b) *The Structural Transformation of the Public Sphere*. Cambridge, MA.: MIT Press.

Habermas, J. (1996) 'The European nation-state: Its achievements and its limits: On the past and the future of sovereignty and citizenship', in G. Balakrishnan (ed.), *Mapping the Nation*. London: Verso.

Habermas, J. (1998) [1984] 'The French path to postmodernity: Bataille between eroticism and general economics', in F. Botting and S. Wilson (eds), *Bataille: A Critical Reader*. Oxford: Blackwell.

Halpern, M. (1962) 'Middle East studies: A review of the state of the field with a few examples', *World Politics*, 15.

Haraway, D. (1991) *Simians, Cyborgs and Women*. London: Free Association Books.

Hardt, M. and Negri, A. (2000) *Empire*. Cambridge, MA: Harvard University Press.

Harré, R. (1979) *Social Being*. Oxford: Blackwell.

Harré, R. (1981) 'Psychological variety', in P. Heelas and A. Lock (eds), *Indigenous Psychologies*. London: Academic Press.

Hart, W.D. (2000) *Edward Said and the Religious Effects of Culture*. Cambridge: Cambridge University Press.

Harvey, D. (1989) *The Condition of Postmodernity*. Oxford: Blackwell.

Harvey, D.L. and Reed, M.H. (1994) 'The evolution of dissipative social systems', *Journal of Social and Evolutionary Systems*, 17 (4): 371–411.

Harvey, P. (1990) *An Introduction to Buddhism*. Cambridge: Cambridge University Press.

Hastings, A. (1997) *The Construction of Nationhood*. Cambridge: Cambridge University Press.

Hastings, A. (2000) 'Communion', in A. Hastings, A. Mason and H. Pyper (eds), *The Oxford Companion to Christian Thought*. Oxford: Oxford University Press.

Hawkes, G. (1996) *A Sociology of Sex and Sexuality*. Buckingham: Open University Press.

Hawkins, M. (1999) 'Durkheim's sociology and theories of degeneration', *Economy and Society*, 28 (1): 118–37.

Hayles, N.K. (1990) *Chaos Unbound*. Ithaca, NY: Cornell University Press.

Hayles, N.K. (1991) *Chaos and Order*. Chicago: University of Chicago Press.

Hayles, N.K. (1999) *How We Became Posthuman*. Chicago: University of Chicago Press.

Hechter, M. (1987) *Principles of Group Solidarity*. Berkeley, CA.: University of California Press.

Heelas, P. (1996) *The New Age Movement*. Oxford: Blackwell.

Heelas, P., Lash, S. and Morris, P. (eds) (1996) *Detraditionalisation*. Oxford: Blackwell.

Hegarty, P. (2000) *Georges Bataille: Core Cultural Theorist*. London: Sage.

Heidegger, M. (1962) *Being and Time*. Oxford: Blackwell.

Heller, A. (1984) *Everyday Life*. London: Routledge.

Hertz, R. (1960) *Death and the Right Hand*. London: Cohen and West.

Hertz, R. (1983) 'St Besse: A study of an Alpine cult', in S. Wilson (ed.), *Saints and their Cults*. Cambridge: Cambridge University Press.

Hervieu-Léger, D. (2000) *Religion as a Chain of Memory*. Cambridge: Polity.

Hill, C. (1966) *Society and Puritanism in Pre-Revolutionary England*. London: Secker and Warburg.

Hillal Dessouki, A.E. (1982) 'The Islamic resurgence', in A.E. Hillal Dessouki (ed.), *Islamic Resurgence in the Arab World*. New York: Praeger.

Hindess, B. (1988) *Choice, Rationality and Social Theory*. London: Unwin Hyman.

Hirst, P. and Wooley, P. (1982) *Social Relations and Human Attributes*. London: Tavistock.

Hjerm, M. (2000) 'Multiculturalism Reassessed', *Citizenship Studies*, 4 (3): 357–81.

Hobbes, T. (1957) [1651] *Leviathan*. Oxford: Oxford University Press.

Hollier, D. (1988) 'Foreword: Collage', *The College of Sociology 1937–39*. Minneapolis: University of Minnesota Press.

Hollier, D. (1998) [1966] 'The Dualist Materialism of Georges Bataille', in F. Botting and S. Wilson (eds), *Bataille: A Critical Reader*. Oxford: Blackwell.

Hollis, M. (2001) 'What truth? For whom and where?', in P. Williams (ed.), *Edward Said*, Vol.I. London: Sage, pp. 303–13.

Holy Bible, Revised Standard Version. (1966) London: Catholic Truth Society.

Howes, D. (1991) *The Varieties of Sensory Experience*. Toronto: University of Toronto Press.

Hubert, H. and Mauss, M. (1964) [1888] *Sacrifice: Its Nature and Function*. London: Cohen and West.

Hughes, R. (1994) *Culture of Complaint*. New York: Time Warner.

Hunter, J.D. (1991) *Culture Wars: The Struggle to Define America*. New York: Basic Books.

Huntington, S.P. (1993) 'The clash of civilisations?', *Foreign Affairs*, Summer edition.

Huntington, S.P. (1996) *The Clash of Civilisations and the Remaking of World Order*. New York: Simon and Schuster.

Iannaccone, L.R. (1997) 'Rational choice: Framework for the scientific study of religion', in L.A. Young (ed.), *Rational Choice Theory and Religion*. New York: Routledge.

Irigaray, L. (1984) 'Sexual difference', in T. Moi (ed.), *French Feminist Thought*. Oxford: Blackwell.

Irigaray, L. (1993) *Sexes and Genealogies*. New York: Columbia University Press.

Jalal al 'Azm, S. (1981) 'Orientalism and Orientalism in reverse'. *Khamsin*, 8: 5–27.

Jameson, F. (1992) *Postmodernism, or, The Cultural Logic of Late Capitalism*. London: Verso.

Janssen, J. and Verheggen, T. (1997) 'The double centre of gravity in Durkheim's symbol theory: bringing the symbolism of the body back in', *Sociological Theory*, 15 (3): 294–306.

Jay, N. (1992) *Throughout Your Generations Forever: Sacrifice, Religion and Paternity*. Chicago: University of Chicago Press.

Jenkins, T. (1998) 'Derrida's reading of Mauss', in W. James and N.J. Allen (eds), *Marcel Mauss: A Centenary Tribute*. Oxford: Berghahn Books.

Jenkins, T. (1999) *Religion in English Everyday Life*. Oxford: Berghahn Books.

Jenks, C. (ed.) (1998) *Core Sociological Dichotomies*. London: Sage.

Jodelet, D. (ed.) (1989) *Les Représentations Sociales*. Paris: Presses Universitaires de France.

Jones, R.A. (1997) 'The other Durkheim: History and theory in the treatment of classical sociological thought', in C. Camic (ed.), *Reclaiming the Sociological Classics*. Oxford: Blackwell.

Jones, R. A. (1999) *The Development of Durkheim's Social Realism*. Cambridge: Cambridge University Press.

Jovchelovitch, S. (2001) 'Social representations, public life and social construction', in K. Deaux and G. Philogène (eds), *Representations of the Social*. Oxford: Blackwell.

Karsenti, B. (1998) 'The Maussian shift: a second foundation for sociology in France?', in W. James and N.J. Allen (eds), *Marcel Mauss: A Centenary Tribute*. Oxford: Berghahn Books.

Kellner, D. (2002) 'September 11, social theory and democratic politics', *Theory, Culture and Society*, 19 (4): 147–59.

Kelly, K. (1995) *Out of Control: The Rise of Neo-biological Civilisation*. Menlo Park, CA: Addison Wesley.

Kennedy, V. (2000) *Edward Said: A Critical Introduction*. Cambridge: Polity.

Kepel, G. (1994) *The Revenge of God: The Resurgence of Islam, Christianity and Judaism in the Modern World*. University Park, PA.: Pennsylvania State University Press.

Kerr, F. (1986) *Theology After Wittgenstein*. Oxford: Blackwell.

Kilminster, R. (1991) 'Structuration theory as a world-view', in C.G.A. Bryant and D. Jary (eds), *Giddens's Theory of Structuration*. London: Routledge.

King, A. (2000) 'A critique of Baudrillard's hyperreality: Towards a sociology of postmodernism', in M. Gane (ed.), *Jean Baudrillard*, Vol. II. London: Sage.

Koopmans, R. and Statham, P. (1999) 'Challenging the liberal nation-state? Postnationalism, multiculturalism, and the collective claims making of migrants and ethnic minorities in Britain and Germany', *American Journal of Sociology*, 105 (3): 652–96.

Korenbaum, M. (1964) 'Translator's preface', to G. Gurvitch, *The Spectrum of Social Time*. Dordrecht: D. Reidel Publishing Company.

Kristeva, J. (1986) 'Stabat Mater', in T. Moi (ed.), *The Kristeva Reader*. Oxford: Blackwell.

Kumar, K. (1995) *From Post-Industrial to Post-modern Society*. Oxford: Blackwell.

Kurasawa, F. (2003) 'Primitiveness and the flight from modernity: sociology and the avant-garde in inter-war France', *Economy and Society*, 32 (1): 7–28.

Lacy, H. (1998) 'Neutrality in the Social Sciences: On Bhaskar's argument for an essential emancipatory impulse in social science', in M. Archer et al. (eds), *Critical Realism: Essential Readings*. London: Routledge.

Lannes, S. (1991) 'La revanche de Dieu – interview with Gilles Kepel', *Geopolitique*, 33.

Lash, S. and Urry, J. (1994) *Economies of Signs and Space*. London: Sage.

Lash, S. and Featherstone, M. (2001) 'Recognition and difference: Politics, identity, multiculture', *Theory, Culture and Society*, 18(2–3): 1–19.

Leach, E. (1982) *Lévi-Strauss*. London: Fontana.

Leavitt, G. C. (1989) 'Disappearance of the incest taboo: A cross-cultural test of general evolutionary hypotheses', *American Anthropologist*, 91 (1): 116–31.

Lefebvre, H. (1971) *Everday Life in the Modern World*. Harmondsworth: Penguin.

Leiris, M. (1950) 'L'ethnographe devant le colonialisme', in *Les temps moderne*. Reprinted in *Brisées*, pp.125–45. Paris: Mercure de France.

Lemert, C. (1995) *Sociology After the Crisis*. Oxford: Westview Press.

Lemert, C. (1999) 'The might have been and could be of religion in social theory', *Sociological Theory*, 17 (3): 240–63.

Lemert, C. (2002) *Social Things*. Boulder, CO: Rowman and Littlefield.

Lemert, C. (2003) 'Schools and scholars: Durkheim's ghosts', *Journal of Historical Sociology*, 16 (3): 303–19.

Levinas, E. (1974) *Autrement qu'être ou au-delà de l'essence*. The Hague: Nijhoff.

Levine, D. (1985) *The Flight From Ambiguity: Essays in Social and Cultural Theory*. Chicago: University of Chicago Press.

Levine, D. (1995) *The Sociological Tradition*. Chicago: University of Chicago Press.

Lévi-Strauss, C. (1963) *Structural Anthropology*. Harmondsworth: Penguin.

Lévi-Strauss, C. (1969) [1949] *The Elementary Structures of Kinship* (*Les Structures élémentaires de la parenté*). London: Eyre and Spottiswoode.

Lévi-Strauss, C. (1971) 'The Family', in H. Shapiro (ed.), *Man, Culture and Society*. London: Oxford University Press.

Lévi-Strauss, C. (1996) [1962] *The Savage Mind*. Oxford: Oxford University Press.

Lévy-Bruhl, L. (1903) *The Philosophy of Auguste Comte*. London: Swan Sonnenschein and Co.

Lévy-Bruhl, L. (1926) *How Natives Think*. London: Allen and Unwin.

Lewis, B. (1976) 'The return of Islam', *Commentary*, 61 (1): 39–49.

Lewis, B. (1990) 'The roots of Muslim rage', *The Atlantic Monthly*, 266.

Lewis, B. (2002) *What Went Wrong? The Clash Between Islam and Modernity in the Middle East*. London: Weidenfeld and Nicolson.

Lindholm, C. (1997) 'Logical and moral dilemmas of postmodernism', *Journal of the Royal Anthropological Institute*, 3 (4): 747–60.

Lockwood, D. (1992) *Solidarity and Schism: The Problem of Disorder in Durkheimian and Marxist Sociology*. Oxford: Clarendon Press.

Løgstrup, K.E. (1997) *The Ethical Demand*. Notre Dame, IN: University of Notre Dame Press.

Lopreato, J. (1984) *Human Nature and Biocultural Evolution*. Boston, MA: Allen and Unwin.

de Lubac, H. (1950) *Catholicism*. London: Burns and Oates.

Luckmann, T. (1967) *Invisible Religion*. New York: Macmillan.

Luhmann, N. (1998) *Observations on Modernity*. Stanford, CA: Stanford University Press.

Lukes, S. (1973) *Emile Durkheim: His Life and Work*. London: Penguin.

Lundby, K. (1997) 'The web of collective representations', in S.M. Hoover and K. Lundby (eds), *Rethinking Media, Religion and Culture*. London: Sage.

Luther, M. (1957) *Christian Liberty*. Philadelphia: Fortress Press.

Luther, M. (1995) 'Address to the Christian nobility of the German nation', in *Readings in World Civilisations*, Vol. II, *The Development of the Modern World*, 3rd edn. New York: St. Martin's Press.

Lyon, D. (1988) *The Information Society*. Oxford: Blackwell.

Lyon, D. (1999) *Postmodernity*. 2nd edn. Buckingham: Open University Press.

Lyon, D. (2000) *Jesus in Disneyland*. Cambridge: Polity.

Lyotard, J-F. (1984) *The Postmodern Condition*. Manchester: Manchester University Press.

Mabille, P. (1977) [1937] *Égrégores ou la vie des civilisations*. Paris: Sagittaire.

MacIntyre, A. (1955) 'Visions', in A. Flew and A. MacIntyre (eds), *New Essays in Philosophical Theology*. London: SCM Press.

MacIntyre, A. (1967) *A Short History of Ethics*. London: Routledge.

MacIntyre, A. (1984) *After Virtue: A Study in Moral Theory*, 2nd edn. Notre Dame, IN: University of Notre Dame Press.

MacIntyre, A. (1988) *Whose Justice, Which Rationality?* London: Gerald Duckworth.

Mack, B. (1987) 'Introduction', in *Violent Origins: Walter Bukert, René Girard and Jonathan Z. Smith on Ritual Killing and Cultural Formation*. Stanford, CA: Stanford University Press.

Macpherson, C.B. (1962) *The Political Theory of Possessive Individualism*. Oxford: OUP.

Maffesoli, M. (1989) 'The sociology of everyday life (epistemological elements)', *Current Sociology*, 37 (1).

Maffesoli, M. (1996) *The Times of the Tribes*. London: Sage.

Malinowski, B. (1927) *Sex and Repression in Savage Society*. London: Kegan Paul.

Malinowski, B. (1930) *Argonauts of the Western Pacific*. London: Kegan Paul.

Mann, M. (1986) *The Sources of Social Power*, Vol. I. Cambridge: Cambridge University Press.

Marett, R. R. (1914) *The Threshold of Religion*. London: Methuen and Co.

Maritain, J. (1939) *True Humanism*. London: Geoffrey Bles/Centenary Press.

Maritain, J. (1986) *Christianity and Democracy*. San Francisco: Ignatius Press.

Martín-Barbero, J. (1997) 'Mass media as a site of resacralisation of contemporary cultures', in S.M. Hoover and K. Lundby (eds), *Rethinking Media, Religion and Culture*. London: Sage.

Marty, M.E. and Appleby, R.S. (1991) *Fundamentalisms Observed*. Chicago: University of Chicago Press.

Marx, K. (1956) *Selected Writings in Sociology and Social Philosophy*. New York: McGraw-Hill.

Marx, K. (1973) *Grundrisse*. Harmondsworth: Penguin.

Maryanski, A. (1987) 'African ape social structure: Is there strength in weak ties?', *Social Networks*, 191–215.

Maryanski, A. (1992) 'The last ancestor: An ecological network model on the origins of human sociality', *Advances in Human Ecology*, 2: 1–32.

Maryanski, A. (1993) 'The elementary forms of the first proto-human society: An ecological/social network approach', *Advances in Human Ecology*, Vol. 2, Greenwich, CT.: JAI Press.

Maryanski, A. (1994) 'The pursuit of human nature in sociobiology and evolutionary sociology', *Sociological Perspectives*, 37: 375–90.

Mathieu, N. (1989) 'Sexual, sexed and sex class identities: Three ways of conceptualising the relationship between sex and gender', in D. Leonard and L. Adkins (eds), *Sex in Question: French Materialist Feminism*. London: Taylor and Francis.

Mauss, M. (1900) 'Sylvain Lévi, La doctrine du sacrifice dans les Brâhmanas', *L'Année sociologique*, III: 293–5.

Mauss, M. (1950) 'Les techniques du corps', *Sociologie et anthropologie*, Part 6. Paris: Presses Universitaires de France.

Mauss, M. (1969) *The Gift: Forms and Functions of Exchange in Primitive Societies*. London: Routledge and Kegan Paul.

Mauss, M. (1973) *Sociologie et anthropologie*. Paris: Presses Universitaires de France.

Mauss, M. (1979) *Sociology and Psychology.* (trans. B. Brewster). London: Routledge and Kegan Paul.

May, C. (2002) *The Information Society.* Cambridge: Polity.

McCormick, J.P. (1998) 'Political theory and political theology: The second wave of Carl Schmitt in English', *Political Theory*, 26 (6): 830–54.

McGrath, A. (1993) *Reformation Thought.* Oxford: Blackwell.

McLellan, D. (1987) *Marxism and Religion.* London: Macmillan.

Mellor, P.A. (1998) 'Sacred contagion and social vitality: Collective effervescence in *Les formes élémentaires de la vie religieuse*', *Durkheimian Studies*, 4: 87–114.

Mellor, P.A. (2000) 'Rational choice or sacred contagion? "rationality", "nonrationality" and religion', *Social Compass*, 47(2): 265–81.

Mellor, P.A. and Shilling, C. (1997) *Re-forming the Body: Religion, Community and Modernity.* London: Sage/TCS.

Mellor, P.A. and Shilling, C. (1998) 'Lorsque l'on jette de l'huile sur le feu ardent: sécularisation, homo duplex et retour du sacré', *Social Compass*, 45 (2): 297–320.

Mestrovic, S.G. (1997) *Postemotional Society.* London: Sage.

Michalski, S. (1993) *The Reformation and the Visual Arts.* London: Routledge.

Milbank, J. (1990) *Theology and Social Theory.* Oxford: Blackwell.

Miles, M. (1989) *Carnal Knowing.* Boston, MA: Beacon Press.

Miles, R. (1989) *Racism.* London: Routledge.

Minh-ha, T.T. (1989) *Woman, Native, Other.* Bloomington, IN: Indiana University Press.

Mizruchi, M.S. and Stearns, L.B. (1994) 'Money, banking and financial markets', in N.J. Smelser and R. Swedberg (eds), *The Handbook of Economic Sociology.* Princeton, N.J./New York: Princeton University Press/Russell Sage Foundation.

Moingt, J. (1996) 'Traveller of culture: Michel de Certeau', *New Blackfriars*, 77 (909): 479; 493.

Moore, A. (2003) *Realism and Christian Faith.* Cambridge: Cambridge University Press.

Morris, B. (1987) *Anthropological Studies of Religion.* Cambridge: Cambridge University Press.

Morrison, K. (2001) 'The disavowal of the social in the American reception of Durkheim', *Journal of Classical Sociology*, 1 (1): 95–125.

Moscovici, S. (1976) *La Psychanalyse son Image et son Public.* Paris: Presses Universitaires de France.

Moscovici, S. (1988) 'Notes towards a description of social representations', *European Journal of Social Psychology*, 18: 211–50.

Moscovici, S. (1989) 'Des représentations collectives aux représentations sociales: Éléments pour une histoire', in D. Jodelet (ed.) *Les Représentations Sociales.* Paris: Presses Universitaires de France.

Moscovici, S. (1993) *The Invention of Society.* Cambridge: Polity.

Moscovici, S. (2001) 'Why a Theory of Social Representations?', in K. Deaux and G. Philogène (eds), *Representations of the Social.* Oxford: Blackwell.

Moscovici, S. and Mugny, G. (eds) (1985) *Perspective on Minority Influence.* Cambridge: Cambridge University Press.

Moss, D. (2001) 'The gift of repentance: a Maussian perspective on twenty years of *pentimento* in Italy', *Archives Européennes de Sociologie*, XLII, 2: 297–331.

Munson, H. (2003) 'Fundamentalism', *Religion*, 33: 381–5.

Nasr, S. H. (1988) *Ideals and Realities of Islam.* London: Unwin Hyman.

Needham, R. (1963) 'Introduction' to E. Durkheim and M. Mauss, *Primitive Classification.* London: Cohen and West.

Nicholson, L. (ed.) (1990) *Feminism/Postmodernism.* London: Routledge.

Nisbet, R. (1993) [1966] *The Sociological Tradition.* Brunswick, NJ: Transaction.

Noyes, B. (2000) *Georges Bataille: A Critical Introduction.* London: Pluto Press.

O'Donovan, O. (1999) *The Desire of the Nations: Rediscovering the Roots of Political Theology.* Cambridge: Cambridge University Press.

Office of National Statistics (2001) 'Ethnicity and religion', National Statistics Online ⟨http://www.statistics.gov.uk/cci/nugget.asp?id=395⟩.

Olson, M. (1965) *The Logic of Social Action*. Cambridge, MA: Harvard University Press.

Ozment, S. (1992) *Protestants: The Birth of Revolution*. London: Fontana.

Park, R.E. and Burgess, E.W. (1921) *Introduction to the Science of Sociology*. Chicago: University of Chicago Press.

Parsons, T. (1951) *The Social System*. London: Routledge.

Parsons, T. (1954) 'The incest taboo in relation to social structure and the socialisation of the child', *British Journal of Sociology*, 5: 101–17.

Parsons, T. (1960) *Structure and Process in Modern Society*. New York: Free Press.

Parsons, T. (1963) 'Christianity and modern industrial society', in E.A. Tiryakian (ed.), *Sociological Theory, Values and Sociocultural Change*. New York: Free Press.

Parsons, T. (1966) 'Religion in a modern pluralistic society', *Review of Religious Research*, 7 (3): 125–46.

Parsons, T. (1968) [1937] *The Structure of Social Action*. New York: Free Press.

Parsons, T. (1969) *Politics and Social Structure*. New York: Free Press.

Parsons, T. (1978) *Action Theory and the Human Condition*. New York: Free Press.

Parsons, T. (1991) 'A tentative outline of American values', in R. Robertson and B. S. Turner (eds), *Talcott Parsons: Theorist of Modernity*. London: Sage.

Pateman, C. (1983) 'Feminist critiques of the public/private dichotomy', in S.I. Benn and G.F. Gaus (eds), *Public and Private in Social Life*. London: Croom Helm.

Patterson, S. (1999) *Realist Christian Theology in a Postmodern Age*. Cambridge: Cambridge University Press.

Payne, D. (2003) 'The clash of civilisations: The church of Greece, the European Union and the question of human rights', *Religion, State and Society*, 31 (3): 261–71.

Payne, J. (1989) *Why Nations Arm*. Oxford: Blackwell.

Paz, O. (1974) *Claude Lévi-Strauss*. New York: Delta.

Pecora, V.P. (2003) 'Religion and modernity in current debate', *Journal for Cultural and Religious Theory*, 4 (2).

Philogène, G. and Deaux, K. (2001) 'Introduction' to K. Deaux and G. Philogène (eds), *Representations of the Social*. Oxford: Blackwell.

Philpott, D. (2002) 'The challenge of September 11 to secularism in international relations', *World Politics*, 55(1): 66–86.

Piaget, J. (1965) *Etudes sociologiques*. Geneva: Droz.

Pickering, M. (1997) 'A new look at Auguste Comte', in C. Camic (ed.), *Reclaiming the Sociological Classics*. Oxford: Blackwell.

Pickering, W.S.F. (1993) 'Human rights and the cult of the individual: An unholy alliance created by Durkheim?', in W.S.F. Pickering and W. Watts Miller (eds), *Individualism and Human Rights in the Durkheimian Tradition*. Oxford: British Centre for Durkheimian Studies.

Pipes, D. (1983) *In the Path of God: Islam and Political Power*. New York: Basic Books.

Pipes, D. (2003) *Militant Islam Reaches America*. New York: W.W. Norton.

Plamenatz, J. (1963) 'Introduction' to Thomas Hobbes, *Leviathan*. New York: Meridian Books.

Poggi, G. (2000) *Durkheim*. Oxford: Oxford University Press.

Polanyi, K. (1971) [1947] *Primitive, Archaic and Modern Economies: Essays of Karl Polanyi*. Boston: Beacon Press.

Polanyi, K. (2001) [1944] *The Great Transformation: The Political and Economic Origins of Our Time*. Boston, MA: Beacon Press.

Polanyi, K., Arensberg, C. and Pearson, H. (1971) [1957] *Trade and Market in the Early Empires: Economics in History and Theory*. Chicago: Henry Regnery Company.

Polanyi. M. (1958) *Personal Knowledge*. London: Routledge and Kegan Paul.

Polanyi, M. (1967) *The Tacit Dimension*. London: Routledge and Kegan Paul.

Pope, W. and Johnson, B. (1983) 'Inside organic solidarity', *American Sociological Review*, 40 (4): 681–92.

Portes, A. (1994) 'The informal economy and its paradoxes', in N.J. Smelser and R. Swedberg (eds), *The Handbook of Economic Sociology*. Princeton, N.J./New York: Princeton University

Press/Russell Sage Foundation.

Prigogine, I. and Stengers, I. (1984) *Order out of Chaos*. New York: Bantam.

The Qur'an (Koran) (1988), trans. A.J. Arberry. Oxford: Oxford University Press.

Radcliffe-Brown, A.R. (1952) *Structure and Function in Primitive Society*. London: Cohen and West.

Rahner, K. (1979) *Theological Investigations*, Vol. XVI: *Experience of the Spirit: Source of Theology*. London: Darton, Longman and Todd.

Rawls, A. W. (2000) '"Race" as an interaction order phenomenon: W.E.B. Du Bois's "double consciousness" thesis revisited', *Sociological Theory*, 18 (2): 241–74.

Rawls, A. W. (2001) 'Durkheim's treatment of practice', *Journal of Classical Sociology*, 1 (1): 33–68.

Rawls, J. (1971) *A Theory of Justice*. Cambridge, MA: Harvard University Press.

Rawls, J. (1993) *Political Liberalism*. New York: Columbia University Press.

Rawls, J. (1999) *Collected Papers*. Cambridge, MA: Harvard University Press.

Reed, M. and Harvey, D.L. (1992) 'The new science and the old: complexity and realism in the social sciences', *Journal for the Theory of Social Behaviour*, 22: 356–79.

Régnier-Bohler, D. (1988) 'Imagining the Self', in G. Duby (ed.), *A History of Private Life. II: Revelations of the Medieval World*. London: Belknap.

Rémond, R. (1999) *Religion in Society in Modern Europe*. Oxford: Blackwell.

Reynolds, V. (1967) *The Apes, the Gorilla, Chimpanzee, Orangutan and Gibbon: Their History and Their World*. London: Cassell.

Richardson, M. (1994) *Georges Bataille*. London: Routledge.

Richman, M. (2003) 'Myth, power and the sacred: anti-utilitarianism in the Collège de sociologie 1937-9', *Economy and Society*, 32 (1): 29–47.

Rieff, P. (1966) *The Triumph of the Therapeutic*. Harmondsworth: Penguin.

Rippin, A. and Knappert, J. (1986) *Textual Sources for the Study of Islam*. Manchester: Manchester University Press.

Rist, J.M. (2002) *Real Ethics*. Cambridge: Cambridge University Press.

Ritzer, G. (1993) *The McDonaldization of Society*. London: Pine Forge.

Ritzer, G. (1998) *The McDonaldization Thesis*. London: Sage.

Ritzer, G. (1999) *Enchanting a Disenchanted World*. London: Pine Forge.

Robertson, R. (1970) *The Sociological Interpretation of Religion*. Oxford: Basil Blackwell.

Robertson, R. (1991) 'The central significance of 'religion' in social theory: Parsons as an epical theorist', in R. Robertson and B. S. Turner (eds), *Talcott Parsons: Theorist of Modernity*. London: Sage.

Robertson, R. (1992) *Globalization*. London: Sage.

Rochlitz, R. (2002) 'Habermas entre démocratie et génétique', *Le Monde*, 20 December.

Roper, L. (1994) *Oedipus and the Devil*. London: Routledge.

Rorty, R. (1989) *Contingency, Irony and Solidarity*. Cambridge: Cambridge University Press.

Rorty, R. (1991) *Essays on Heidegger and Others*. Cambridge: Cambridge University Press.

Rorty, R. (1992) 'Cosmopolitanism without emancipation: a response to Lyotard', in S. Lash and J. Friedman (eds), *Modernity and Identity*. Oxford: Blackwell.

Rose, N. (1996) 'The death of the social? Refiguring the territory of government', *Economy and Society*, 25: 327–56.

Roth, G. (2003) 'The near-death of liberal capitalism: Perceptions from Weber to the Polanyi brothers', *Politics and Society*, 31 (2): 263–82.

Rousseau, J-J. (1983) *The Social Contract and Discourses*. London: Dent.

Rubin, G. (1975) 'The traffic in women: Notes on the "political economy" of sex', in Rayna R. Reiter (ed.), *Toward an Anthropology of Women*. New York: Monthly Review Press.

Ruel, M. (2002) 'Christians as believers', in M. Lambek (ed.), *A Reader in the Anthropology of Religion*. Oxford: Blackwell.

Rumford, C. (2003) 'European civil society or transnational social space', *European Journal of Social Theory*, 6 (1): 21–43.

Rupp, E.G. (1975) 'Luther and the German Reformation to 1529', in G.R. Elton (ed.), *The*

Reformation, The New Cambridge Modern History, Vol. 2. Cambridge: Cambridge University Press.

Said, E. (1978) *Orientalism*. London: Routledge and Kegan Paul.

Said, E. (1993) *After the Last Sky: Palestinian Lives*. London: Vintage.

Said, E.W. (1994) *Representations of the Intellectual: The 1993 Reith Lectures*. London: Vintage.

Said, E.W. (1997) *Covering Islam*. London: Vintage.

Said, E.W. and Ashcroft, B. (2001) 'Conversation with Edward Said', in P. Williams (ed.), *Edward Said*, Vol.I. London: Sage.

Sawyer, R.K. (2002) 'Durkheim's dilemma: Toward a sociology of emergence', *Sociological Theory*, 20 (2).

Sayer, A. (2000) *Realism and Social Science*. London: Sage.

Scheff, T.J. (1990) *Microsociology*. Chicago: University of Chicago Press.

Scheler, M. (1961) *Ressentiment*. New York: Free Press.

Schmitt, C. (1996a) *Roman Catholicism and Political Form*. Westport, CT: Greenwood.

Schmitt, C. (1996b) *The Leviathan in the State Theory of Thomas Hobbes*. Westport, CT: Greenwood.

Schmitt, C., Schwab, G., Strauss, L, Lomax, H.J., and Strong, T.B. (eds) (1996) *The Concept of the Political*. Chicago, IL: University of Chicago Press.

Schurtz, H. (1902) *Alterklassen und Männerbünde*. Berlin: Georg Reimer.

Schutz, A. (1962) *The Problem of Social Reality*. The Hague: Nijhoff.

Schwan, G. (1998) 'The "healing value" of Truth-telling: Chances and Social Conditions in a Secularized World', *Social Research*, 65 (4): 725–40.

Scott, J. (1995) *Sociological Theory: Contemporary Debates*. Aldershot: Edward Elgar.

Seligman, A.B. (1992) *The Idea of Civil Society*. Princeton, N.J.: Princeton University Press.

Sennett, R. (1977) *The Fall of Public Man*. London: Faber and Faber.

Serres, M. (ed.) (1995) *A History of Scientific Thought*. Oxford: Blackwell.

Shepard, W. (1987) 'Fundamentalism, Christian and Islamic', *Religion*, 17 (4): 353–78.

Shilling, C. (2003) *The Body and Social Theory*. 2nd edn. London: Sage.

Shilling, C. and Mellor, P. A. (1996) 'Embodiment, structuration theory and modernity', *Body and Society*, 2 (4): 1–15.

Shilling, C. and Mellor, P.A. (2001) *The Sociological Ambition*. London: Sage.

Shils, E. (1981) *Tradition*. London: Faber.

Siedentop, L. (2000) *Democracy in Europe*. London: Penguin.

Simmel, G. (1971) [1908] 'The problem of sociology', in D. Levine (ed.), *Georg Simmel on Individuality and Social Forms*. Chicago: University of Chicago Press.

Simmel, G. (1997) *Essays on Religion*. London: Yale University Press.

Skidmore, D. (1998) 'Huntington's clash revisited', *Journal of World-Systems Research*, 4 (2): 180–8.

Slater, D. (1998) 'Public/Private', in C. Jenks (ed.), *Core Sociological Dichotomies*. London: Sage.

Smart, B. (2000) 'On the disorder of things: Sociology, postmodernity and the "end of the Social"', in M. Gane (ed.), *Jean Baudrillard*, Vol. I. London: Sage.

Smelser, N.J. and Swedberg, R. (1994) 'The sociological perspective on the economy', in N.J. Smelser and R. Swedberg (eds), *The Handbook of Economic Sociology*. Princeton, NJ/New York: Princeton University Press/Russell Sage Foundation.

Smith, J.Z. (1987) 'The domestication of sacrifice', in *Violent Origins: Walter Bukert, René Girard and Jonathan Z. Smith on Ritual Killing and Cultural Formation*. Stanford, CA: Stanford University Press.

Smith, W.C. (1978) *The Meaning and End of Religion*. London: Society for Promoting Christian Knowledge.

Sollers, P. (1998) [1968] 'The roof: Essays in systematic reading', in F. Botting and S. Wilson (eds), *Bataille: A Critical Reader*. Oxford: Blackwell.

Solnic, S. and Hemenway, D. (1996) 'The deadweight loss of Christmas: comment', *American Economic Review*, 86(5):1298–1305.

Song, R. (1997) *Christianity and Liberal Society*. Oxford: Clarendon Press.

Soskice, J. M. (1987) 'Theological Realism', in W.S Abraham and S.W. Holtzer (eds), *The Rationality of Religious Belief*. Oxford: Clarendon Press.

Southern, R.W. (1962) *Western Views of Islam in the Middle Ages*. Cambridge, MA: Harvard University Press.

Spivak, G. (1990) *The Post-Colonial Critic: Interviews, Strategies, Dialogue*. London: Routledge.

Stark, R. (1997) 'Bringing theory back in', in L.A. Young (ed.), *Rational Choice Theory and Religion*. New York: Routledge.

Stark, R. and Bainbridge, W.S. (1985) *The Future of Religion*. Berkeley, CA: University of California Press.

Stark, R. and Bainbridge, W.S. (1987) *A Theory of Religion*. New York: Peter Lang.

Stedman Jones, S. (2001) *Durkheim Reconsidered*. Cambridge: Polity.

Stehr, N. and Grundmann, R. (2001) 'The authority of complexity', *British Journal of Sociology*, 52 (2): 313–29.

Steiner, F. (1956) *Taboo*. New York: Philosophical Library.

Stiglitz, J.E. (2001) 'Foreword' to K. Polanyi, *The Great Transformation*. Boston, MA: Beacon Press.

Strathern, M. (1998) 'The concept of society is theoretically obsolete: For the motion (1)', in T. Ingold (ed.), *Key Debates in Anthropology*. London: Routledge.

Strenski, I. (1997) *Durkheim and the Jews of France*. Chicago: University of Chicago Press.

Strenski, I. (1998) 'Durkheim's bourgeois theory of sacrifice', in N.J. Allen, W.S.F. Pickering and W. Watts Miller (eds), *On Durkheim's Elementary Forms of Religious Life*. London: Routledge.

Strenski, I. (2002) 'Durkheim, Judaism and the afterlife', in T.A. Idinopulos and B.C. Wilson (eds), *Reappraising Durkheim for the Study and Teaching of Religion Today*. Leiden: Brill.

Tabataba'i, S.M.H. (1987) *The Qur'an in Islam*. London: Zahra Publications.

Taylor, C. (1989) *Sources of the Self*. Cambridge: Cambridge University Press.

Taylor, C. (1994) 'The politics of recognition', in A. Gutmann (ed.), *Multiculturalism: Examining the Politics of Recognition*. Princeton, NJ: Princeton University Press.

Temple, D. and Chabal, M. (1995) *La Réciprocité et la Naissance des Valeurs Humaines*. Paris: Editions L'Harmattan.

Thompson, K. (1971) 'Introductory essay' to G. Gurvitch, *The Social Frameworks of Knowledge*. Oxford: Blackwell.

Thompson, K. (1993) 'Wedded to the sacred', in W.S.F. Pickering and W. Watts Miller (eds), *Individualism and Human Rights in the Durkheimian Tradition*. Oxford: British Centre for Durkheimian Studies.

Thurnwald, R. (1932) *Economics in Primitive Communities*. London: Humphrey Milford/Oxford University Press for the International Institute for African Languages and Culture.

Tiryakian, E. (1995) 'Collective effervescence, social change and charisma: Durkheim, Weber and 1989', *International Sociology*, 10 (3): 269–81.

Tiryakian, E. (2003) 'Durkheim, solidarity and September 11', in J. Alexander and P. Smith (eds), *The Cambridge Companion to Durkheim*. Cambridge: Cambridge University Press.

Toffler, A. (1970) *Future Shock*. London: Bodley Head.

Tönnies, F. (1957) *Community and Association*. Michigan: Michigan State University Press.

Toren, C. (1998) 'The concept of society is theoretically obsolete: For the motion (2)', in T. Ingold (ed.), *Key Debates in Anthropology*. London: Routledge.

Torrance, T.F. (1982) 'Theological realism' in B. Hebblethwaite and S. Sutherland (eds), *The Philosophical Frontiers of Christian Theology*. Cambridge: Cambridge University Press.

Torrance, T.F. (1984) *Transformation and Convergence in the Frame of Knowledge*. Belfast: Christian Journals Limited.

Torrance, T.F. (1985) *Reality and Scientific Theology*. Edinburgh: Scottish Academic Press.

Torrance, T.F. (1998) *Divine and Contingent Order*. Edinburgh: T & T Clark.

Touraine, A. (1969) *La société post-industrielle*. Paris: Editions Denoël.

Touraine, A. (1989) 'Is Sociology still the study of society?' *Thesis Eleven*, 23: 5–34.

Touraine, A. (1995) *Critique of Modernity*. Oxford: Blackwell.

Touraine, A. (2003) 'Sociology without Societies', *Current Sociology*, 51 (2): 123–31.

Trigg, R. (1998) *Rationality and Religion*. Oxford: Blackwell.

Turner, B.S. (1990) *Theories of Modernity and Postmodernity*. London: Sage.

Turner, B.S. (1991) *Religion and Social Theory*. London: Sage.

Turner, B.S. (2002) 'Sovereignty and emergency: Political theology, Islam and American conservatism', *Theory, Culture and Society*, 19 (4): 103–19.

Turner, B.S. and Rojek, C. (2001) *Society and Culture*. London: Sage.

Turner, J.H. (1996) 'The evolution of emotions in humans: A Darwinian Durkheimian analysis', *Journal for the Theory of Social Behaviour*, 26 (1): 1–33.

Turner, S. (1983) 'Durkheim as methodologist', Part 1: 'Realism, teleology and action', *The Philosophy of Social Science*, 13: 425–50.

Turner, V. (1967) *Forest of Symbols*. New York: Cornell University Press.

Turner, V. (1969) *The Ritual Process*. London: Routledge.

Turner, V. (1974) *Dramas, Fields and Metaphors*. New York: Cornell University Press.

Twitchell, J.B. (1987) *Forbidden Partners: The Incest Taboo in Modern Culture*. New York: Columbia University Press.

Tylor, E.B. (1888) 'On a method of investigating the development of institutions, applied to laws of marriage and descent', *Journal of the Royal Anthropological Institute*, 18: 245–69.

Urry, J. (2000) *Sociology Beyond Societies*. London: Routledge.

Urry, J. (2003) *Global Complexity*. Cambridge: Polity.

Van Baal, J. and Van Beek, W.E.A. (1985) *Symbols for Communication*. Assen: Van Gorcum.

Van den Berghe, P. (1981) *The Ethnic Phenomenon*. New York: Elsevier.

Van Gennep, A. (1909) *Les Rites de passage. Étude systématique des Rites*. Paris: Émile Nourry.

Van Kley, D.K. (1996) *The Religious Origins of the French Revolution: From Calvin to the Civil Constitution, 1560-1791*. London: Yale University Press.

Vertigans, S. and Sutton, P. (2001) 'Back to the future: "Islamic terrorism" and interpretations of past and present', *Sociological Research Online*, 6 (3): U55–U60.

Vertovec, S. (1996) 'Berlin multikulti: Germany, "foreigners" and "world-openness"', *New Community*, 22: 381–99.

Virilio, P. (1984) *L'Horizon negatif*. Paris: Galilée.

Virilio, P. (1994) *The Vision Machine*. Bloomington, IN: Indiana University Press.

Virilio, P. (1996) *Cybermonde, la politique du pire*. Paris: Editions Textuel.

Virilio, P. (1997) *Open Sky*. London: Verso.

Virilio, P. (2000) *The Information Bomb*. London: Verso.

Virilio, P. (2002) *Ground Zero*. London: Verso.

Virilio, P. and Lotringer, S. (1997) *Pure War*. New York: Semiotext(e).

Voll, J. (1987) 'Islamic renewal and the "failure of the West"', in R.T. Antoun and M.E. Heegland (eds), *Religious Resurgence: Contemporary Cases in Islam, Christianity and Judaism*. New York: Syracuse University Press.

Wagner, P. (2001) *A History and Theory of the Social Sciences*. London: Sage/TCS.

Waldron, J. (2002) *God, Locke and Equality*. Cambridge: Cambridge University Press.

Waldrop, M.M. (1992) *Complexity*. London: Viking.

Walhout, M. (2001) 'The *Intifada* of the intellectuals: An ecumenical perspective on the Walzer–Said exchange', in P. Williams (ed.), *Edward Said*, Vol.I. London: Sage.

Walzer, M. (1994) *Thick and Thin: Moral Argument at Home and Abroad*. Notre Dame, IN: University of Notre Dame Press.

Wanner, C. (2003) 'Advocating new moralities: Conversion to evangelicalism in Ukraine', *Religion, State and Society*, 31 (3):273–87.

Warner, R.S. (1993) 'Work in progress toward a new paradigm for the sociological study of religion in the United States', *American Journal of Sociology*, 98 (5): 1044–93.

Warner, R.S. (1997) 'Convergence toward the new paradigm', in L.A. Young (ed.), *Rational Choice Theory and Religion*. New York: Routledge.

Watts Miller, W. (1996) *Durkheim, Morals and Modernity*. London: UCL Press.

Weber, M. (1965) *The Sociology of Religion*. London: Methuen.

Weber, M. (1978) *Economy and Society*. London: University of California Press.

Weber, M. (1991) *The Protestant Ethic and the Spirit of Capitalism*. London: Harper Collins.

Webster, F. (1995) *Theories of the Information Society*. London: Routledge.

Weintraub, J. (1997) 'The theory and politics of the public/private distinction', in J. Weintraub and K. Kumar (eds), *Public and Private in Thought and Practice: Perspectives on a Grand Dichotomy*. Chicago: The University of Chicago Press.

Werbner, P. (2003) 'Divided loyalties, empowered citizenship? Muslims in Britain', *Citizenship Studies*, 4 (3): 307–24.

Wernick, A. (1992) 'Post-Marx: Theological themes in Baudrillard's America', in P. Berry and A. Wernick (eds), *Shadow of Spirit: Postmodernism and Religion*. London: Routledge.

White, L. A. (1948) 'The definition and prohibition of incest', *American Anthropologist*, 50: 416–35.

Williams, M. and May, T. (1996) *Introduction to the Philosophy of Social Research*. London: UCL Press.

Williams, R. (1989) 'Resurrection and peace', *Theology*, XCIII (750): 481–90.

Williams, R. (2000) *Lost Icons: Reflections on Cultural Bereavement*. Edinburgh: T&T Clark.

Wilson, B.C. (2002) 'Altars and chalkstones: The anomalous case of Puritan sacred space in light of Durkheim's theory of ritual', in T.A. Idinopulos and B.C. Wilson (eds), *Reappraising Durkheim for the Study and Teaching of Religion Today*. Leiden: Brill.

Wilson, S. (1995) 'Fêting the wound: Georges Bataille and Jean Fautrier in the 1940s', in Carolyn Bailey Gill (ed.), *Bataille: Writing the Sacred*. London: Routledge.

Winnicott, D.W. (1965) *Playing and Reality*. Harmondsworth: Penguin.

Wrong, D. H. (1994) *The Problem of Order*. Cambridge, MA: Harvard University Press.

Yang, M.M. (2000) 'Putting global capitalism in its place: Economic hybridity, Bataille and ritual expenditure', *Current Anthropology*, 41 (4): 477–509.

Yeatman, A. (2003) 'Globality, state and society', Citizenship Studies, 7 (3): 275–90.

Young, F. W. (1967) 'Incest Taboos and Social Solidarity', *American Journal of Sociology*, 72: 589–600.

Young, I. M. (1990) *Throwing Like a Girl and Other Essays in Feminist Philosophy and Social Theory*. Bloomington, IN: Indiana University Press.

Young, L.A. (1997) *Rational Choice Theory and Religion*. New York: Routledge.

Zafirovski, M.Z. (2000) 'Spencer is dead, long live Spencer: Individualism, holism and the problem of norms', *British Journal of Sociology*, 51(3): 553–79.

Zaretsky, E. (1995) 'The birth of identity politics in the 1960s: Psychoanalysis and the public/private division', in M. Featherstone, S. Lash and R. Robertson (eds), *Global Modernities*. London: Sage/TCS.

Zelizer, V. (1994) *The Social Meaning of Money*. New York: Basic Books.

Zizek, S. (1989) *The Sublime Object of Ideology*. London: Verso.

Zizek, S. (2000) *The Fragile Absolute or, Why is the Christian Legacy Worth Fighting For?* London: Verso.

Zizek, S. (2002) *Welcome to the Desert of the Real*. London: Verso.

Zohar, D. and Marshall, I. (1994) *The Quantum Society*. New York: William Morrow.

Index